# ANTHROPOLOGY,
# SPORT, AND CULTURE

# ANTHROPOLOGY, SPORT, AND CULTURE

EDITED BY

## Robert R. Sands

Foreword by Kendall Blanchard

**BERGIN & GARVEY**

Westport, Connecticut • London

**Library of Congress Cataloging-in-Publication Data**

Anthropology, sport, and culture / edited by Robert R. Sands ;
   foreword by Kendall Blanchard.
       p.    cm.
    Includes bibliographical references and index.
    ISBN 0–89789–599–1 (alk. paper)
    1. Sports—Anthropological aspects.   I. Sands, Robert R.
   GV706.2.A58   1999
   306.4′83—dc21        98–20128

British Library Cataloguing in Publication Data is available.

Library of Congress Catalog Card Number: 98–20128
ISBN: 0–89789–599–1

First published in 1999

Bergin & Garvey, 88 Post Road West, Westport, CT 06881
An imprint of Greenwood Publishing Group, Inc.

Printed in the United States of America

The paper used in this book complies with the
Permanent Paper Standard issued by the National
Information Standards Organization (Z39.48–1984).

10 9 8 7 6 5 4 3 2 1

This book is dedicated to Dr. Alyce Cheska and Dr. Beluh Drom
Pioneers in the study of sport and culture

# Contents

# Foreword

## *Kendall Blanchard*

The Superbowl! It is mid-January on a Sunday afternoon. The attention of the world is drawn to what may well be the major sporting event of the year. Football enthusiasts and loyal fans have fought and paid big money for a chance to see the game live. Others are glued to their television sets in anticipation. Everywhere there are parties, large and small, as people take advantage of the occasion to get together with friends. Advertisers have paid as much as $1 million per minute for commercial time on the television broadcast of the event. As the teams are introduced, the crowd roars; the sound is deafening. Television announcers shout above the noise of the crowd, working their audience into a frenzy and bringing the emotional intensity of the stadium into living rooms, dens, and sports bars everywhere. The Superbowl illustrates the extremes to which sport has invaded all areas of modern life. However, it is only one event and one sport among many. Americans--indeed, people throughout the world--are often consumed by sport. It is no wonder that some refer to sport as the "New American Religion" (e.g., Peake 1998: 6).

For such reasons, social scientists can no longer afford to ignore sport as a subject of serious research and discussion. Sport is not just an American religion; it is passion that has gripped most of the world. It is a universal phenomenon. It is shaping cultures, driving economies, and molding politics. It is a metaphor for modern life. Its impact is global, facilitating communication among nations while, at the same time, underscoring national, regional, and ethnic identities. It is a major mode of international relationships as American ping-pong players compete in a mainland China still off-limits to Americans, American wrestlers wrestle in an Iran still hostile and virtually closed to Americans, Japanese martial artists visit Malaysia, and Thai kick boxers tour Japan.

Even before the dawn of written history, it is likely that sports were culturally conditioned institutions that, along with material artifacts, social customs, and ideologies, were transported across cultural lines. Physically combative games developed by one group were adopted by neighbors, reshaped to fit the new cultural context, and gradually institutionalized. During the last century, the so-called major sports of the world have moved freely and quickly from one country or culture to another: European soccer, American baseball, Japanese martial arts, and Native American lacrosse. Even more interesting, though, is the rate at which even minor sports are internationalizing. Consider the recent case of Philip Boit, a Kenyan who represented his country in the Nagano Winter Olympics in the 10-kilometer cross-country skiing event yet who had never even seen snow until two years earlier.

This universal fascination with sport and sport competition is, in many ways, giving a new ecumenical globalism to the phenomenon. It is ubiquitous. The games go on and as never before imagined. But why? What does this say about human nature psychologically, socially, culturally? What does it say about human relationships, values, and modes of communication? What does it say about postmodernism, the new technology, and expectations for the twenty-first century? This is what is important about this work and the chapters that Robert Sands has assembled. *Anthropology, Sport, and Culture* brings together some of the most important articles written about sport by social scientists, humanists, and athletes themselves. All of the articles are analytical in nature. As a collection, the works brought together here explore the universal characteristics of sport, treat sport as a cultural given, and employ various anthropological perspectives to address the type of questions raised earlier. The answers they provide to these questions are both interesting and thought provoking. As a whole, the collection illustrates the nature and importance of studying sport as a universal phenomenon that both shapes and is shaped by its cultural context. Whether you love them, hate them, or are ambivalent on the matter, sports have become a fundamental component of modern human life. *Anthropology, Sport, and Culture* helps us understand how and why.

## REFERENCE

Peake, Charles F. "Economic Icons of Religious Beliefs." *National Forum* 78, no. 1 (1998): 5-6.

# Preface

I have always been enamored with sport as an anthropologist, participant and observer, and as an athlete and fan. Twelve years ago I combined sport and anthropology and undertook an ethnography of black and white collegiate basketball players for my M.A. thesis at Iowa State University; field studies on sprinters and college football players soon followed. I had always known that sport commandeered my life and those closely around me, my father, brothers, and friends, even my mother, who recounted passionate afternoons watching college football with my father. For days at a time, while I was caught in the spring of my life (be it the World Series, the summer long quest of the Chicago Cubs to finish above 500, Gale Sayers and the Chicago Bears the trials and tribulations of University of Illinois football and basketball, the Olympics--you name it), we did more than watch sport-- we absorbed it. If we weren't watching it, we were playing it, from summer baseball, to winter basketball; from playgrounds, to city parks; from tennis courts, to golf courses.

As I finished my participant-observation of college basketball players, playing and watching basketball in the dead of winter in Ames, Iowa, I realized that for so many Americans, no matter the culture, ethnicity, or even gender, interest and involvement in sport do not diminish with "growing up." Indeed, interest often deepens as sons and daughters continue the same pattern followed by parents; soccer moms have been touted to be an influential demographic factor in national politics, and fathers and mothers now play catch with both sons and daughters. An emergent, wildly successful fundamentalist interest group, the Promise Keepers, grew out of the mind of a college football coach, and standing-room-only crowds now flock to football and baseball stadiums to witness and take part in centering the family once again around the male.

As my research in sport and anthropology continued through graduate programs, I realized that interest in sport was high in many other cultures as well; rites of passage were tied to participation, tribal identity was reified by sporting events, culture contact and change were precipitated and carried in competitions. It is not an overstatement to say that, indeed, now more than ever, sport is a pervasive human behavior that is made to order for anthropological study and the holistic, cross-cultural, and ethnographic traditions that still define such an endeavor. As well, these traditions, which have set anthropology apart from other disciplines, are now being borrowed by other social sciences as the natural boundaries of academe blur and dissolve in the face of postmodernism and cultural studies. Nowhere is this phenomenon more visible than in the study of sport, where sociologists and cultural studies people are the ethnographers of sport and culture. As much as I am a traditionalist, anthropology is best done by those trained in anthropology, the present and future of culture study dictate interdisciplinary research. Yet, I am of the mind that anthropology should be the leader in this area. This volume presents an eclectic array of sport and culture research, from anthropology, to the diverse fields of sociology and cultural studies, from the far different disciplinary perspectives of positivism and symbolic interactionism. The common denominator that binds all selections together in a coherent, cohesive work is the study of sport, not so much as it relates to a culture of athletes and sporting behavior but, more importantly, as it relates to what light and cultural illumination sport can shed on contemporary issues of ethnicity, identity, ritual, and culture change. In tapping into contemporary work, I selected research that included a comparative, cross-cultural perspective, the hallmark of anthropology; sport used as a means of addressing larger issues of culture change and identity, not an end in itself; and, lastly, a look at human behavior that has been a hallmark of traditional focus in anthropology, ritual, qualitative fieldwork, the effect of environment and genes (physical and biological anthropology), symbolization, and culture change, and places that behavior in a contemporary focus.

There are five sections for *Anthropology, Sport, and Culture*, each section focusing around a central theme in contemporary and traditional anthropology that relates to the relationship between culture and sport. Within each section, contributed works present research and/or case studies that highlight that specific theme.

Anthropology, by its very nature, provides a forum for broad-based research as well as offers the opportunity to specify a narrow focus on a cross-cultural "stage." That is what this volume presents; taking the relationship of one facet of human behavior, sport, and looking at the similarities and differences in that behavior expressed in Western and non-Western cultures.

Much of what is presented in this volume is very current and/or original research. Some chapters offer a look back at research presented within the last two decades that still has validity to ongoing research in the field (Ness, Gmelch, Dundes). There is also a mix of more traditional anthropology and research by non-anthropologists that uses an anthropological approach (Sands, Jackson and Meier, Jackson and Andrews, Cole, Crawford, Bale, and Malec). There are selections that have been published in nonacademic publications that offer a more popular view of sport and culture that should not be ignored due to the use of that particular medium (Burfoot, Hoberman). Anthropology cannot afford to ignore or look beyond popular work that uses tools of anthropology or offers a look at the nature of changing cultural order in global society.

# Acknowledgments

I would like to acknowledge the support, interest, and help of the following people. My agent, Linda Petersen of Zola Peters Agency, spent an inordinate amount of time querying publishers and editors and then spent more time obtaining permissions to reprint selections. I would also like to acknowledge the help of a lifelong colleague, Dr. Jackie Eller, who has continually provided me a sounding board and a channel to vent frustration over my chosen field of study, not if frustration came, but when it came. Acknowledgments also to Dr. F. K. Lehman for his help in reading selections and offering constructive comments.

I would also like to thank those who contributed to this first-ever volume on anthropology and sport; they were prompt and professional in providing me with their selections so that the laborious job of editing was made relatively pain-free. Special acknowledgment goes to Dr. Steven Jackson for his excitement and enthusiasm during this project and to Raymond Rich, who allowed me the use of his office and computer while my office was being furnished.

Last, but not least, by any means, I would like to thank my wife, Linda Sands, for her continued support and understanding during a very trying time of research and writing; research and writing continue, as does her support; may it never wane.

# ANTHROPOLOGY, SPORT, AND CULTURE

# PART I

## Theory and Method in Anthropology of Sport

# chapter 1

## Anthropology and Sport

### Robert R. Sands

The study of sport and anthropology is a relatively recent field of inquiry in which little interest and research have been generated by the rank and file in anthropology. In the middle to late 1800s, anthropologists had no time for such small, trivial looks at human behavior such as sport; their interest lay in generating grand theories of cultural diffusion and evolution and the origin of religion. For over 100 years, what interest in physical activity generated in the discipline's infancy was devoted to the study of "games" and gamelike behavior.

For this chapter and the other chapters in this volume, I define sport as a cultural universal having the following features: a human activity that is a formal and rule-directed contest ranging from a gamelike activity to a highly institutionalized structure; competition between individuals or teams or can result in internal competition within an individual; a basis in physical skills, and strategy, chance or a combination of all three; and potential tangible rewards for the participants, monetary, material, or status.

Sport is, indeed, not only universal but perhaps one of the best indicators or expressions of culture; as I tell my cultural anthropology students, sport reflects culture. Behavior in sport can be applied to that of the surrounding culture; in other words, the sport behavior we see in American football is far different from what we see in Trobriand cricket. A closer look at the sports and related behavior produces a blueprint of those important and valued behaviors that are the foundation of the larger culture in which the sport is embedded. That is an example of only one arm of cultural anthropological inquiry: to derive and identify behavior of a culture. We can proceed to the next more valuable step in anthropological inquiry. Using the notion of sport as a human constant, we can generate a cross-cultural comparison and produce a "cognitive" map of human behavior. The violent, pololike Afghani stan sport of Buzkhanzi can then be compared to not only Western polo but in the same research breath the more sedate sport of lawn bowling.


## HISTORY: THE EARLY PERIOD

One of the first anthropologists to pursue the study of games was E .B. Tylor. "In particular, he [Tylor] realized that activities such as sports might provide the anthropologist with important clues about the nature of prehistoric cultural contact between geographically distant groups of people" (Blanchard 1985: 285). In keeping with the times, Tylor's work (Tylor 1896, 1879) was distinctly theoretical; building theory of diffusion and culture contact based on, for example, similarities between Hindustani pachisi and the Mexican game of patolli (Tylor 1896).

Along with Tylor, in those early years a few scholars turned their focus to games and sport. Most notable were Stewart Culin's many works on North American Indians. At the turn of the century, Culin was the first ethnologist to produce a comprehensive and systematic look at the many games and sport activities of 225 different Native American tribes (Blanchard and Cheska 1985; Blanchard 1985). The first half of the twentieth century featured little research done by anthropologists examining the role of sport and culture.

Raymond Firth's (1931) "A Dart Match in Tikopia: A Study of the Sociology of Primitive Sport" probed the relationship of competitive dart throwing and social organization and religious beliefs of the Tikopian, and, in the end, Firth suggested that sport deserved more attention and had the potential to be a fruitful avenue of research. Perhaps the best example of early work on game and sport activity is Alexander Lesser's monograph (1933) *The Pawnee Ghost Dance Hand Game*. Not only is Lesser's analysis a first-rate treatment of the relationship of a specific game's role in Pawnee culture, but it is also a brilliant piece of anthropological work.

Yet despite these rare works, the study of games, sport, and culture during this early period lay on the fringe of anthropology. Classic ethnographies, at best, only mention game or sport activity; the majority fail to treat the subject as a significant feature of cultural activity.


## THE CONCEPTUAL PERIOD

The 1960s brought a radical restructuring of Western society and the academic disciplines that looked at the comparison of non-Western and Western societies. Anthropological research on sport and culture entered a less benign atmosphere where the "old guard" traditional anthropologists were being replaced by younger, less traditional anthropologists who were open to new arenas of academic inquiry and who were extending the boundaries of what passed as legitimate areas of anthropology research. For the area of sport and culture, the research that was pivotal in establishing the legitimacy of such an area was the seminal treatise by John Roberts, Malcom Arth and Robert Bush (1959) "Games in Culture," which appeared in *American Anthropologist.* "This was one of the first systematic attempts to put definable parameters around the concept of games. It served to stimulate productive theoretical debate regarding the special role of sport in human society among anthropologists" (Blanchard 1985: 288).

If research in the early period was a trickle, the conceptual period resembled a spring thaw. During the next 20 years, the study of sport and culture grew up around disciplines outside anthropology as much as within anthropology. Leslie White in his 1964 presidential address before the *American Anthropological Association* suggested that anthropology could lend a credible model for the study of sport, especially for baseball, "which he saw as a vital expression of the American cultural system itself" (White 1965 in Blanchard 1985: 289).

Disciplines such as sociology, psychology, history, and physical education also laid claim to sport as a means of expressing social systems. "The primary reason for its [sport] respectability in sociology rather than in anthropology is the fact that sport is more likely to be a major element in the social systems that sociologists study than those treated by anthropologists" (Blanchard 1985: 292).

No more was this apparent than with the radical social upheaval in the 1960s and 1970s involving race, power, and social inequality. The ills of American society were played out on the highly visible fabric of western sport: hegemony, racism, social inequality could be seen on the televised playing fields of America and the international athletic arenas. Sociological publications that explored these areas included *Sport, Culture, and Society* (Loy and Kenyon 1969) and *Games, Sport and Power* (Stone 1972).

While sociology led the sport and society research movement, anthropologists were involved in developing cross-cultural views of the impact of sport on cultural systems through ethnographic investigation. Baseball was the sport of choice for several pioneering pieces of research on sport and culture. Navajo baseball and the use of magic were chronicled in Robin Fox's widely read 1961 article, "Pueblo Baseball: A New Use for Old Witchcraft." George Gmelch's (1972) "Baseball Magic" provided an entertaining, yet insightful, example of Malinowski's observations of magic in Trobriand society with superstition and ritual in American baseball (a revised version of this piece appears in this volume). Blanchard's work on Navajo culture and basketball and Alyce Cheska's research on Native American sport, games, and ritual also supplied looks at the relationship of sport and non-Western society.

Perhaps the work that best fitted into the traditional scope of mainstream anthropology of the times was Clifford Geertz's (1972) look at Balinese cockfighting, "Deep Play: Notes on the Balinese Cockfight." This selection was more a part of a larger work on the evolution of anthropology as more of a fluid, symbolic expression of human variation, which proved to be revitalizing to anthropology theory, and less a specific piece on the nature of sport and culture.

Without a doubt, the most influential anthropologist in bringing attention to sport and culture during this conceptual period was Edward Norebeck. Norebeck was a catalyst in the 1974 development of the Anthropological Association for the Study of Play (TAASP) which was created from a 1973 American Anthropology Association symposium. TAASP, later shortened to TASP, was a cadre of scholars from not only anthropology but history, sociology, psychology, physical education, kinesiology, cultural studies, and other fields Annual meetings were held in conjunction with Popular Culture Associations through the 1980s, and yearly edited volumes were produced from these meetings.

In 1985, Kendall Blanchard and Alyce Cheska published the first-ever text on the anthropology of sport, *The Anthropology of Sport*. It was designed as an introductory text and was a survey of literature and research as well as a serious attempt at introducing a rigorous methodological approach to the study of sport and culture.1

That same year (1985), Blanchard contributed a chapter in an edited volume on sport and culture calling for the use of sport studies in anthropology curricula. "In recent years," Blanchard wrote, "the number of anthropologists dealing with sport in their research, writing and classroom instruction has increased. No longer is sport simply a topic of idle conversation and pastime activity among anthropologists; it has become a legitimate subject of serious study" (Blanchard 1985: 293).

## POSTCONCEPTION: THE 1990s

The 1990s has produced a plethora of sport and culture research, yet, most notably, anthropology has contributed little to this area of study. Very few anthropology departments offer undergraduate or graduate courses in anthropology of sport. However, physical education, kinesiology, sociology, and psychology departments offer a wide variety of courses, both undergraduate and graduate, that deal with sport. Several journals focus on sport, society, and/or culture, none of them anthropological. There are numerous academic works ( edited volumes and sole authored) on sport and society, including ethnographies yet, recently, very little on sport and culture and only a handful written by anthropologists (Bale and Sang 1996; Brownell 1995; Henning et al. 1998; Klein 1993,1993 a, b; MacClancy 1996; Sands 1991,1994, 1995).

## SPORT AND ANTHROPOLOGY

Sport is one of those enterprises, global and universally participated in, that are ready-made laboratories for studying pressing issues of a changing world order and has captured the imagination of any number of social sciences, like sociology, psychology, and history, but have so far escaped the scrutiny of American anthropologists, save for a few.

For over a century and a half, anthropologists have been describing cultures in minutiae, interlocking behavior, institutions, and material expressions in a holistic mural of representation, yet, sport, even features of play and games, have been overlooked or ignored as being either nontangential or non-existent in non-Western "small scale society as it is modern, more complex systems" (Blanchard 1985: 290). Still, with the traditional focus in anthropology on integrated views of culture, to excuse such oversights is a stretch. Malinowski's seminal work on Trobriand society is complete, yet description of sport, even games, is lacking.

Blanchard offers other potential reasons for the neglect of sport in a cultural and social context by anthropologists. Traditionally, the most studied facets of culture were economics, social structure, kinship, and political and religious systems, and these areas still carry the most weight in contemporary anthropology, often to the exclusion of other areas, belying the inclusive holistic and integrated nature of the discipline. According to Blanchard, early "fathers" of the discipline were not active in sport in their childhood, especially sports of the masses, and this could have created an avoidance or, at least, minimization of the importance of sports in cultures studied during the infancy of anthropology.

Today, sport commands the attention of cultures, nations, even the world, and only a handful of anthropologists have published on sport and culture. Recent work by anthropologists includes work on bodybuilding, female athletes in China, lacrosse, baseball groupies, black sprinters, and junior college football, to name a few. Yet, regional and national meetings such as those of the American Anthropological Association (AAA) do not feature symposiums on current topics in sport and culture; in fact, two years ago, a proposed and well-organized section on sport for the AAA meetings was canceled, prompting some criticism.

Nonanthropologist scholars doing work in the field of sport and culture question the noninvolvement of anthropologists in such a compelling subject. Toby Miller, editor of the *Journal of Sport and Social Issues*, asks, "What might explain the continuing marginality of sports to anthropology and social theory even as it is central to popular, folk and commodified life?" (Miller 1997: 115). To add to Blanchard's speculations, I can only agree and suggest that mainstream anthropologists operate under the misguided notion that sport is somehow frivolous and does not represent or offer a viable field of study. This I find difficult to accept with one of the foundational canons of anthropology that separates it from other social sciences is of a holistic and integrated field of study. As well, another reason may be that the study of sport in anthropology and other fields does not adhere to the rigorous method and analysis found in the ethnography and anthropology of non-Western cultures. One need only look at contemporary studies such as Klein (1993a, 1997) or Brownwell (1995) or even my own (Sands 1991, 1995 ) to see that the method that lies at the heart of these studies is very traditionally focused, powerful ethnography.

Possibly yet another reason for contemporary lack of interest in sport is the recent paradigmatic struggle between postmodernism and positivism that is currently polarizing anthropology theory.

## A STATE OF FLUX IN ANTHROPOLOGY

This volume represents a serious effort to bring to the study of sport a critical perspective, what James Peacock, president of the *American Anthropological Association*, referred to as crucial to the future of anthropology, a "holistic and comparative insight into human diversity and commonality with such practices as participant observation" (Peacock 1996: 11).[2]

Anthropology is a discipline in academic turmoil, searching for its place in academe as interdisciplinary studies draw interest to the state of individual and global culture. Human issues such as sex, ecology, gender, religion, and sport are being addressed by nonanthropologists. Peacock urged the discipline to keep up with the changing world, reinvent the sacred truths that have ruled the discipline since before World War II, and focus on things that concern humankind, not the abstract mix of theory and description that many have fallen back on in the face of this interdisciplinary onslaught. Anthropology should be the discipline of the twenty-first century, banking on its strengths, not the starving child it is. "With our humanistic aspects, we need to probe the human experience, in its variety, but also in its abiding unity, not only in pop culture, but also in the sustaining strengths (healing, belief, epic, movements etc.) and prevailing structures (race, class, gender and kinship). We need not abandon the search for pattern and regularity in human life" (Peacock 1996: 14).

Roy Rappaport is another anthropologist who sees the necessity of delving into more issue-oriented areas of research in contemporary society and culture by anthropology. "Grappling with contemporary [issues]," wrote Rappaport, "may not only help society to enlarge its understanding of its own difficulty, but also enlarge anthropological theory and method" (Rappaport 1994: 2). It is clear that a number of individual anthropologists have been affected by matters posed by the changing nature of global culture and society, this author included, yet the discipline as a whole is extremely conservative in its move toward embracing such contemporary studies.

In response to globalization and culture change and the diminishing geographical and cultural distance between peoples, old disciplines are being forced to shift focus, and new disciplines, like cultural studies, are evolving. As through time, paradigm shifts continue; postmodernism and literary criticism, the latest theoretical revolution, have swept through the social sciences; and traditional elements of anthropology have been challenged and, in some cases, modified (Blanchard 1985: 293). "Anthropologists have been transformed by their recent emphasis concerning matters as problematic to society as gender, oppression, ethnic identity, cultural pluralism, class and inequality" (Rappaport 1994: 2).

In 1985, Blanchard warned anthropology and anthropologists, perhaps foreshadowing Peacock's admonition a dozen years later, to branch out into areas of human interest, that the popularity of sport makes it impossible to ignore. "It is especially evident in contact societies," Blanchard wrote, "where culture change often involves the transmission of modern sports (e.g. basketball, soccer, baseball) into traditional social setting." Another reason given by Blanchard for the attention of anthropologists to sport is the dwindling number of specialties left to study: "Sport represents one of the few remaining frontiers in the discipline," he wrote (1985: 293).

For anthropologists who remain above and beyond the multidisciplinary fray, researching areas that share little relevance with contemporary scholarly focus, research in sport and culture is another example of the encroaching popular culturalists. However, for anthropologists wanting to connect with human diversity in the context of a rapidly changing cultural milieu as well as grounded in the traditional methodology and theoretical focus, the study of sport and culture represents timely research an academic tonic prescribed by Peacock; anthropology turning outward, addressing the larger needs and objectives of the coming century and millennium.

For anthropology to survive and prosper, the student must be able to connect this very traditional discipline, with contemporary and extensive research on the modern human condition. Features of this temporal hybrid anthropology that continue to set it apart from other social inquiry are a holistic perspective that highlights the interdependence of culture; a cross-cultural, comparative view of human behavior; and the traditional, long-term, participant-observation (ethnographic) fieldwork method, where anthropologists bury themselves in the ebb and flow of cultural behavior and extract a highly detailed insider's view of that group's lifeways. Even in the more contemporary "shotgun," issue-driven ethnographic approach, the anthropologist is often a member of, or has some familiarity with, that group and proceeds to focus on specific elements of cultural behavior.

To assist in the enterprise of ethnography and of immersion into the population being studied, participation in local recreation and sports offers an informal method of crossing over the often rigidly adhered to boundary of ethnographer and those being studied and bringing to the table a more relaxed and trusting relationship. A good example of the use of sport as a means of developing the depth of the relationship between ethnographer and those being studied involves research I was doing on cultural identity and alternate lifestyles (Sands 1994). I was looking at lesbians and lifestyles, extracting salient features of identity, and I was in the process of identifying, contacting, and developing "informants." Finding out that a few of those I wanted to interview played in a competitive softball league, I began attending games and taking part in their practices and also for a while played in a coed league with them as well. By no means was the team or league all gay, and, even though the softball experiences provided some data on identity, the study itself did not revolve around softball, but, above all, this time spent "playing" provided a powerful mechanism of entry into their "culture" and allowed me time spent with my informants in a relaxed and nonthreatening manner.

Lastly, anthropology looks at cultural expression as it varies from culture to culture, but, in the end, the application of theory drives the science of human behavior to extract similarities between groups of peoples; ultimately, what makes us humans are the commonalities, not the differences.

Anthropology as a discipline needs to apply its "holistic" and cross-cultural perspective to those areas of interest in contemporary academe, or else face either an unwelcome assimilation into other multidisciplinary fields or gradual extinction. The area of sport and culture is a ready-made vehicle to help bring anthropology into "compliance" with the suggestions offered by Peacock.

## ANTHROPOLOGY, SPORT, AND CULTURE

You would be hard-pressed to find a social scientist who would not agree that Western sport and non-Western sport play a large role in contemporary intercultural interaction, Western sport in terms of international games and athletic events, non-Western sport in terms of the reification of cultural tradition and identity. This volume, in part, exploits this larger arena of global change and the smaller arenas of cultures adapting to this shifting world order. Unique to most work done on sport and society, an anthropological perspective focuses on sport yet applies it not only in a cross-cultural fashion but in the traditional cross-discipline nature of anthropology.

In keeping with Peacock's urging not to avoid areas that fall into "pop" culture, "anthropologists must think and communicate beyond the discipline and beyond the academy" (Peacock 1996: 14), this volume also includes selections that originate from nonanthropological and popular sources yet have intrinsic value to understanding the human condition and cultural diversity. There have been publications done by anthropologists on the topic of sport and some aspect of anthropological research, but this is the first edited reader/volume proposed by an American anthropologist that brings a systematic approach to the field and considers sport from the many different aspects of anthropology.3

In addition, in keeping with the canons of anthropology, the study of sport can be a vehicle for developing statements concerning the nature of human culture (theory) and then by its application put theory into practice. In this vein, following Peacock, research in this volume and other research offer an "effective synergy: reflective practice and connected research" (Peacock 1997: 14).

Although anthropological in nature, this volume provides timely, popular, and scholarly research for the multidisciplinary look at the field of sport, society, and culture. Many nonanthropologists' research offers a cross-cultural look at sport or uses an ethnographic method. This volume offers this cadre of sport scholars a publication based on anthropology theory and method. Recent research in sport and culture not only brings together a cross-cultural collection of work that reflects an anthropological perspective, but also provides the beginning of a formal academic treatment of what Blanchard, 10 years ago, called for, but has never emerged, an anthropology of sport. Anthropology, Sport, and Culture does so in a highly readable fashion, mixing grounded academic work with innovative and popular studies. By no means is this volume an exhaustive compilation of current research. It is, instead, an array of studies that provide a representation of work being currently done in the field. As well, it is a concerted effort to bring focus and structure to an avenue of anthropology that has been generally ignored by anthropologists.

Sport has been and will always be a significant element of cultural behavior, in our own backyard as well as in emerging Third World countries and long-standing tribal societies. Sport also reflects the enormous amount of cultural change through the impact of Westernization occurring in every corner of the globe. In essence, sport has become both a barometer of social change and a leading agent of social change. Witness the meaning of South Africa's world rugby title in 1996 to a society and culture in the throes of social, economic, and, more importantly, cultural upheaval. A black president once jailed by the apartheid government, extolling the virtues of South African nationhood through a rugby team, once banned from international competition due to racial policies of its government, with only one black player on the team. Sport, indeed, is a phenomenon driven by power and politics, but it is also an extremely large window in which to peer into the tickings and cultural variation of the humankind. As I tell my introductory students in cultural anthropology, anthropology seeks not the differences but the similarities that lurk beneath that highly visible cultural expression and that make us all members of the human species. The study of sport is no different; sport reflects culture, and culture reflects sport.

Using the field of anthropology of sport, the new emerging world order, where cultural contact between Western and emerging Third World cultures and reconstructed nations is, in major part, through sport, becomes more accessible to the human consciousness. Anthropology offers a formal and theoretical orientation to studying this reconstruction of world order, and the study of sport and culture becomes a necessity.

By involving a cross-cultural approach, including anthropology fieldwork, the place of Western sport in society can be compared with non-Western sport and culture. The study of sport should not be an end in itself. Sport is just one facet or cultural expression of human lifeways. The beauty of anthropology is its ability to view singular traits, such as sport, in the context of the larger cultural "gestalt." Ethnography of sport, as I have shown in earlier work, provides a valuable perspective on other cultural facets. As Blanchard wrote, no longer can the anthropologist avoid the importance of sport. And no longer can the study of sport ignore anthropology.

## NOTES

1. Blanchard and Cheska's work rose out of the early success (1970s and 1980s) of TAASP, later shortened to the Association for the Study of Play (TASP). Annual TAASP meetings produced conferences that were well attended and an edited proceedings on each conference. TASP is still in existence as a 250-member association, with quarterly a newsletter headed by Stuart Reifel at the University of Texas, Austin.

2. For a discussion of this most current paradigm shift see Rappaport 1994, Peacock 1996; Sands 1991, 1995.

3. Jeremy MacClancy, a British anthropologist, has recently (1996) edited a volume of research done by British and European anthropologists, *Sport, Identity, and Ethnicity*, that looks at sport and ethnicity from a cross-cultural perspective. But it is a treatment of just one aspect of sport, and it is not widely distributed in the United States.

## REFERENCES

Bale, John, and Joe Sang. *Kenyan Running: Movement Culture, Geography and Global Change*. London: Frank Cass, 1996.

Blanchard, Kendall. "Sport Studies and the Anthropology of Sport." In *American Sport Culture: The Humanistic Dimensions*, edited by Wiley Umphlett. Lewisburg, PA: Bucknell University Press, 1985.

Blanchard, Kendall, and Alyce Cheska. *The Anthropology of Sport: An Introduction*. Westport, CT: Bergin and Garvey, 1985; reprinted 1995.

Brownell, Susan. *Training the Body for China: Sports in the Moral Order of the Peoples Republic*. Chicago: University of Chicago Press, 1995.

Eichberg, Henning, John Bale, Chris Philo, and Susan Brownell. *Body Cultures: Essays on Sport, Space and Identity*. New York: Routledge, 1998.

Firth, Raymond. "A Dart Match in Tikopia." *Oceania* 1 (1931): 64-97.

Fox, J. R. "Pueblo Baseball: A New Use for Old Witchcraft." *Journal of American Folklore* 74 (1961): 9-16.

Geertz, Clifford "Deep Play: Notes on the Balinese Cockfight." In *The Interpretation of Cultures*. New York: Basic Books, 1972.

_____.*Works and Lives*. Palo Alto, CA: Stanford University Press, 1990.

_____. *After the Fact: Two Countries, Four Decades, One Anthropologist*. Cambridge: Harvard University Press, 1995.

Gmelch, George. "Magic in Professional Baseball." In *Games, Sports and Power*, edited by Gregory P. Stone. New Brunswick, NJ : Dutton, 1972.

Klein, Alan. *Little Big Men: Bodybuilding Subculture and Gender Construction* . Albany, NY: SUNY Press, 1993a.

_____. *Sugarball: The American Game, the Dominican Dream*. New Haven, CT: Yale University Press, 1993b.

_____. *Baseball on the Border: A Tale of Two Laredos*. Princeton, NJ: Princeton University Press, 1997.

Lesser, Alexander. The Pawnee Ghost Dance Hand Game: A Study of Cultural Change Columbia University Contribution to Anthropology, 16. New York: Columbia University Press, 1933

Loy, John W., Jr., and Gerald Kenyon, eds. *Sport, Culture, and Society: A Reader of the Sociology of Sport*. New York: Macmillan, 1969.

MacClancy, J., ed. *Sport, Identity, and Ethnicity*. London: Berg, 1996.

Miller, Toby. "...The Oblivion of the Sociology of Sport..." *Journal of Sport and Social Issues* 21, no. 2 (1997): 115-119.

Peacock, James. "The Future of Anthropology." *American Anthropologist* 99, no.1 (1996):9-29.

Rappaport, Roy. "The Anthropology of Trouble." *American Anthropologist* 94, no. 2 (1994): 359.

Roberts, John M., Malcom J. Arth, and Robert R. Bush. "Games in Culture." *American Anthropologist* 61 (1959): 597.

Sands, Robert R. "An Ethnography of Black Collegiate Sprinters: A Formal Model of Cultural Identity and the Identity Complex." Ph.D. diss., Department of Anthropology, University of Illinois, 1991.

_____. "Cultural Identity and Cultural Groups: The Changing Social Landscape of Ethnic Relations in the United States." Paper given at the Western Social Science Conference, Albuquerque, NM, April 1994.

_____. *Instant Acceleration: Living in the Fast Lane*. The Cultural Identity of Speed. Lanham, MD: University Press of America, 1995.

_____. *Gutcheck! : An Anthropologist's Wild Ride into the Heart of College Football* ,n.d.

Stone, Gregory P. ed. *Games, Sport and Power*. New Brunswick, NJ: Dutton, 1972.

Tylor, Edward B. "On American Lot Games as Evidence of Asiatic Intercourse before the Time of Columbus." *International Archives for Ethnographia*, Supplement to vol. 9 (1896): 55-67.

_____. "The History of Games." *Fornightly Review*, 25 (January 1-June 1 1897): 735-47.

White, Leslie. "Anthropology 1964: Retrospect and Prospect." *American Anthropologist* 67 (1965): 629-37.

# chapter 2

## Experiential Ethnography: Playing with the Boys

### Robert R. Sands

The power of ethnography lies in its keen eye for the ordinary. Where other social sciences have no time for the subtle nuances of human behavior that unfold in micro-increments over macro-periods of time, the ethnographer revels in pattern and repetition. (Robert Sands 1995: 7)

I am an experiential ethnographer, participating in every subtle nuance and behavior of the population in which I am studying. In the end I become one of them and draw no boundaries between us. I offer no caveats of explanation to the duality of roles of studier and studied. I do not share in the journey, filtering experience as it glides by me....life flow through me. My experience is not a metaphor for the experience of others. In a way, I have crossed the final bridge that spans the chasm of researcher and those studied. Self and other marry in a resonance of authorship that decries negotiation and instead offers the reality of meaning in the "eyes of others" (Robert Sands 1995: 8)

This was Gonzo ethnography and this was college football. Jump on the wagon, lose yourself in the action, express it, record it, watch it, ask way too many questions, listen, hurt--ride the bull till it bucks you off, climb back on and hang on for dear life while your knuckles turn white and the wind peels back your face. (Robert Sands n.d.)

## INTRODUCTION

This chapter focuses on the research methodology I used in two sport ethnographies, one about black collegiate sprinters, *Instant Acceleration: Living in the Fast Lane. The Cultural Identity of Speed*, and the second concerning junior college football in Southern California, *Gutcheck!: An Anthropologist's Wild Ride into the Heart of College Football*. The application of participant-observation and the adoption of an intensive method of research were instrumental in forming a proper field of inquiry. I acknowledge that features of interpretive, symbolic-interactionist, and classical ethnography were present in both studies. Ethnography does not have a set procedure for data acquisition or analysis; however, this chapter introduces a general orientation of research that includes a flexibility of research design that allows for a variety of field situations one may encounter.

Recent anthropological theory and methodology have been and still are in a state of flux (Marcus and Fisher 1986; Sperber 1985; Farndon 1990; Geertz 1994; Aunger 1995; Roscoe 1995; Shokeid 1997; O'Meara 1997); there is no dominant school or paradigm. What has occurred, instead, is a diverse array of competing models of not only what passes as traditional ethnographic goals of discovery and description of cultures and peoples and the search for underlying universal similarities in humanity but also how the anthropologist interacts with cultural subjects and the many levels of interpretation and meaning that lies between the ethnographer, those being studied, and the cultural text (see Geertz 1973) generated from the shared experience of both researcher and "native" (see Shokeid 1997; Aunger 1996; Gottlieb 1995; for a recent discussion on the roles of ethnographer and those studied).

In this chapter, I advance a form and style of ethnography that mediates the chasm between postmodernists and positivists. The form of participant-observation used in this study sets it apart from the classic ethnographies (Malinowski 1965; Mead 1928; Radcliffe-Brown 1964) and the interpretive and interactionist ethnographic orientation (see Blumer 1969; Bruner 1984; Clifford and Marcus 1986; Marcus and Fisher 1986; O'Meara 1997--for critique of interpretive anthropology see Ellen 1984; Farndon 1990). Instead of grounding inquiry in a rigid empirical positivism or a negotiated narrative, the "experiential ethnography" I describe advocates complete immersion into the population over a long period of time, where the ethnographer travels through a series of "doors" or stages, each door providing a deeper understanding of the culture and requisite behavior of that population. Unlocking each door is similar to successive rites of passage. Usually, opening these "doors" takes on trappings of rites of passage, subtle or overt, direct or indirectly acknowledged by both anthropologist and the members of the population.

Utilizing Goodenough's (1970) notion of the ethnographer's competence of acting and performing successfully in that culture as being a measure of the validity of the worldview advanced by the ethnographer and an overt, systematic effort at cognitively "challenging" members of the population to themselves construct their own worldview, the ethnographer and anthropologist can then, after a period of time, faithfully reconstruct the cultural and social components of that population and ultimately describe the collective worldview of that population. The ethnographer becomes another "voice" and subject to add to the choir of voices of the population but, in addition, becomes a valuable instrument in determining the validity of information being accessed through participation and observation.

This view is different from the reflexivity of postmodernists (Fisher and Marcus 1986; Marcus 1994; Geertz 1988) and more recent attempts to marry post-modernism with a revamped and altered data gathering technique of a positivistic anthropology (Aunger 1996; Roscoe 1997).

I agree that modern ethnography must include some aspects of reflexivity; "the reader's ability to interpret the quality of ethnographic statements must be increased by clues to the origin and nature of ethnographic statements provided" (Aunger 1996: 98), and includes messages detailing the process of acquisition and accessing such messages (Meyerhoff and Ruby 1982: 2). However, in postmodern-ism, the reader is presented with the "raw" (Aunger 1996: 98) ethnographic data, supposedly involving the reader more intimately in the ethnographic experience. Without the actual experience or context, the reader, therefore, must rely on the ethnographer to provide insight and interpret the findings. In this case, reflection involves a myriad of relationships, and each level removes further the reader from the study.

In the method I advance, reflection is not negotiated in the act of observation or in the rendering of a faithful representation of the population under study (see later; Sperber 1985; Bowlin and Stromberg 1997 for discussion of representation and truth). Instead, reflection is the process of transformation in the ethnographer's position as *outsider* to involved *insider*. This process is not only guided by the population but acquired in a learning process by the ethnographer, which any other member of that population would undergo upon entry into that "culture." Ethnographers naturally must "situate" themselves in the ethnographic process (see Aunger 1995 for a discussion of "situationalism"), but the novelty, uniqueness, and "contamination" of the ethnographer's role in the social dynamics of the population are significantly reduced, to the point of being negligible within the context of lived experience. Other than being a shared, "negotiated" narrative between anthropologist and those studied as proposed by postmodern ethnography or the dry, etic, and objective voice of classical ethnography, the length of fieldwork and intensity of experience operate to situate the ethnographer in a position of cultural understanding, experiencing the surrounding experience as Malinowski suggested, "through the eyes of the native."

This is not a unique perspective; recently, Aunger (1995) and Shokeid (1997) suggest similar practices; Aunger used informants to help gather data in the acquisition process, and Shokeid was challenged by a key informant in his perception of constructing the cultural reality of the population. Through a long-term process of give-and-take, the informant became a silent and occasionally bothersome "coauthor" of the ethnography.

The method proposed in this chapter is different from the shared, jointly constructed narrative of interpretive ethnography as the ethnographer describes cultural reality from the "native's point of view, both experienced and elicited. This type of research is admittedly difficult, switching roles from observer to participant, in my case, from ethnographer to athlete and back again, and was at times both emotionally and physically draining. "And as an anthropologist, I had more than a first row seat. I was there, as a player, as an ethnographer, a describer of culture. More often than not, each role got lost in the other. But that was one of the pitfalls of doing ethnography; trying to figure out where science ended and real life began" (Sands nd).

However, it is my contention that the rewards, in the nature and validity of the data and resultant description of the population of athletes, were culturally specific and an accurate representation. Finally, I suggest that this type of experiential ethnography is limited in its application. In many cases, the ethnographer, due to obvious constraints of gender and age, for example, will not be able to fully become a member of the population, but the implicit goal of experiencing all facets of cultural life should not be disregarded.

## ETHNOGRAPHY--A PROCESS

Simply put, ethnography is a description of a people, population, or culture. "Ethnography is the primary data-gathering part of sociocultural anthropology, that is field work in a given society" (Kottack 1972: 12). To Dobbert, "The main aim of ethnographic research is to discover and describe the culture of a people or an organization" (1982: 39). "Ethnography is a research process in which the anthropologist closely observes, records and engages in the daily life of another culture--an experience labeled as the fieldwork method--and then writes an account of this culture, emphasizing descriptive detail" (Marcus and Fisher 1986: 18).

It is a mistake to think of ethnography as anything but an operation, a collection, analysis, and writing and result of itself; it is not a theory or a paradigm. In short, in a Kuhnian sense, a paradigm can be thought of as a way of *doing* science, complete with method, rules, guidelines, practices, and experience. In this sense, ethnography can be thought of as part of a paradigm. Yet it is obvious that the concept of paradigm and/or theory has taken on a more elastic and pejorative meaning. It is a research tool and a collection of observations, generalizations, interpretations, and meanings. In this respect, ethnography is a process, a vague and loose structuring of guidelines one follows and it is a thing, tangible; when finished, it is a description of data. "The main task of ethnography is to make intelligible the experience of particular human beings as shaped by the social group in which they belong" (Sperber 1985: 34).

Ethnography's arrangement may be subject to a personalized cognitive formulation and analysis; the recent genre of interpretive anthropology argues that an ethnographer interprets the native experience so that it becomes comprehensible and meaningful to those who read it. I suggest that the postmodernist school--of which the interpretive anthropology of Rabinow, Clifford, Marcus, Geertz, Fisher and Tyler is a part--introduces levels of interpretation that distort the natives' cognitive description of their reality, which is contrary to the process of ethnography, the description of a population and its cultural experience from a *native's point of view* (see later for a more detailed discussion). To experience the native's reality is beyond the belief that what people say is actually the same thing they have in their mind. What you hear is only the first step to understanding the conceptual knowledge that is carried in what the native says but can be ascertained only with a more thorough understanding of the native's reality.

What has distinguished anthropology from other social sciences, from its early beginnings to the present, is the use of participant-observation in the ethnographic process, a long-term, labor-intensive process to elicit data (Stocking 1983; Gonzalez, Nadar, and Ou 1995). Early ethnography featured participant-observation as a part of a normative or empirical positivism to analyze and form theories of cultural experience. Data were gathered, institutions and cultural practices were described, and then fitted into a theoretical orientation. Recent and current interpretive and interactionist ethnography has denied the positivistic perspective, postulating that description leads directly to interpretation, and through the various levels or "filters" of interpretation cultural meaning becomes illuminated.

Anthropology is under siege by competing paradigms, and the process of ethnography and the data elicited have become a prisoner of that paradigmatic struggle. What lies at the heart of this titanic struggle are the nature of anthropological knowledge and the ultimate quest of the anthropologist.

## COMPETING WORLDVIEWS: POSTMODERNISM AND POSITIVISM

Postmodern anthropology posits that description of cultural phenomena can be done only through interpretation of such phenomena. Evans-Pritchard, over forty years ago, suggested the only possibility of interpretation was a translation of foreign cultures into the idiom of the anthropologist. Clifford Geertz (1973) and more recently, James Clifford, George Marcus, Stephen Tyler and Paul Rabinow have advanced a similar view which is a result of the symbolic interactionist school of George Mead and Herbert Blumer. In this view culture is a system of meaning, composed of signs, icons, and messages and description is carried out in cultural "texts."

They continue by suggesting the dichotomy of anthropologist/native begs the primary reason for interpretation: "One of the key contemporary justifications for anthropological knowledge has derived from this us/them comparative side of ethnography, and it, too is undergoing important revision" (Marcus and Fisher 1986: 23).

In brief, interpretive anthropology is the elicitation of description in the form of ethnographic texts (see Geertz 1973; Bruner 1984) and what can be done with such a description of cultural phenomena. "The critical question is what this evocative metaphor of interpretation as the reading of texts by both the observer and the observed stands for in the cultural process of research" (Marcus and Fisher 1986: 26).

It is important to realize that what one is after is meaning of cultural phenomenon and that this meaning is arrived at by the anthropologist through not one but two levels of interpretation, how the native interprets the phenomena and the interpretation of the native's interpretation by the ethnographer. "This has led to the present dominant interest within interpretive anthropology about how interpretations are constructed by the anthropologist, who works in turn from the interpretation of his informants" (Marcus and Fisher 1986: 26).

The focal point of the interpretive genre in anthropology is not the data itself or in part, the process that yields the data. It is the role of the anthropologist *vis-a-vis* the native, which is played out in the dialogue between meaning and interpretation of this meaning. This dialogue is contained in the analysis of cultural texts, the description of that culture. While concentrating on this dialogue, interpretive anthropologists, at the same time, reflect on the process of ethnography and the suspect historical and colonial or neocolonial legacy of nineteenth- and twentieth-century anthropology "targeting anthropology's insensitivity or ineffectiveness in dealing with issues of historical context and political economy" (Marcus and Fisher 1986: 34).

In essence, what is involved is the deconstruction and the reconstruction of texts. "The textualists have argued that classic ethnographies incorporate linguistic devices that tend to obscure the uncertain and personal nature of ethnographic statements regarding particular features of social life or cultural beliefs in the group under study. This all implies that the knowledge produced in the field is necessarily incomplete, distorted, tentative, speculative, and thus essentially contestable" (Aunger 1995: 97).

What is proposed by the interpretists is an "experimental ethnography" that includes autobiographical accounts of the ethnographer, multiple voices, the use of historical texts, and so on. In effect, the anthropologist and the native together create a text of shared meaning. It is a process that must involve two aims or perspectives or, as Marcus and Fisher label them, justifications: "One is the capturing of cultural diversity, the other is a cultural critique of ourselves" (Marcus and Fisher 1986: 20). Herein lies the primacy of interpretive anthropology: one looks at cultural diversity to understand more about oneself, and the final aim is the reflection and the interpretation of that meaning upon the ethnographer.

To capture this meaning, one must, as Geertz first argued (1973), "negotiate" what will become the shared meaning, and this is where the exchange of information between researcher and studied becomes a dialogue. "Dialogue has become the imagery for expressing the way anthropologists (and by extension, their readers) must engage in an active communicative process with another culture. It is a two-way and two-dimensional exchange, interpretive process being necessary for communication internally within a cultural system and externally between systems of meaning" (Marcus and Fisher 1986: 30).

It is apparent that interpretive anthropology is a marriage of several processual orientations, symbolic interactionism, hermeneutics, symbolic anthropology, and the related, cross-disciplinary field of literary criticism. In each of these orientations, reflexive interpretation becomes the primary means of couching elicited manifestations of cultural phenomena into an ethnographic discourse. How one arrives at the shared meaning (interpretation of the native and interpretation of the ethnographer) is not dependent on total immersion into the native culture. In fact, reliance on participant-observation minimizes the significance of translation within the negotiation process.

In establishing a foundation for interpretive anthropology, Marcus and Fisher argue that it is grounded in a more complex form of relativism, founded in the 1920s and 1930s, stemming the tide of eugenics and social Darwinism. Interpretive ethnography is now a means of opposition in the struggle against neocolonialism and global, Westernized structures of "political and economic power" (Marcus and Fisher 1986: 33). It becomes a mediating or equalizing construct, reducing the impact of Western hegemony, and if this means, at the same time, denying the inherent and historic legacy of anthropology to "generalize and affirm universal values," so be it.

> Ethnography, as the practical embodiment of relativism and interpretive anthropology, challenges all those views of reality in social thought which prematurely overlook or reduce cultural diversity for the sake of the capacity to generalize and affirm values usually from the still-privileged vantage point of global homogenization emanating from the West. (Marcus and Fisher 1986: 33)

## ANTHROPOLOGY: AN UNEASY SCIENCE

Sperber suggests that the interpretist's view of anthropology is a science only in the respect that it is an "interpretive" science. "Like any other science, anthropology aims at an objective and general knowledge. However, the special character of the description it uses makes it somewhat less ambitious in this respect than the natural science" (1985: 10). As discussed later, I suggest that Sperber's declaration that interpretive anthropologists would argue that their view in one of a scientific nature is suspect (see Marcus and Fisher 1986: 26-27; Clifford and Marcus 1986).

Sperber goes on to suggest another view of anthropological knowledge, a somewhat uneasy alliance between interpretation and the ultimate quest for theory in anthropology. "The task of theoretical anthropology is to account for variability of culture. Like any other science, it must answer the question: what is empirically possible? And hence: what is empirically impossible" (Sperber 1985: 10).

The alliance is indeed tenuous, as to Sperber, ethnography and anthropology tend to be mutually exclusive. "I argue that ethnography aims at interpretation and anthropology at explanation; in order better to achieve these aims, and to entertain more fruitful relationships the two disciplines should distance themselves from one another" (1985: 7).

Roscoe sees a similar dichotomy between the interpretist school of thought and that of the positivists. The difference revolves not so much from mechanical modifications in method but from what determines the data that spring from the method: social facts, such as "norms, institutions, networks of actual existing relations," versus actions and "utterances" (1997: 499).

## ANTHROPOLOGY AS SCIENCE: USING ETHNOGRAPHY TO VALIDATE

I suggest that Sperber's attempt at forming an alliance out of contradiction is perpetuating the myth that interpretive ethnography is a process generating interpretation from description. At the same time, I suggest that even more fundamental in nature than what is involved in the interpretive process of ethnography is the absence or, in this case, avoidance of the ultimate priorities of anthropology (what is and has been implicit in the study of culture and peoples), beyond description of such cultural phenomena ["preoccupation with genres of description rather than with usually more prestigious and totalizing theoretical discourse" (Fardon 1990: 3)], which is that of the inherent, traditionally based search for how these culturally unique phenomena suggest general models or views of human nature.

Marvin Harris reasserts this premise of a "theoretical" anthropology in a scathing treatment of Tim O'Meara's 1997 article on the failure of a science of society when he states that "the basic premise of empirical science is that there are things outside the observer whose nature can be known only by interacting with them through observation, logical manipulation and experiment" (1997: 413).

In essence, this is the comparative nature of our "science," and at this point I argue that science does not mean an empirically positivist method of the natural sciences but, rather, an epistemological flexibility that allows data to be discovered and described and advanced as primary means of testing or validating models of reality (in this case, reality is not an empirically correct phenomenon; it is, instead, models of perception or how people form their existentialism). It is not positivism to suppose that there exists a world around us and that it is something that can be observed. Observation of this world can never be culture-free or mindlessly objective. It is possible, however, that we can test, attempt to refute, and refashion our ideas in attempting to achieve a modest amount of relative objectivity--including descriptive and explanatory adequacy, relative to competing hypotheses.

Aunger sees the ethnographic process as being a combination of the postmodern "textualist" approach and positivism: "I argue that a particular two-step approach is necessary and sufficient to provide a scientific explanation of processes affecting cultural domains" (1995: 98).

Fardon suggests that a successful field experience leads to an analysis of what he labels "experiential positivism" where "the facility of experience outweighs the anticipation of theory" (Fardon 1990: 5).

In fact, Ellen writes that observation in itself constitutes an appropriate means of carrying out a "positivist" anthropology. Yet when one becomes a participant, it precludes an active research goal of normative scientific research.

> From the point of view of the theoretical notions of positivist anthropology, as well as from the point of view of its aim of being scientific, participation is highly problematic; and from the methodological point of view, rather uneasy part of fieldwork. Far from being in itself, methodologically describable, the anthropologist's participation violates the separation of observer and observed phenomenon (characterization of observation in natural sciences) and this goes contrary to the scientific canons of anthropology. It makes problematic the basic belief that the object of the research exists in an external world in the same sense as the object of scientific inquiry it has knowable characteristics which must not be disturbed in the process of observation. (Ellen 1984: 26)

Ellen sees a way around this dilemma by concluding that the disturbing nature of participation can be eliminated or, at least, minimized by undergoing an extended period of time in the field: "the longer the stay, the less disturbing the effect of the ethnographer" (1984: 26).

Postmodernists like Clifford and Marcus (1986) and Marcus and Fisher (1986) reject the positivism of empirical science: "Under the hegemony of positivist social science, this practice (that of reflexivity on the centrality of ethnography) has been masquerading, relatively unreflected upon by anthropologists or others, as a method like any other" (Marcus and Fisher 1986: 26).

In other words, the recent interest in this genre is due to the internal reflexivity of the anthropologist, which gets at the nature of "ethnographic reporting." At this time, interpretation and reflexivity have commandeered the literature in interpretive anthropology. To restructure and reformulate a process of inquiry, however, following the critique of interpretive anthropology (Fardon 1990; Sperber 1985; Ellen 1984), the data that such a process or method yields remain inconsistent with what is needed to validate or even form theoretical suppositions about the nature of cultural phenomena.

Sperber argues that the inconsistency or nature of interpretive data denies this access to a theoretical orientation. Interpretive data do not fulfill these conditions of validity and/or reliability. Due to the current lack of an operating paradigm in anthropology, there are relatively few hypotheses in need of validating, and the nature of interpretive data and the large amount of massed recent ethnographic data are "twice devoid of scientific usefulness" (Sperber 1985: 11).

It is my contention that ethnography is a process, an analytical tool that is not an end in itself. Richard Fardon writes along similar lines.

> Our attitude betrays a fundamental presupposition of our history: that theory is not determinant of ethnography, or at least, it is not determinant of anthropologists ethnographies. In short, the argument for our privileged status among reporters holds that theory cannot entirely determine ethnographic writing because it cannot determine the ethnographer's experience in the field. (Fardon 1990: 3)

I argue, following Fardon (1990), Stocking (1983), Aunger (1995), Harris (1997) and others, that even though anthropology is in a state of flux (lacking a primary theoretical orientation), an anthropologist should not lose sight of the history and tradition of anthropology to explain the general condition of humankind by the use of theory and models, substantiated by the description and comparison elicited from fieldwork. In this respect, interpretive ethnography can be considered only a revolution in, and restructuring of, process.

In the two studies I conducted, I suggest that formal, testable models deal with the nature of individual and group identity and that, contrary to what Sperber suggests, an ethnographic process yields the level of reliability that constitutes evidence for validation or nonvalidation of the models (see section on participant-observation).

## POSITIVISM, EXPERIENTIAL PARTICIPATION, AND THE DENIAL OF POSITIVISM

Since Malinowski's groundbreaking study on the Trobriand Islanders, participant-observation has been the means by which one could break down cultural phenomena and institutions, analyze the constituent facets, and reconstruct and present to the rest of the world. The process of ethnography has recently been explored and described in detail, and several works on how to do ethnography have been published. Spradley (1979, 1980), Spradley and McCurdy (1972), Ellen (1984), Dobbert (1982), Sanjek (1990), Werner and Schoeppfle (1988), among others. Stocking (1983) looked at the making of past ethnographies; Farndon (1990) looked at the regionalization of ethnographies, Geertz (1973, 1980), Bruner (1984), Marcus and Fisher (1986), and Clifford and Marcus (1986) looked at the interpretive orientation in ethnography.

> Participant-observation may be labeled the classical ethnographic method (Dobbert 1982: 102).

> Both for the practitioners and outsiders, a distinguishing feature of modern ethnography is the commitment to fieldwork by "participant-observation" (Stocking 1983:7 )

> While fieldwork is carried out in other behavioral sciences, anthropology is seen by many as having imparted a special quality to "the field" tied up

with the intensive, all-encompassing character of participant-observation
(Sanjek 1990: 17)

Both anthropologists themselves as well as philosophers of science
consider the unique method of yielding data through long-term participant observation as distinguishing anthropology from other social
sciences (Ellen 1984: 25)

My two studies are no different from the preceding descriptions; both
utilized a participant-observation process as the primary method of data acquisition.
The aim of any participant-observation is a balance of participant and observer (see
Russell 1988; Ellen 1984; Werner and Schoepfle 1988), an objective, academic
voice to equalize the subjective feelings of being a part of what one is studying. "It
involves establishing rapport in a new community; learning to act so that people go
about their business as usual when you show up; and removing yourself every day
from cultural immersion so you can intellectualize what you have learned, put it into
perspective and write about it convincingly" (Russell 1988: 148).

## UNLOCKING THE DOORS OF CULTURAL EXPERIENCE

Both of my studies are an example of a contrasting view of what actually
constitutes participation and suggest that participation is composed of multiple levels
of involvement within the native culture and that it is imperative that one experience
(participate) on all levels--or what is meant by being a member of a population (one
must be able to experience the ideational sphere and the observable, behavioral
sphere and "know" when the two spheres do not coincide). In other words, instead
of looking at participation as a line of research that one crosses or enters into a
compromising (contaminating--see Ellen 1984) position vis-a-vis objectivity, I argue
that all levels of participation act to open "doors" of experience needed, that at each
level, the prior experiences in which the researcher has participated coalesce to form
a more complete understanding of the experiences up to that level and act to guide
or map the researcher into "deeper" levels of experience. As well, each of the stages
represents further acceptance by the population of the participant-observer into the
network of social relations and cultural identity of that population (Sands 1991,
1995). Witnessed by some or all of the athletes, uncelebrated, and only indirectly
acknowledged, passage through each of these doors can be considered, in a loose
way, a rite of passage. As it relates to track and field and football, my acceptance
was based, in a large measure, on physical prowess and demonstrated skills and on
a measure of manhood.

In my experience with college football, more than track and field, the
physical nature of the sport produced identifiable stages or doors that marked
entrance into "deeper" levels of understanding of the culture of football. My first
football practice, my first hit, my first injury, my first game, my first selections as
cocaptain, my first start, my first completion, my first after-game party all not only

produced further acceptance by the players into that culture but also further reduced the effects of the researcher-informant/anthropologist-player dichotomies. To really experience organized football, one has to journey from the grandstands to participate in touch or tackle football games in the park.

It is the contention of this study that each level represents an unlocking of cultural experience one must tap to incorporate a comprehension of the cultural existence of the native. This is similar to the work of Frake, Spradley, Good enough, Keesing, and Chomsky, where competence in cultural performance is the test of validity, to be able to participate as a cultural member.

## INTENSIVE PARTICIPATION AND PASSIVE OBSERVATION

The ethnographic method I used presents a deviation from the traditional method of participant-observation, not only in the way participant-observation is carried out but in the cognitive orientation of the researcher (participant). I label this method as intensive participation; in this process:

1.  The researcher participates as one of the population in *every* aspect of their interaction;
2.  The researcher must travel through numerous layers of participation from a passive observation and participation at the outset, to extensive participation and becoming one of the population, not only in behavior but in a cognitive understanding of that cultural universe (see Keesing 1970 and Lehman 1985 for a more complete discussion of cognitive and behavioral levels of understanding);
3.  The stay in the field is extended for a lengthy period of time (in one study my research extended over a period of three years; the second study, 24 months), which obviously gives the researcher control over social fluctuations in interaction that occur infrequently and allows a more stable and complete picture of that population to emerge (see Ellen 1984; Sanjek 1990; Stocking 1983; Foster et al. 1979; Smith and Kornblum 1989; Kottack 1983);
4.  Observation becomes integrated within the participation; in other words, intensive participation is at once participation and observation;
5.  Interaction forms an important part of validation (this suggests adherence to the competence theory of cognitive science).

Data acquisition is handled in a way that one of the population studied would acquire these data, as in learning about how one should act and understand cultural experience, as if just entering the population, moving through "deeper" and "deeper" levels of experience. This is in direct contrast to the process of negotiation and interpretation and shared meaning advocated by interpretive anthropology; interpretation distances one from the levels of cultural experience "experienced" by the native. The voice of the participant *is* the voice of the native (see Rose 1987 for a description of fieldwork that was complete immersion into a black southside Philadelphia neighborhood by a white researcher). Reflection, in this light, does not produce a middle ground where the cognitive worlds of the researcher and native meet to form a created (or a reality that is neither one nor the other) interpreted reality. Instead reflection becomes internal; the researcher experiences the cultural reality of the native. In fact, this process is so complete that the researcher's reflection leads to an identical worldview to that of the native (obviously, individual variation creates a range of cultural experience available to the native; see Keesing 1970 for a more complete discussion). Thus, the experiences of the participant are devoid of levels of interpretation, negotiation, or narrative dialogue. One literally assumes, interacts, and understands the social identities, statuses, and roles of the actors within that population. Representations of the ethnographer's experience can then stand as an accurate cognitive map of cultural reality or cultural truths.

Bowlin and Stromberg (1997) argue that representations derived by ethnographers hinge on the true beliefs of those studied. As any ethnographers worth their salt know, there are collisions of true beliefs between studier and studied. Beyond this collision, leading to the age-old problem of how much of a cultural relativist an anthropologist should be, however, is a more pressing problem for theory construction: are there any universally true beliefs? They suggest an epistemological humility based on common sense; true beliefs are based on reasons that justify their existence as beliefs and, instead of being intractable, are relative and situated in the current surrounding environment. "And since what we have good reason to believe today may turn out to be false tomorrow, all that we believe must be considered revisable, even the most certain truths" (Bowlin and Stromberg 1997: 129).

Good reasons, then, become the best "path" to truth discovery, but since good reasons ultimately derive from the human mind, the "path" may not always lead to the mountaintop. In essence, even group members may not hold beliefs that are true but, instead, cherish mistaken false beliefs whose existence is based on, at least to them, very good reasons. Thus, truth is grounded in reason, and an ethnographer must be humble enough to give into the fact that others' reasons may "track" the truth better than his or her beliefs. "At the heart of ethnographic inquiry is a desire for truth: the truth about what others think and feel and do, the truth about the reasons that justify their thoughts and actions, and the truth about our relations with them" (Bowlin and Stromberg 1997: 130).

As I traveled deeper and deeper in acquiring cultural knowledge of the athletes, as I literally became one, representations of cultural reality became, instead, truth, fueled by the same "good" reasons of my counterparts. Yet, for representations to become truths, the good or "false" reasons for holding truths had to be more than explained or described; language can describe but fail to carry "meaning" if the reasons that undergird the cultural system are not experienced by both the sender and the receiver. However, if experience of physical and social actions, including language, is experienced by the ethnographer for an extended period of time in an intensive manner, then meaning is not a quest but is *lived*.

Ellen (1984) suggests that participant-observation becomes a "theory of its *cognitive* availability through participation in the construction of its meaning, which implies a research procedure in which the notion of participation in the subject's activities replaces the notion of their simple observation as the main data yielding technique" (1984: 29; emphasis added).

> In my field study of college sprinters, immersion into that population was involved and comprehensive. From that day [the first day of the fall season, 1986], and for over three years, I missed only four practices. Every day I was a willing participant, taking part in all the workouts and competing in most of the meets (I competed unattached as all of my four year college eligibility had long disappeared) It was not long before I was accepted as part of the workout. They [the sprinters] soon realized I was undergoing as much pain and effort as they were. They accepted my presence and did not exclude me from conversation, activities, or being considered part of the "team." Soon I became one of them, thinking, talking and behaving like a sprinter. (Sands 1995: 10)

As I argued earlier, understanding (meaning) is arrived at through active participation, not through observation. This contradicts the tenets of empirical positivism. "Such a procedure defies the role of the researcher, not as that of participant-observer but of observing participant, and it consciously eliminates the distinction between the observer and the observed phenomenon and this radically departs from the scientific attitude of the positivistic paradigm" (Ellen 1984: 29).

Yet, as suggested before, the data derived from active participation are the cognitive orderings of social identities and their respective relationships and statuses within that population. What is experienced as a participant becomes the cognitive understanding of how the patterns and arrangements within social interaction are formed but, more importantly, how those cognitive patterns coalesce into roles.

> My positions assumed within the team (sprinter, older sprinter--I turned thirty the first year of my research on sprinters--teammate, and roomate-- lived with two of the sprinters for two years) were no different than positions shared by other sprinters. In other words, many of the positions I filled were not dependent on my unique filling of those positions. The impact of my individual personality (that of older and more educated, not to forget researcher) was lessened considerably by those who filled similar positions on the team. (Sands 1995: 10)

For my ethnography of junior college football, participation was complete. At age 38 and a professor of anthropology, I became a member of the Santa Barbara City College football team. To do so, I had to become a student/athlete. I took 12 units a semester for four consecutive semesters, participating not only in the in-season practices and games and off-season spring and summer workouts but also as a student. The length and depth of fieldwork acted to slow down and enrich the process of accessing the cultural reality of the players.

> One *must* actively experience everything and experience was best translated using a shotgun approach, experience and behavior were caught in a snapshot, frozen by he flash and the field research becomes an immensely long roll of film. It was an exhaustive and emotionally draining process--you had to purposely lose the identity of anthropologist and become for all practical purposes, one of the boys. It was like making a feature length film, but you didn't direct it, you just lived the story-line. (Sands n.d.)

For a model of this type of method, I borrowed from journalism and Hunter S. Thompson. "Early on, Thompson tested the limits of journalism, deciding on intense participation and an overthrow of conventionality. To report on life was an exercise in stretching the bounds of normalcy. 'Gonzo journalism' is based on William Faulkner's idea that the best fiction is far more true than any kind of journalism," said Thompson (in Sands n.d.).

Thompson's classic work on the 1972 presidential campaign was an intensely experienced, two-year journey, an ethnography of grassroots politics and politicians. "My idea," Thompson wrote, "was to provide a big fat notebook and record the whole thing as it happened then send in the notebook for publication without editing. The way I felt, the eye and mind of the journalist would be functioning as a camera" (in Sands n.d.).

In Thompson's quest for realism and the bottom line, he was part of the story because necessity dictated it. "True Gonzo reporting needs the talents of a master journalist, the eye of an artist/photographer and the heavy balls of an actor because the writer must be a participant in the scene," he said (in Sands n.d.).

In football, like other sports, social and sport action can be lightning-quick or crawl at the pace of a tortoise. Thompson's first work on the Hell's Angels (Thompson 1989) was also an in-depth look at the infamous outlaw culture; he lived, rode, and took part in rituals of manhood and membership with the bikers and reproduced a brutal look at life on the road. Although he did not dictate action, Thompson was ever-present and, similar to what I experienced, was treated with repetition of ritual and experience. Long-term participation allows second and third chances to access those moments. Intensive participation (Ellen refers to it as "total soaking") allows as close as possible access to cultural experience in long range fieldwork, removing the formal and informal barriers of researcher-informant. Thompson ultimately became closely associated with Sonny Barger, president of the Angels. As well, enduring the same physical and emotional pain of competition, rescheduling my life around track and football, and dealing with the same problems of intensive participation created for me a role similar to that of the athletes and allowed me the same view of cultural reality.

Form and content of such formal/cognitive data can be used to validate, predict, and model cultural behavior; this seems to support Sperber's notion of a theoretical anthropology, and the participation yielding such data becomes similar to his "descriptive comment" (see also LeVine 1984; Shweder and LeVine 1984).

Data that could be elicited from alternate field techniques, like interviews, life histories, and biographies, anecdotes, and stories, can also be ascertained through normal channels that are a part of identity relationships and the interaction between various identities within a population. The participant can assume a series of positions within that population that a newcomer would develop. Instead of producing an artificial environment of forced interaction, the participant, through the opening of "experiential doors," is exposed to information about the members of that population, their background, emotions, and perceptions, by asking questions similar to those the network would ask about the cultural experience associated with the category (in this case, collegiate sprinters).

The length of time that one spends in the field is instrumental in minimizing the "attitude" that Ellen perceives is created toward the participant and reduces the impact the researcher has on "shaping the social reality being studied" (Ellen 1984: 29). Interpretive anthropology, specifically, hermeneutics, argues that the relationship between researcher and informant/subject is crucial in shaping shared reality (see Harris 1983). In my case, the actual participation in practices and meets and games extended the period of fieldwork and seemed to control conscious or unconscious shaping of that social reality. I became, in the eyes and perceptions of sprinters and football players, similar to the dichotomy expressed by Ellen; instead of a sprinting anthropologist or football-playing anthropologist, I was first a sprinter or a football player, then a researcher; "the roles of the participant-observer and of the observing participant are not simply mirror images of one another" (Ellen 1984: 29).

In this case, that seems to be an understatement; the latter connotes a cognitive alignment with the native, while the former introduces the added problems of cultural transmission, translation, and interpretation. Translation and interpretation not only act as a filter between researcher and native but actively corrode the cognitive alignment that this method seeks (interpretation, in this sense, can be thought of as a misalignment between researcher and the native's "cultural grammar," between the cognitive view and the actual observation of interaction).

The "dialogue" that is an essential feature of interpretive anthropology becomes a methodological hindrance to establishing a cultural reality that is "real" to the researcher *and* those studied. While this form of participation necessitates an almost virtual cognitive realignment of the participant/ethnographer, interpretive ethnography moves in the other direction, distancing the researcher from understanding the cultural experience from the "native's point of view." Negotiation with dialogue and interpretive reflection introduce an added dimension not part of the "praxis of the population" (Ellen 1984: 29).

## INTENSIVE PARTICIPATION--THE SCOPE

This form of intensive, experiential participation is best utilized within a small population and over an extended period of time. It is imperative that the researcher establish or, in a sense, create a series of positions that are subsumed into the network and that make up that cultural category. It is also important that the interactions that constitute the corresponding relationships in which the researcher becomes a part have an established sequential history and a future. The researcher must be seen as one who participates and will continue to participate within that network in order to facilitate the cultural bonding that exists between group members and, in turn, aid the process of moving from level to level in cultural experience. At the same time, the researcher, being a participating member of that group, becomes, in essence, an informant who can use experience to validate or "check out" the experiences provided by the other members of that group. In this case, the researcher represents an added dimension of validation not available to traditional participant-observation. What occurs is that the researcher experiences the duality of cognitive and behavioral spheres within the cultural (variation between individuals is within the cultural or populational "limits" of the "cultural grammar" (see Sands 1991, 1995--cognitive precepts and sequences of behavior are not only observed but experienced).

The researcher continues to be a part of the process of validation during fieldwork and analysis after leaving the field. Shokeid's (1997) ethnographic experience of a gay Jewish synagogue did not end at the culmination of fieldwork but entered a more intense introspection and analysis during the two years he prepared his monograph. In a critique of Shokeid's collaborative method, Esther Newton believes this type of research is needed; it diminishes power differentials between anthropologist and those studied and humbles the "buccaneering anthropologist" (Nussbaum 1998: 56). However, there are dangers in doing ethnography by committee. "I don't think that works, that kind of nonhierarchical thing. I want to hear a point of view! I want an analysis of the data! Someone has to pick up the reins and get the Pony Express going. Then it's your responsibility and your glory" (Newton in Nussbaum 1998: 56). In both studies, I continually allowed and, even more so, actively sought out sprinters and football players, to read and reread field notes and passages of representations of cultural reality and suggest a reordering of material, if need be.

During the three years of my track study, "I was constantly checking and rechecking with sprinters about what I was experiencing and continoulsy took part in group interactions to insure what I was experiencing and perceiving was cognitively and behaviorally 'in tune' with the other sprinters" (Sands 1995: 11). "To the extent that the anthropologist's labor carries authority in representing another reality, it must also stand the test of its subjects. Can they identify themselves in the ethnographic hall of mirrors, as distorted as that image might be in their own eyes? This is probably a far more crucial test of the reliability, morality, and usefulness of our work" (Shokeid 1997: 631).

Like Shokeid, I encouraged sprinters and football players to read and reread notes and, after taking life histories, had those gone over as well. "In this way I was actually challenging them to form and model their own perceptions of the social interaction and universe of the college sprinter" (Sands 1995: 11). The danger of running into what Shokeid encountered can be minimized by the anthropologist's being the last voice that produces the final product.

## WHOSE VOICE, ANYWAY?

Where the roles of researcher, observer, participant, informant, and group member come together is in the "text." Being a participant and being a group member are not synonymous; to participate in social and physical action is one thing, and to actively become involved in the identity of the "culture" is far more encompassing and far more time-consuming (see Sands 1995 for a discussion of identity and roles in group interaction). The body of knowledge, at least in my two studies, was presented, in part, in a linear journey of discovery; fieldwork, indeed, is measured not only in amount of knowledge gained or accessed but in the time one is present in the population. Knowledge of the culture cannot be gleaned from an office on a campus or through the Internet; it can be gained only by physically being there. The more time spent in research/experience, the more that chance of discovery is possible.

The main "voice" of the ethnographies is mine, yet the traditional "me as source, or I the expert" authoritative voice--objective, removed, and concise--is absent. Instead, the voice of the experience blends multiple personalities and those of the teams but retains a definitive personality to anchor the journey of discovery.

Shokeid raises a number of questions dealing with ethnographic authority and collaboration of informants. In support of Shokeid's collaboration with multiple informants, he leans on W. F. Whyte's 50-plus years of ethnographic experience by reasking the questions, "Whose voice does the researcher use when reporting results that were collectively generated? and "Can the researcher ever represent anyone but the ethnographer?" (in Shokeid 1997: 637).

To Whyte and Shokeid, the second query is more than a possibility; it is just good ethnography, a matter of actively involving those being studied. To the first question, which is just as crucial to contemporary ethnography, the answer is, indeed, problematic. The research experience gives rise to multiple viewpoints, more than occasionally competing in authority and information; mix in the ethnographer, and one is left, on the surface, with a choir of voices singing a selection with no harmony. It is obvious that this process of reducing the field experience to a text is crucial to the authenticity of the experience and the resultant description.

Yet quieting the choir to a solo and producing an authentic voice are more than problematic; they border on impossible. To avoid the postmodern method of shared narrative and interpretation by the ethnographer, which does meld disparate voices but produces little representation of the "native," I wanted to reproduce what it felt like to be an athlete, the types of social interactions that took place in a team, the dynamics of the athlete-coach relationship, the joy and pain of competing--all these factors combined to make up the identity of a football player or a sprinter. Observation, passive participation, and interpretation would not replicate or give me the experience of living those features, and the voice that emanated from the experience was through the "eyes of a native" from a "native."

Whyte's second question begs the process; my ethnographic experience suggests that in addition to the material, the "data" I gathered from my "teammates," the ethnographic voice was, indeed, from more than one person, from multiple viewpoints, and in many cases it was from one person with multiple viewpoints, myself.

Shokeid suggests that the practice of writing the ethnography to more than one audience is a way to deal with this second question, which will always confront and confound the ethnographer. Success is not just publication through peer review but, as well, through the acceptance of the work in nonacademic readers, especially the culture that was written about. "The emergence of such new readers, including those from the 'colonized object of study,' may also effect change within the publishing world.as a new audience of readers develop, publishers will increasingly take their new customers' special sensitivities into account. This will inevitably affect the ethnographic project" (Shokeid 1997: 638).

In the end however, as fieldwork becomes less of an ivory tower adventure, collaboration becomes more of a necessity. The final product has to come from one pen. "But when it comes down to writing the final report, the anthropologist's collaboration must come to an end: No matter how many caveats and cautions spice the stew of a modern ethnography, no matter how many viewpoints are mingled together in the final dish, only one hand actually stirs the pot" (Nussbaum 1998: 53).


## A SUCCESSFUL ETHNOGRAPHY: SOMEWHERE BETWEEN A DESCRIPTION AND AN AUTOBIOGRAPHY

My fieldwork centered around the desire to uncover the contemporary mechanics of identity attribution (see Sands 1991, 1995). How does one ascribe identity to oneself and others, and are features of race and ethnicity being replaced by a more inclusive, less traditional means of self-determination, such as occupation, social group membership, common interest groups, sport, and so on. Using sports that have a high degree of racial and ethnic diversity, do athletes see themselves and other athletes as sprinters or football players before any other identity, and is this attribution of "athlete" all-encompassing or contextual?

Identity is based on accessing and controlling social knowledge. I postulated the existence of knowledge domains, cognitive structures that "house" pertinent sensory, social, and cultural information concerning an identity such as "sprinter" or "junior college football player." The accessing of this "domain" and the exchange of features within the domain between identity or group members not only operate to define a particular identity to group members and nonmembers but also act as a continuing litmus test for who is and who is not considered a group member.

To this end, I constructed a formal model of cultural identity incorporating features of cognitive anthropology, cultural grammar (syntax and rules that govern the "grammar"), cultural competence, mental and cultural universals, and linguistic analogy. As I tapped into the knowledge domain of a sprinter, I learned what it took to be a sprinter.

> As I was accessing that I suggest that a cognitive domain can be thought of as an individual culture, accessed in response to interaction between identities. And herein lies the key: I did not access or retrieve that knowledge of sprinter from books or running practices by myself. The [cultural knowledge] domain of sprinters is accessed through the interaction of individuals in a cultural identity and this knowledge is represented in how the individuals perceive the content of that particular identity. Knowledge only becomes knowledge through the relations of cultural identities and this knowledge is made available though universal cognitive rules that are expressed in the order and arrangement of positions within an identity. Ultimately we can see how our mind works in the way we order and arrange our social relations through the process and mechanics of identity. (Sands 1995: 20)

Using the recent work on artificial intelligence and cognitive science in many fields of the social sciences, I was able to construct a formal model and then applied this model to the data acquired from my ethnographic research, but just as important to my experience of doing ethnography were assuming and interacting through the more intimate roles of athlete, group or team member, competitor, informant, and, finally, anthropologist. In these two studies, observation and participation were one and the same. "With this assumption [model construction and testing] we have the second part of ethnographic research, advocated by Malinowski, using the descriptions [and experience] of a culture to help prove or disprove more general models of human behavior" (Sands 1995: 20).

Thus, in the end, the features of interpretive ethnography would have not only delivered the wrong kind of data but framed the entire ethnographic process in a way that would have not allowed for the right kind of data. Dauber (1997) argues that in the ethnographic process, "good" data are information that is not only collected but managed properly. Citing Malinowski's scientific preoccupation with analysis, Dauber argues that ethnographic authority derives not only from voice but from analysis.

> The past two decades have seen a flood of work on the construction in anthropological texts of ethnographic authority. These critiques have produced valuable insights, but they fail to account fully for the way in which ethnographers overcome the real weakness imposed by the exigencies of fieldwork--including ignorance, temporary status and the overwhelming mass of information it is necessary to supplement a focus

on literary/charismatic authority with an examination of the bureaucratic practices--among them filing, cross-referencing and drawing diagrams. These practices have been overlooked in literary critiques of ethnography, yet they are at the heart of the ethnographer's ability to produce knowledge that can compel assent not simply from ignorant outsiders but also from the "natives" themselves. (Dauber 1997: 75)

These descriptive and analytical measures propel an ethnographic experience shaped by multiple voices and a shared reflective narrative into a tool for potential comparative and ultimately theoretical construction and/or validation. "Texts are a peculiar and potent kind of object. Once produced, they can be transported, juxtaposed with other texts, sorted in a way that objects outside this 'paper world' cannot" (Dauber 1997: 76).

Indeed, the end result of an ethnographic experience is a text, but stopping short of an anthropologist's being able to use that text for further comparative analysis is like building a bridge to span a river and completing only the skeleton, never laying the road or path allowing passage from one side to the other. The text provides that path or road connecting riverbanks or studies done separated by time and/or space. Situating the ethnographer in the center of daily and event activity allows for a more richly and descriptive text--not to mention, a more entertaining one--and then allows the reader of that text to follow and even step inside the shoes of the ethnographer as the text takes him or her further into the "webs of cultural significance" (Geertz 1973) of that population. Interpretation, by reader and ethnographer alike, falls by the wayside as the text lays bare lived experience.

The value of the text does not solely lie in its descriptive power but finds strength in the use of that text as a representation of cultural reality. As much as the application of science, scientism, and method to the fields of social sciences has come under increasingly hostile "fire" from the ranks of the postmodernists and even some positivists, texts become the vehicle for the validation of the scientific method. Science tests reality; it does not create reality. A cognitive rendering of identity attribution by athletes was posited by my two studies, one that was "discovered" by becoming an athlete. Simply put, 12 sprinters and 90 football players saw the expression of their identity in the sport they participated in; for the length of practice and social interaction both on and off the track/field, meets, and games, these athletes were first sprinters and football players before other facets of identity, race, ethnicity, student, and so on. They were football players to themselves, to each other, to coaches, girlfriends, parents, even teachers. Yet, the model also suggests that context forms the basis for selecting identity--when they stop being football players, at the end of the day, on a date, when their playing season ends, when their career ceases, other, more pertinent identities surface and manifest--and this context becomes the target for testing such a model. It is the text (s) that delivers the fuel for the positivistic testing engine.

## NOTES

I would like to thank Dr. F. K. Lehman for his comments on the manuscript.

1. Tom Gatewood (in *Directions in Cognitive Anthropology*, edited by Janet Doughtery, Champaign: University of Illinois Press, 1985) advanced a similar position concerning participation, that such an activity is a rich source of data about what one needs to know cognitively to behave in an orderly fashion.

## REFERENCES

Aunger, Robert. "On Ethnography: Storytelling or Science?" *Current Anthropology* 36, no. 1 (1996): 97-127.

Blumer, Herbert. "Society as Symbolic Interaction" In *Symbolic Interactionism*, edited by Herbert Blumer. Englewood Cliffs, NJ: Prentice-Hall, 1969.

Bowlin, John R., and Peter G. Stromberg. "Representation and Reality in the Study of Culture." *American Anthropologist* 99, no.1 (1997): 123-34.

Bruner, Edward, (ed.) *Text, Play and Story*. Washington, DC: American Ethnological Society, 1984.

Clifford, James, and George Marcus. *Writing Culture: The Poetics and Politics of Ethnography*. Berkeley: University of California Press, 1986.

Dauber, Kenneth. "Bureaucratizing the Ethnographer's Magic." *Current Anthropology* 16, no. 1 (1995): 75-102.

Dobbert, Marion. *Ethnographic Research*. New York: Praeger, 1982.

Ellen, Roy F. *Ethnographic Research: A Guide to General Conduct*. London: Academic Press, 1984.

Farndon, Richard. *Localizing Strategies: Regional Traditions of Ethnographic Writings*. Washington, DC: Smithsonian Institutional Press, 1990

Foster, George, et al. *Long Term Field Research in Social Anthropology*. New York: Academic Press, 1979.

Geertz, Clifford. *The Interpretation of Cultures*. New York: Basic Books, 1973.

_____. *After the Fact: Two Countries, Four Decades, One Anthropologist*. Cambridge: Harvard University Press, 1995.

Gonzalez, Roberto J., Laura Nadar, and C. Jay Ou. "Between Two Poles: Bronislaw Malinowski, Ludwik Fleck, and the Anthropology of Science." *Current Anthropology* 36, no. 5 (1995): 866-869.

Goodenough, Ward. *Description and Comparison in Cultural Anthropology*. Chicago: Aldine, 1970.

Gottlieb, Alma. "Beyond the Lonely Anthropologist: Collaboration in Research and Writing." *American Anthropologist,* 97 no. 1 (1995): 21-24.

Harris, Marvin. "Comment to Tim O'Meara." *Current Anthropology* 38, no. 3 (1997): 410-415.

Keesing, Roger. "Towards a Model of Role Analysis." In *Handbook of Method in Cultural Anthropology,* edited by Raoul Narroll and M. Cohen. New York: Columbia University Press, 1970.

Kottack, Conrad. *Cultural Anthropology*. New York: Random House, 1982.

Lehman, F. K. "Cognition and Computation: On Being Sufficiently Abstract." In *Directions in Cognitive Anthropology,* edited by Janet Doughtery. Champaign: University of Illinois Press, 1985.

LeVine, Robert A. "Properties of Culture: An Ethnographic." In *CultureTheory: Essays on Mind, Self and Emotion,* edited by Schweder and LeVine. Cambridge: Cambridge University Press, 1984.

Malinowski, Bronislaw. *Argonauts of the Western Pacific.*

Marcus, George, and Michael J. Fisher. *Anthropology as Cultural Critique.* Chicago: University of Chicago Press, 1986.

Mead, Margaret. *Coming of Age in Samoa.* New York: William Morrow, 1928.

Nussbaum, Emily. "Return of the Natives." *Linguafranca* 8, no. 1 (1998): 53-56.

O'Meara, Tim. "Causation and the Struggle for a Science of Culture." *Current Anthropology* 38, no. 3 (1997): 399-415.

Radcliffe-Brown, A. R. *The Adaman Islanders.* New York: Free Press, 1964.

Roscoe, Paul B. "The Perils of 'Positivism' in Cultural Anthropology." *American Anthropologist* 97, no. 3 (1995): 492-504.

Rose, Dan. *Black American Street Life: South Philadelphia 1969-1971.* Philadelphia: University of Pennsylvania Press,1987.

Sands, Robert R. *"An Ethnography of Black Collegiate Sprinters: A Formal Model of Cultural Identity and the Identity Complex. "* Ph.D. diss., Department of Anthropology, University of Illinois, 1991.

_____.*Gutcheck! : An Anthropologist's Wild Ride into the Heart of College Football,* n.d.

_____.*Instant Acceleration: Living in the Fast Lane. A Cultural Identity of Speed.* Lanham, MD: University Press of America, 1995.

Sanjek, Roger. *Fieldnotes.* Ithaca, NY: Cornell University Press, 1990.

Shokeid, Moshe. "Negotiating Multiple Viewpoints: The Cook, the Native, the Publisher, and the Ethnographic Text." *Current Anthropology* 38, no. 4 (1997): 631-45.

Smith, Carolyn, and William Kornblum. *In the Field: Readings on the Field Research Experience.* New York: Praeger, 1989.

Sperber, Dan. *On Anthropological Knowledge.* Cambridge: Cambridge University Press, 1985.

Spradley, James. *Culture and Cognition: Rules, Maps and Plans.* San Francisco: Chandler, 1972.

Spradley, James, and David W. McCurdy. *The Cultural Experience: Ethnography in Complex Society.* Chicago: Science Research Associates, 1980.

Stocking, George. *Observers Observed.* Madison: University of Wisconsin Press, 1983.

Thompson, Hunter S. *Hell's Angels: A Strange and Terrible Saga.* New York: Ballantine Books, 1989.

_____. *Fear and Loathing on the Campaign Trail.* New York: Warner Books, 1992.

Werner, Oswald, and Mark Schoepfle. *Systematic Fieldwork: Foundations of Ethnography and Interviewing.* Newbury Park, CA: Sage, 1988.

Whyte, William F. "Encounters with Participatory Action Research." *Qualitative Sociology* 18 (1995): 289-300.

# *chapter 3*

# Understanding Cultural Performance:
# Trobriand Cricket

## *Sally Ann Ness*

The film *Trobriand Cricket: An Ingenious Response to Colonialism* was made in 1973 by anthropologist Jerry W. Leach and filmmaker Gary Kildea. As the interpretive camp in anthropology grows, and as interest in the way different peoples *perform* their culture increases, the importance of film as a tool in anthropological education expands as well. Film offers the sort of text most appropriate for the study of cultural performance; however, the use of film in anthropology generally fails to develop its full potential. A major impediment to the use of available ethnographic films is the lack of supplementary materials. "The key to understanding an ethnographic film, or gaining information from it," according to Karl G. Heider, "is not just repeated viewings but the availability of written materials which can fill in what the film leaves ambiguous" (Heider 1976: 130). Ideally, all films used in connection with anthropology would be accompanied by such supplementary materials.

Movement analysis focuses on some of the visible aspects of ethnographic film that are often left unrecognized in the film narrative, resulting in a more profound ethnological appreciation of its contents. The appreciation is *ethnological* as opposed to *ethnographic* because the analysis allows the description of a particular cultural performance--an ethnographic account--to be compared to those of other performances in other cultures for the purpose of generalizing about human nature and human culture. Movement analysis is especially valuable for films such as *Trobriand Cricket* that focus intentionally on cultural performance.

*Trobriand Cricket* was praised in *American Anthropologist* as a film of "exceptional vitality and power," a film that made a "significant anthropological contribution" (Weiner 1977: 506). David MacDougall, too, in "Ethnographic Film: Failure and Promise," cited *Trobriand Cricket* as an example of illustrative ethnographic film at its best, providing an analysis of behavioral patterns evident in a formalized event" (MacDougall 1978: 413). S. J. Tambiah called it a "marvelous film" and used the contents of the film to show the value of Levi- Strauss' ideas about the relationship of ritual to play (Tambiah 1979: 118). *Trobriand Cricket* has generally been regarded as one of the finest examples of ethnographic film.

Also important is the particular subject matter of the film. Several anthropologists at the University of Washington who have used the film in their anthropological classes agree that it is one of the only films available that focus on the issue of culture contact, and it is especially valuable as a teaching tool for that reason (Ottenberg 1986; Dumont 1986; Harrell 1986). *Trobriand Cricket* is seen as a film that reveals the genius of the Trobriand culture in transforming a sporting event, British cricket, into a Trobriand ritual of exchange (Harell 1986). The particular focus of the film is especially advantageous because games create worlds unto themselves. The Trobriandization" of cricket, then, allows a more complete or holistic glimpse of the Trobriand cultural if identity than might be available in almost any other context (Ottenberg 1986). The film was found to be especially useful with respect to teaching the anthropology of art because it provides clearly designed, symbolic forms. Among them are visual metaphors--for example, performances when men, in the dancing that takes place during the cricket game, become airplanes. These metaphors serve as excellent subjects for class discussions about the artistic beliefs and practices of a given culture (Ottenberg 1986).

The consensus among anthropologists concerning *Trobriand Cricket*, then, is that it is a documentary film of special value for the study of culture. It is one not to be overlooked by those who are concerned with the anthropology of art, sport, ritual, identity, or performance--which intersects with all the other branches. As such, *Trobriand Cricket* deserves critical examination, so that its full potential as a teaching tool and as an anthropological text can be realized.

*Trobriand Cricket* has an advantage over many ethnographic films because of the availability of supplementary materials. It focuses on the culture about which Malinowski's anthropological classic *Argonauts of the Western Pacific* (1922) was written. However, few supplementary materials are available that pertain directly to the film itself. Aside from the review published in *American Anthropologist* (Weiner 1977: 506-507) and another published in the *Royal Anthropological Institute Newsletter* (Leach 1975: 6), no written materials are available concerning the film.

Heider identifies two types of necessary supplementary information: (1) contextual information about the historical and contemporary background of the film's contents and (2) visually relevant information that explains or clarifies action presented in the film footage, either from the native's point of view or from the anthropologist's point of view (Heider 1976: 70, 73). In the case of *Trobriand Cricket*, the film narrative is devoted primarily to information of the first type, concerning itself mainly with the historical context of the cricket game in the Trobriands. The history of the early mission games, the stories behind various transformations of the game over the years, and the sources of inspiration for various dances and costumes constitute a large part of the film's narration. Contemporary context is also given some attention when background information relating to the current social setting of the games and their consequences in the communities involved are discussed.

Visually relevant information is presented almost entirely from the native informant's point of view. Interviews with informants explain the action, emphasizing the essential changes made in playing the game and their respective meanings. They discuss the reasons for making changes in batting and ball-pitching style, for example, as well as reasons behind changes made in scoring and the addition of various dances during breaks in the action.

What is given little attention is the anthropologist's ethnological analysis of the action. Instead, the filmmaker attempts to let the action "speak for itself." Apart from the informants' comments, there are relatively few observations made about the visual contents of the film. The omission of this sort of information need not be seen as a shortcoming of the film. Indeed, it may more likely be seen as an asset, since it strengthens the film's visual impact and avoids overloading the viewer with narration. The absence of visually relevant narrative, in fact, may be one reason for the film's enduring popularity, since the lack of a specific analytical perspective allows viewers of the film to act later as analysts. The absence of narration necessitates its presentation elsewhere, because this sort of information is essential for an anthropological understanding of the film.

*Trobriand Cricket*, however, need not be a film that concerns itself *only* with Papua New Guinea and British colonialism. As anthropologists who have used *Trobriand Cricket* point out, this film makes a visual statement about the inventiveness of human adaption, about the capacity of human groups to distinguish themselves from others. It is a film directly addressing the subject of ethnic identity and depicting the use of ethnic markers.

In order to address these issues in relation to the film, further narrative focusing on how the action in the film relates to human action in all its innovative diversity is needed. One method that is uniquely suited to this task is Laban movement analysis (LMA). The LMA system focuses on the form, rhythm, organization, and sequencing of the performance of movement (see Davis 1979: 182). Human action thus appears as an unfolding structural process, as opposed to a mode of being functionally productive per se.

LMA differs from other methods of analyzing nonverbal behavior in both its complexity and its flexibility with respect to macro- and microbehavioral analysis. Observations are always made with respect to three general aspects of movement: (1) how the body (which may be viewed either literally, as an individual's physical body, or figuratively, as a group's, a society's, or a culture's collective "body") as a system of body parts is organized in movement; (2) how space is made visible both through the body's changing shape and through the external trace forms (the outlined pathways) created by the movement; and (3) how the energy inspiring the movement manifests itself in various dynamic characteristics and sequences. LMA can be used to record and analyze the subtle changes in movement during short spans of time, as do microbehavioral analysts such as Ray Birdwhistle (1970), William S. Condon (1982), Albert E. Scheflen (1982), and Adam Kendon (1982;

also see Davis 1982). It can also be used to record and analyze grosser forms of movement, capturing in a single phrase, for example, the style of a political uprising in the Philippines, the movement of economic reform in China, or the major features of a cultural dance style.

The following analysis focuses on the visual contents of *Trobriand Cricket* from a movement analyst's perspective, examining what the film shows visually but does not recognize in words. The analysis presented here cannot even begin to approach completeness; only a few of the most outstanding movement characteristics are reported and discussed in relation to the film narrative. Although I cannot give an exhaustive survey of the movement presented in *Trobriand Cricket* here, I can suggest what sort of insights may be gained from movement analysis and the value of those insights in bringing out the larger anthropological significance of an ethnographic film.

The cultural identity of the Trobrianders emerges in the contrast between Trobriand and British cricket play. The film narrative says only that the British sport is "known for its slow pace"; also given is some information about how the body is used, such as underarm throwing style and several rules relating to running, throwing, and batting. The film, however, relies mainly on footage of British games to establish the basis of comparison with Trobriand cricket style, and several of the main features of performance shown in this footage are left undefined. For example, one aspect of the game's movement left completely unaddressed is spatial form: the trace forms that are revealed in the play of each style and their respective relationships to both the dynamic quality of the game's performance and the players' bodily situations.

The movement characteristics of fielding are particularly important. While batting, players operate in relatively similar ways in both Trobriand and British cricket styles. However, the fielding strategies, the ways of *coping with*, as opposed to *producing,* the central actions of the game--the hit and run--differ in extreme. The cultural identity of the Trobrianders becomes visible in a particular movement context of forming a world of people--a team on a field--that can deal effectively with the act of an individual aggressor. In designing a group-oriented fielding strategy for both defeating the efforts of an opposing team member and celebrating the success of that defeat, the Trobrianders create a model of the culture's tradition of adaptive survival.

As the film clips of British cricket show, the British fielding team sets itself up to receive hit balls in terms of clearly defined linear relationships that form various rectangular and triangular configurations among players. The nature of the defense is geometric in the sense that the invasion of the ball into the field is dealt with through a system of points, lines, surfaces, and planes. The appearance of this network on the playing field reveals a distinctive mentality of preparedness--a collective posture of controlled anticipation. These lines by their very nature as lines exist within a huge "vacant" spatial area, the field itself. The bird's-eye shots of British cricket presented in the film convey the idea that the presence of large, open areas around and among the players is a definitive feature of the British game. The fielders appear as a small set of dots scattered--though not scattered randomly--over a huge, empty domain.

Careful positioning of the players creates a clear set of spatial relationship or tensions on the field, which is organized in such a way as to make the space that is not "taken up" by or between players appear as "open areas." The players act as nodes maintaining the vertices of various intersections. Their "places" on the field-- places that are imaginary insofar as the given constraints of the field are concerned-- become significant as positions that hold constant a linear construct. The bodies of the individual players serve as pins planted in the field, pins that track down the lines of tension that do not change in direction or in size throughout the game.

The clear relationships in space established among the players themselves and the relationship established between the team and the field, then, have a distinctive character that places constraints upon the dynamics that a British cricket match might possibly develop. When a ball is hit into this network, the lines between the fielders are temporarily distorted or even severed while someone "leaves his place" to field the ball. The importance of the players' relative positions is demonstrated in the film when a clip is shown of a fielding team's celebrating an "out" suffered by the opposing team, in this case an out that occurred when a player struck out, missing the ball for his last allotted time. The players on the fielding team, expressing their sense of victory, jumped, as one body, into the air, extending their arms high over their heads, in a simultaneous collective action of extreme extension. However, they did not leave their positions on the field for a moment to manifest their collective response more fully. Instead, they remained a scattered bunch, holding down the network of linear tensions that stabilized the field. While the individuals transformed themselves in their jubilation, the world of the cricket field not only remained intact but also kept the same shape and the same size. The importance of maintaining a complex spatial configuration over a constant area prevailed.

There is, then, an interplay between the space, the dynamics of play, and the bodily actions of the players in British cricket that develops from the geometric world created by the fielding team. The staid character of the game (see Weiner 1977: 506) results from this interplay, as does the game's "slow pace."

The Trobriand fielding style, in contrast, does not create a world in which "empty" space is assigned a constant volume that is determined by measured positioning. One of the most outstanding features of the Trobriand style, which is often brought out in discussion of the film, is the continual growing and shrinking of the collective form, the field created by the fielding team. This repeated collection and dispersal of the players that serves to condense and expand the activity field occur on the occasion of every out. During a single game, the field may grow and shrink more than 100 times--about every two minutes for a period of four hours or more.

A central, dense point governs the spatial world created in the Trobriand game, in contrast to the British game, where a number of points on various edges or peripheries are held at a distance from the center of play. In the Trobriand style, a single locus exercises its influence on the entire team, drawing the players in for a show of strength and then releasing them to prepare for another engagement. The players do not operate as nodes describing vertices; instead, they work together to form a cluster of points, all responding to the center of the field much as filaments of iron will respond to a magnet when it is placed in their midst. The sense of balance conveyed in the Trobriand game is at once less stable and more organic than that manifest in the British game, while being no less abstract. It is a balance created through rhythm and change rather than through a stable configuration. Morever, the pattern of growing and shrinking is apparent at several levels of performance: at the subindividual (in the movement design of isolated body parts), individual, and collective levels.

The film is designed to highlight this movement pattern at the group level, presenting as its initial image a sense of the fielding team gathering for the celebration of an out. It makes no verbal comment, however, about this spatial pattern. Nevertheless, this pulsing spatial form that creates within itself a sense of process of transformable magnitudes, a responsiveness to the continual change in a certain gravitational field, is the key feature of the Trobriand game style. The pattern determines the relationship between play and dance as manifest in the game, a relationship that itself determines various rules of Trobriand cricket play and distinguishes it from British play.

The relationship between dynamic energy and spatial organization appears more closely bound in the Trobriand playing style than in the British. That is, the relationship between moving inward and moving outward is characterized by a distinctive qualitative pattern. The players collect in haste. The film shows them running toward the center of the field immediately upon an out. The gathering is followed by a show of force: the groups dance and chant, using synchronized body movements that are designed to be loud and strong. This display reaches its conclusion in a brief moment of confusion that is followed by a change in direction, when the group disperses, traveling outward. The rhythm, then, has both spatial and dynamic characteristics that are interrelated. Moving toward the dense center is associated with urgency and eventually with strength, while moving away is related to a loss of focus and release from the center point's magnetic pull. Interestingly, the same pattern appears at a microlevel in the step-style of the individual players as they perform their team dances. Steps are delivered toward the earth, toward gravity, in movements that begin in haste and gather force, climaxing in intensity at the moment of impact with ground: the feet then reverse their direction, although without clear spatial intent, exhibiting a quality of release.

What the film makes obvious, without giving it specific recognition, is the manner in which the phrasing of growing and shrinking--gathering and scattering-- dominates the Trobriand cricket game. Under the influence of this integrative phrasing pattern, the boundary between what is play and what is "secondary" activity contingent upon play appears to dissolve, changing fundamentally the definition of what can now be seen only marginally as a "game" in the competitive British sense. Profound differences that relate to the Trobriand process of winning the game--changes in scoring in terms of both rules for keeping score and also strategies for making scores--appear to spring directly from a more basic interest in continually re-creating and reinvesting the reversible pattern of collective contraction and expansion that goes on between playing and celebrating outs. For example, "slowing the play," as the film explains, is likely to bring angry reactions from the crowd and the players alike. The main effect of slowing the play is its retarding of the out sequences, thus affecting the rhythm of growing and shrinking which is dependent on the celebration of outs. The extension of a batter's time at bat, which might result in a better score, results in a time lag that belabors a more important issue: the repeated collection of the team for out celebrations and their dispersion for batting play. The efficiency of the batter is sacrificed to maintain the rhythm of the game. The world of the cricket match is a world that must respirate in order for action to acquire the meaning that holds the interest of all involved.

This performance characteristic is intimately related to one of the major functional changes instituted by the Trobrianders--their formalization of the designation of winner. As the film explains, the determination of the winner and the loser is made before the game begins. The host is destined to win, and the visiting team to lose. The rhythm of the Trobriand match, as manifest in the changing spatial configuration, is a function of the game's having become a predetermined form. The whole event is a formality, and the distinctive shaping and sizing of the formality take precedence over the win-lose indeterminacy so important to the British game. Playing is not a matter of winning but of conforming to a rhythmic pattern climaxed by the performance of dances at each out. Play merges with dance, becoming phases of the dominant performance unit: the phases of collection and dispersal. The repetition of these units and the creation of a series of phases constitute the real "subject" of Trobriand cricket.

The footage of the British and Trobriand cricket games shows that two very different worlds are created on the respective playing fields. The ability to outline geometric forms contrasts sharply in the British style with the ability to perpetuate a vibrant gravitational field in the Trobriand style. The British world is defined in terms of spatial design, set up as though dissociated from energy forces. The Trobriand world is defined in terms of fluctuating density that exercises its own influence upon the collective emotions of its inhabitants. The players' bodies in the British game distinguish themselves, one from another, in terms of the particular field position they assume, while the bodies of the Trobriand players contribute to a collectivity that does not identify distinctive, individual roles.

The construction of both of these worlds is closely related to the issue of winning, which is treated very differently in each cultural context. Winning is an open question in the British game, and as such it is given top priority insofar as decisions about how the action of the play develops. In the Trobriand game winning is a settled issue, a definitive statement made before the game begins. Therefore, winning does not determine strategies of action in the game. The differences between British and Trobriand cricket style reveal different models of organizing worlds full of people. How these respective models might operate in other domains of British and Trobriand life is open to question. The differences in the mentality of fielding, however, may well be the same differences that appear in such realms of activity as politics, economics, and religion.

One of the more misleading aspects of the *Trobriand Cricket* narrative is its emphasis on the imitative aspects of the dancing performed during the cricket matches. Resemblances between certain dances and the phenomena for which they are named take up most of the descriptive commentary. The Airplane Dance, the Rowing Dance, and the Seabird Dance are reported simply as the personification in dancing of these various subjects. Even in regard to dances that are not expressly mimetic, the focus of the commentary is on those imitative features of performance that link the dancing to other dances. In sum, the only way the narrative attempts to come to terms with the moment of the dances is through the notion of resemblance. This strategy is misleading. It conveys to the viewer the impression that abstract, nonimitative processes are not operating in the movement and are not significant features of the dance performance. The dances, however, do exhibit nonimitative processes that must be considered as indicators of cultural identity.

For example, one outstanding feature of the dances shown in *Trobriand Cricket*--a feature that serves as an integral part of all the imitative dances presented without being imitative itself--is the emphatic phrasing of individual action. This feature is apparent in the musical accenting of the team chants as well as the movement of the players while they dance.

Emphatic phrasing is a general type of movement patterning that occurs when a sequence of action is marked or accented at its end. The activity is performed with a final burst of energy serving as the main accent of the entire sequence. Activities such as hammering a nail or pounding a gavel to call a meeting back to order tend to manifest themselves in emphatic movement phrases. This type of phrasing has a character very different from that created, for example, by impulsive phrasing, which occurs when a sequence of activity is accented at its beginning. Emphatic phrasing "ends with a bang," and impulsive phrasing "starts with a bang." Many of the activities of a cricket game rely on impulsive phrasing. When a fielder makes a dash for a ball hit into his vicinity, for example, his retrieval of the ball is typically phrased impulsively. His initial burst of energy in response to the ball's movement is the main accent of his activity sequence.

While phrasing patterns are closely related to functional issues, they are not determined completely by them. The difference in batting style in British and Trobriand cricket is partly a matter of phrasing, even though the function of the movement is identical in both games. The British tend to swing the bat using an emphatic movement phrase, a sequence of rapid and subtle changes accented at the end of the swing. The Trobrianders, in contrast, use impulsive phrasing to swing the bat, accenting the beginning of the swing so intensely that the movement usually sweeps them off their feet. The function of the swing in both cases is to send the ball as far afield as possible. The choice of phrasing, however, reveals a different approach toward accomplishing this end.

The leg movements used in this imitative Airplane Dance and the arm movements of the imitative Rowing Dance, as well as the leg movements of the nonimitative PK Dance shown in *Trobriand Cricket* all exhibit emphatic phrasing, which serves no imitative function. That is, it does not serve to make the visual metaphors "I am an airplane" or "I am a seabird" more accurate in any way. Nevertheless, the phrasing characteristics are a pervasive and outstanding feature of the Trobriand dance style. Its presence, however, is completely ignored in the film's narrative, while imitative features are emphasized, even in regard to dances where they are of only minor significance.

The importance of emphatic phrasing becomes somewhat clearer at the level of group movement phrasing. As the film footage of entrance dances illustrates, emphatic phrasing is used to structure entire dance sequences that are performed by the teams as a preparation to assuming positions in the field at the start of the inning. These dances share a general organization sequence that begins by proceeding through a spatial figure encompassing the playing field and then staging the climax of the performance at its end with a "ritual charge"--as it is described in the film. The phrasing of the entire sequence "ends with a bang," a charging inward that places a final accent at the end of the performance.

This phrasing serves no functional purpose and is not imitative. Its very abstractness indicates that the patterning may have a very general and profound meaning in Trobriand life. The appearance of emphatic phrasing at the subindividual, individual, and group levels is important as an organizing feature of the dancing. It merits more attention than the more minor imitative relationships that are brought out in the film's narrative.

The bias toward descriptive commentary that focuses on imitative aspects of the dancing detracts somewhat from the film's overall instructiveness. The viewer ought not come away from the film with the idea that cricket match dancing is mostly about being like something else. The dancing may be concerned overtly with establishing a similarity through visual metaphors, but it is also something inventive, a form of celebration with abstract as well as concrete associations that are markers of cultural identity.

The analysis is not designed to answer all the questions about the meaning and function of the performance observed. It is designed to clarify perceptions of the performance process, revealing how action is patterned, sometimes at several levels. In regard to the formation of questions concerning function and meaning, then, LMA observations prove most valuable.

For example, the analysis of *Trobriand Cricket* raises several questions concerning the function and meaning that patterns observed in the cricket matches might acquire in other domains of activity. It would be useful to reexamine tensions that have existed in British and Trobriand political relations in terms of their respective performances on the cricket field. Is the organizing design of the Trobriand cricket match--the growing and shrinking spatial form--also an organizing metaphor in other domains of Trobriand life? Does a wife, for example, become a locus of power around which a family collects and disperses? Or does a husband serve in that capacity? Or is it at the level of village organization that chiefs gather and scatter whole families in continual patterns of concentration and dispersal? Or is it perhaps not an individual but a planted field that serves as a locus of communal attraction and release? Or maybe the pattern shown in cricket is not, in fact, an organizing metaphor in any other physical activity. Perhaps it manifests itself in mental processes instead, creating an organizing framework for the formation of visual designs, such as those used in the body painting and instrument decoration shown in the film. Or the pattern could serve as the organizing metaphor used to represent linguistically the passage of time, as the linear forward/backward spatial dimension is used in connection with the formation of tenses in the English language. In a more narrow application, the relationship of emphatic phrasing to other phrasing types exhibited in the cricket game also raises questions about the use of emphatic phrasing in other activities of Trobriand culture.

While further research is necessary to answer these questions, the fact that they have come to light at all demonstrates the value of the movement analysis. Had the understanding of the performance remained entirely dependent on imitative relationships, the cricket match would appear simply as a hybrid lumping together of two otherwise unrelated activities--sport and dance--each conveying meaning with respect to separate functional and aesthetic activity domains. In fact, the integration of the activities in the performance process, which is visually apparent but left unnarrated in the film, takes place in a distinctive style that imitative references alone fail to capture. This pattern provides insight into Trobriand lifestyle and culture.

*Trobriand Cricket* is not unusual in its unbalanced presentation of descriptive commentary. The reliance on the informant's point of view almost exclusively, supported by the ethnographer's reference to imitative aspects of human movement, is a common approach to anthropological research on cultural performances that involve dance. The emphasis upon overt relations of resemblance, upon finding meaning in human movement only insofar as it is intentionally imitative of something else, is widespread in the study of ritual dancing (see Schieffelin 1976; Ortner 1978; Brown 1976).

While the recognition of imitative associations is important to understanding how ritual movement in general and dancing in particular are designed, it is by no means sufficient for a full appreciation of the performance process and its relationship to the culture in which it has developed. It is equally important to observe the abstract, nonimitative processes exhibited in movement that "in-form" the imitative content, making it spatially and temporally familiar and comprehensible. The more pervasive, subtle patterning, which comes across less obviously in the processing of various kinds of action, is recognizable in terms of the relations of time, space, energy, and force processed through the complex (though concrete) entity of the human body. With respect to the articulation of this processing of functional and aesthetic activity the LMA approach becomes valuable as an analytical tool for the anthropology of ritual, sport, art, and, of course, dance.

The cultural interpretation of any performance--no matter how transparently the performance is represented to the observer (as it is so effectively in ethnographic film)--relies on the kind of close observation that organizes several details of performance into a system. It is not simply growing and shrinking that are at issue in the Trobriand design, not simply linear formations that are at stake in the British style. The relationship of those features to other features, the relationship of growing and shrinking to force and speed and clusters of bodies, the relationship of lines to individudal bodies and to a stabilizing energy field bring out distinctive patterns. The value of movement analysis lies in its ability to construct an articulate representation of particular and even peculiar performances in terms of the very general features that all movement processes share so that various patterns of association can be traced throughout the action of a given culture and between performances of various cultures. A system like LMA can abstract principles of conduct and can represent them accurately in their full complexity and peculiarity.

The type of analysis presented here, then, is particularly helpful in relation to cultural identity--one of the main subjects mentioned in connection with *Trobriand Cricket*. Movement analysis allows the viewer to distinguish one cricket style from another rather than leaving the perception of differences on an entirely visual, nonanalytical level of awareness. For similar reasons, the analysis is also useful in regard to the relation of art to the rest of the culture, allowing viewers to grasp central characteristics of Trobriand performance style. Finally, the method is valuable because it reveals the limitations of the narrative of *Trobriand Cricket*. This is not to say that *Trobriand Cricket* is less than an excellent ethnographic film or that the film should be anything other than what it is. The focus on mimesis and the informant's point of view is both appropriate and effective, given the design and style of the film. Nevertheless, these are severe constraints concerning the anthropological "statement" made by the film.

Movement analysis has its own limitations. By itself it cannot go beyond descriptive interpretations into explanatory statements of origin, function, and meaning. However, the approach, as this chapter has demonstrated, may yield valuable insight in the initial stages of understanding performance, information that is all too often overlooked or misrepresented by other methods of observation. These insights can serve as a basis for more extended interpretive analysis. The method shows promise not only in the specific case of *Trobriand Cricket* but also for the understanding of ethnographic films in general.

## NOTE

"Understanding Cultural Performance: Trobriand Cricket" by Sally Ann Ness, *The Drama Review* 32, no. 4 (1988):135-147. © 1988 by New York University and Massachusetts Institute of Technology. Reprinted with permission.

## REFERENCES

Birdwhistell, Ray. *Kinesics and Context: Essays on Body Motion*. Philadelphia: University of Pennsylvania Press, 1970.

Brown, Donald N. "The Dance of Taos Pueblo." *CORD Dance Research Annual* 7 (1976): 189-272.

Condon, William S. "Cultural Microrhythms." In *Interaction Rhythms*, edited by Martha Davis. New York: Human Sciences Press, 1982.

Davis, Martha. "Laban Analysis of Nonverbal Communication." In *Nonverbal Communication: Readings with Commentary*, edited by Shirley Weitz. New York: Oxford University Press, 1979.

_____ ed. *Interaction Rhythms*. New York: Human Sciences Press, 1982.

Dumont, Jean-Paul. Interview with author, Seattle, April 9, 1986.

Harrell, Stevan. Interview with author, Seattle, April 17, 1986.

Heider, Karl G. *Ethnographic Film*. Austin: University of Texas Press, 1976.

Kendon, Adam. "Coordination of Action and Framing in Face-to-Face Interaction." In *Interaction Rhythms*, edited by Martha Davis. New York: Human Sciences Press, 1982.

Leach, Edmund. *Royal Anthropological Institute Newsletter*, 1975.

MacDougall, David. "Ethnographic Film: Failure and Promise." *Annual Review of Anthropology* 7 (1978): 405-25.

Malinowski, Bronislaw. *Argonauts of the Western Pacific*. New York: Dutton, 1922.

Ortner, Sherry. *Sherpas through Their Rituals*. Cambridge: Cambridge University Press, 1978.

Ottenberg, Simon. Interview with author, Seattle, April 30, 1986.

Scheflen, Albert L. *The Sorrow of the Lonely and the Burning of the Dancers*. New York: St. Martin's Press, 1976.

Tambiah, S. J. "A Performative Approach to Ritual." *Proceedings of the British Academy* 65 (1979): 113-169.

Weiner, Annette B. "Trobriand Cricket: An Ingenious Response to Colonialism." *American Anthropologist* 79, no. 2 (1977): 506-7.

# PART II

Sport, Culture, Race, and Running

## *chapter 4*

# African Speed, African Endurance

## *Amby Burfoot*

This month in Barcelona, for the first time in the history of the Olympic Games, runners of African heritage will win every men's running race. West Africans, including American blacks of West African descent, will sweep the gold medals at all distances up to, and including, the 400-meter hurdles. East Africans and North Africans will win everything from the 800 meters through the marathon.

These results won't surprise any close observer of the international track scene. Ever since America's Eddie Tolan won the 100 meters at the 1932 Los Angeles games, becoming the first black gold medalist in an Olympic track race, black runners have increasingly dominated Olympic and World competitions. An analysis of the three World Championships paints the clearest picture. In 1983, blacks won 14 of the 33 available medals in running races. In 1987, they won 19. Last September in Tokyo, they won 29.

What's more surprising is the lack of public dialogue on the phenomenon. The shroud of silence results, of course, from sour societal taboo against discussing racial differences-a taboo that is growing stronger in these politically correct times.[1]

A good example: *Sports Illustrated*'s changed approach to the subject. In early 1971, *Sports Illustrated* published a landmark story, "An Assessment of 'Black Is Best'" by Martin Kane, which explored various physical reasons for the obvious success of black athletes on the American sports scene. African American sociologists, particularly Harry Edwards, wasted little time in blasting Kane's article. Wrote Edwards, famed for orchestrating black power demonstrations at the 1968 Olympics: "The argument that blacks are physically superior to whites is merely a racist ideology camouflaged to appeal to the ignorant, the unthinking and the unaware."[2]

Edwards was right to question arguments attributing sport success primarily to physiology. American blacks fear that such an overemphasis on their physical skills may call into question their mental skills. Besides, sport success clearly demands more than just a great body. It also requires desire, hard work, family and social support, positive role models, and, often, potential for financial reward.

For these reasons, the University of Texas' Bob Malina,[3] the country's leading expert on physical and performance differences among ethnic groups, has long argued for what he calls a "biocultural approach." Nature (the overall cultural environment) is just as important as biology (genetics).

Because Edwards and others attacked so stridently, mere discussion of the subject grew to be regarded, ipso facto, as a racist activity and hence something to be avoided at all cost. In 1991 *Sports Illustrated* returned to the fertile subject of black athletes in American sports, devoting dozens of articles to the topic in a multi-issue series. Not one of these articles made even a passing mention of physical differences between blacks and whites. Likewise, *USA Today* barely scratched the surface in its own four-day special report "Race and Sport: Myths and Realities."

When NBC television broadcast its brave "Black Athletes: Fact and Fiction" program in 1989, the network had trouble locating a scientist willing to discuss the subject in the studio. Instead, host Tom Brokaw had to patch through to two experts attending a conference in Brussels. In beginning my research for this story, I contacted one of America's most respected sports scientists. He didn't want to talk about the subject. "Go ahead and hang yourself," he said," but you're not going to hang me with you."

Fear rules. Why? Because this is a story about inherited abilities, and Americans aren't ready for the genetics revolution that's sweeping over us. In the next 10 years, scientists worldwide will devote $3 billion to the Human Genome Project. In the process they will decipher all 100,000 human genes, cure certain inherited diseases (like cystic fibrosis, Tay-Sachs, and sickle-cell anemia), and tell us more about ourselves than we are prepared to know, including, in all likelihood, why some people run faster than others.

> Tom Brokaw, moderator of "Black Athletes: Fact and Fiction," talking with geneticist Claude Bouchard: "A lot of people, when I told them we were doing this program, kept saying to me: 'Why would you even want to do this?' So let me ask you: What do we gain from these studies of blacks and caucasians?"
>
> Dr. Bouchard: "Well, I have always worked with the hypothesis that ignorance fosters prejudice. And that knowledge is the greatest safeguard against prejudice."

## SPORT: THE ILLUSION OF FAIRNESS

Many casual sports fans mistakenly believe that athletic competitions are fair. In fact, this is one reason so many people enjoy sports. Politics and corporate ladder-climbing may be rotten to the core, but sports at least provide a level playing field.

This simple notion of fairness doesn't go very far. Just ask any female athlete. Women excel in law school, medical practice, architectural design, and the business world, but they never win at sports. They don't even want to compete side by side with men in sports (as they do in all other areas of social, cultural, and economic life). Why not? Because sports success stems from certain physical strengths and abilities that women simply don't have. We all acknowledge this.

But we have more trouble understanding that what is true for women is also true for some male groups. In some sports, certain racial groups face overwhelming odds. The Japanese are passionate about sports and surely rank among the world's most disciplined, hardest working, and highest achieving peoples. These qualities have brought them great success in many areas and should produce the same in sports.

Yet the Japanese rarely succeed at sports. They fall short because, on the average, they *are* short. Most big-time sports require size, speed, and strength. A racial group lacking these qualities must struggle against great odds to excel.

Of course, a few sports, including marathoning, gymnastics, and ice-skating, actually reward small stature. You've heard of Kristi Yamaguchi and Midori Ito, right? It's no mistake that the Japanese are better at ice-skating than, say, basketball. It's genetics.

> On their trip to the 1971 Fukuoka Marathon in Japan, Kenny Moore and Frank Shorter asked athlete coordinator Eiichi Shibuya why the Japanese hold the marathon in such high regard. "We made the marathon important because it is one event in which a man needs not be tall to be great," Shibuya said. "In the marathon we can do well against the world."

> In a recent "first," molecular biologists discovered a single amino acid, just a small part of a gene that controls the eye's ability to see the color red. In Olympic archery events, competitors with this gene presumably have an advantage over those without it.

## TRACK: THE PERFECT LABORATORY

A scientist interested in exploring physical and performance differences among different racial groups couldn't invent a better sport than running. First of all, it's a true worldwide sport, practiced and enjoyed in almost every country around the globe. Also, it doesn't require any special equipment, coaching, or facilities. Abebe Bikila proved this dramatically in the 1960 Olympic Games when shoeless, little coached, and inexperienced he won the marathon.

Given the universality of running, it's reasonable to expect that the best runners should come from a wide range of countries and racial groups. We should find that Europeans, Asians, Africans, and North and South Americans all win about the same number of gold medals in running events. This isn't, however, what happens. Nearly all the sprints are won by runners of West African descent, and nearly all the distance races are won, remarkably, by runners from just one small corner of one small African country Kenya.

Track and field is the perfect laboratory sport for two more important reasons. First, two of the most exciting events the 100 meters and the marathon represent the far reaches of human physical ability. A sprinter must be the fastest, most explosive of humans. A marathoner must be the most enduring. Any researcher curious about physical differences between humans could look at runners who excel at these two events and expect to find a fair number of differences. If these differences then broke down along racial lines well, so be it.

Second, since running requires so little technique and equipment, success results *directly* from the athlete's power, endurance, or other purely physical attributes. This explains why drug testing is so important in track. If a golfer, tennis player, gymnast, or even basketball player were to take steroids or to blood dope, we'd be hard-pressed to say that the drugs helped the athlete. In these sports, too much else--rackets, clubs, specialized moves--separates the athlete's physiology from his or her scoring potential.

Runners find, on the other hand, that if they improve the body (even illegally), the performance has to improve. Some scientists even acknowledge that a simple running race can measure certain physical traits better than any laboratory test. The results we observe in Olympic Stadium are as valid as they get.

On the all-time list for 100 meters, 44 of the top 50 performances are sprinters of West African origin. The highest ranking white, Marian Woronin of Poland, stands in 16th place. At the Seoul Olympics, Kenyan men won the 800 meters, the 1500 meters, the 3000 meter steeplechase and the 5000 meters. Based on population percentages alone, the likelihood that this should have happened is 1 in 1,600,000,000 (one billion, six hundred million).

## HUMAN PHYSIQUE: THE DIFFERENCES

The evidence for a black genetic advantage in running falls into two categories: physique and physiology. The first refers to body size and proportions, and the second to below-the-surface differences in the muscles, the enzymes, the cell structures, and so on. To appreciate the significance of either, you must first understand that very small differences between two racial groups can lead to very dramatic differences in sports and performance. For example, two groups, A and B, can share 99 percent of the same human genes and characteristics. They can be virtually identical. Nevertheless, if the 1 percent of variation occurs in a characteristic that determines success at a certain sport, then group A might win 90 percent of the Olympic medals in that sport.

Over the years, numerous studies of physique have compared blacks of West African heritage with white Americans and consistently reached the same conclusions. Among these conclusions: blacks have less body fat, narrower hips, thicker thighs, longer legs, and lighter calves. From a biomechanical perspective, this is an impressive package. Narrow hips allow for efficient, straight-ahead running. Strong quadriceps muscles provide horsepower, and light calves reduce resistance.

Speaking a year ago at the American College of Sports Medicine's symposium on "Ethnic Variation in Human Performance," Lindsey Carter observed: "It appears that the biomechanical demands of a particular sport limit the range of physiques that can satisfy these demands." Carter, a San Diego State professor who has conducted a series of studies of Olympic athletes, concluded: "If all else is equal, can a difference in ethnicity confer advantages in physical performance? From a biomechanical point of view, the answer is yes."

A number of direct performance studies have also shown a distinct black superiority in simple physical tasks such as running and jumping. Often the subjects in these studies were children (e.g. fourth graders in the Kansas City public schools), which tends to mute the criticism that blacks outrun and out jump whites because society channels black youngsters into sports.

A few studies have even looked beyond simple muscle performance. In one of the first, Robert L. Browne of Southwestern Louisiana Institute showed that black college students had a significantly faster patellar tendon reflex time (the familiar knee-jerk response) than white students. Reflex time is an important variable to study for two reasons: many sports obviously require lightning reflexes, and classic biological theory holds that faster reflexes will tend to create stronger muscles, which will tend to create denser bones. All of these have been observed in blacks, whose denser bones may make it particularly hard for them to succeed in one major Olympic sport—swimming.

> From a 1934 edition of a black-owned newspaper, the *California Eagle*:
> "We had no colored swimmers in the last Olympic games or the ones before that. Isn't it high time we show the Fact: No black swimmer has ever qualified for the U.S. Olympic swim team.

## MUSCLE FIBERS: SOME SLOW, SOME FAST

Since the study of black-white differences frightens off many U.S. scientists, it's no surprise that the best research on the subject comes from other laboratories around the world. In the last decade, scientists from Quebec City, Stockholm, and Cape Town, South Africa, have been leading the way.

Claude Bouchard of Laval University in Quebec City is perhaps the world's leading sports geneticist, as well as a foremost expert in the genetics of obesity.

When the the *New England Journal of Medicine* published a Bouchard study on human obesity two years ago, it made headlines around the world for its finding that the degree of fatness and locale of fat deposition (hips, waist, etc.) were largely determined by heredity.

Bouchard achieved these and many other remarkable results through carefully controlled studies of twins who live in and around Quebec City. From such experiments he has determined the "hereditability" of many human traits., including some relating to athletic performance. Bouchard has shown, for example, that anaerobic power is from 44 to 92 percent inherited, while max $VO_2$ is only 25 percent inherited. From these findings, we might quickly conclude that sprinters are "made," which, loosely, is what track observers have always thought about sprinters and distance runners.

What "makes" distance runners, of course, is their training, and Bouchard has also investigated "trainability." It's surprisingly easy to do. You simply gather a bunch of out-of-shape people, put them on the same training program, and follow their progress according to certain key physiological measures. The results are astonishing. Some subjects don't improve at all or take a long time to improve; some improve almost instantly and by large amounts. This trainability trait, Bouchard has found, is about 75 percent inherited.

This means that potential for distance-running success may be just as genetically determined as potential for sprinting success- which is why many coaches and physiologists have been saying for years that the best way to improve your marathon time is to "choose your parents carefully."

Bouchard is now examining physiological differences between white French Canadians and black West Africans, both culled from the student population at Laval. In one study, the only one of its kind ever performed between these two groups, the researchers compared muscle fiber percentages. The West Africans had significantly more fast-twitch fibers and anaerobic enzymes than the whites. Exercise physiologists have long believed that fast-twitch muscle fibers confer an advantage in explosive, short-duration power events such as sprinting.

Two Bouchard disciples, Pierre F. M. Ama and Jean-Aime Simoneau, next decided to test the two groups' actual power output in the lab. On a 90-second leg extension test (basically the same exercise we all do on our weight benches), the black and white subjects' performed about equally for the first 30 seconds. Beyond 30 seconds, the whites were able to produce significantly more power than the blacks.

This experiment failed to show what the researchers expected-that West African blacks should be better sprinters. It may, on the other hand, have shown that these blacks generally wouldn't perform well in continuous events lasting several minutes or longer.

Of course, a leg extension test isn't the same thing as the real world of track and field. In particular, it can't account for any of the biomechanical running advantages that blacks may have--which could explain the curious findings of David Hunter.

Two years before An and Simoneau published their study, Hunter completed his Ph.D. requirement in exercise physiology at Ohio State University by writing his thesis on "A Comparison of Anaerobic Power between Black and White Adolescent Males." Hunter began by giving his subjects-high schoolers from Columbus-two laboratory tests that measure anaerobic power. These tests yielded no difference.

Then he decided to turn his subjects loose on the track. There the blacks sprinted and jumped much better than the whites. These results apparently disturbed Hunter, an African American, whose dissertation concluded that the laboratory results (no differences) were more significant than the real-world results (big differences).

In attempting to balance his results, Hunter noted that a 1969 study in the journal *Ergonomics* found that blacks actually had less *anaerobic* power than whites. What he failed to point out, and perhaps even to recognize, was that the *Ergonomics* study compared a group of Italians with a group of *Kenyans*. Indeed, many of the Kenyan subjects came from the Nandi and Kikuyu tribes, famed for their distance running but scarcely noted for their sprinting (anaerobic power). From running results alone, we would expect these Kenyans to score low on any test of anaerobic power.

I mention this only because I believe it highlights an important point: the word "black" provides little information about any one person or any group. Of the 100,000 genes that determine human makeup, only 1 to 6 regulate skin color, so we should assume almost nothing about anyone based on skin color alone. West Africans and East Africans are both blacks, but in many physical ways they *are more unlike each other* than they are *different from most whites*.

When it comes to assumptions about Africans, we should make just one: the peoples of Africa, short and tall, thick and thin, fast and slow, white and black, represent the fullest and most spectacular variations of humankind to be found anywhere.

> Stanford track coach Brooks Johnson: "I'm going to find a white Carl Lewis. They're all over the place."

> Sports columnist Scott Ostler in the *Los Angeles Times*: "Dear Brooks-Pack a lunch. And while you're out there searching, bring back a white Spudd Webb, a white Dominique Wilkens, a white O. J. Simpson, a white Jerry Rice, a white Bo Jackson and a white Wilt Chamberlin."

## ENDURANCE: THE MUSCLE COMPONENT

Tim Noakes, director of the Sport Science Centre at the University of Cape Town Medical School, has spent the last 30 years researching the limits of human endurance, largely because of his own and, indeed, his whole country's passion for the 54-mile Comrades Marathon. Noakes' book *Lore of Running* (1991) stands as the ultimate compilation of the history, physiology, and training methods of long-distance running.

In recent years, Noakes has been trying to learn why South African blacks, who represent only 20 percent of their road-racing population, nevertheless take 80 percent of the top positions in South African races. (South African blacks are related to East African blacks through their common Bushmen ancestors. West African blacks, representing the Negroid race, stand apart.)

In one experiment, Noakes asked two groups of white and black marathoners to run a full marathon on the laboratory treadmill. The two groups were matched for ability and experience. While they weren't among South Africa's elite corps of distance runners, subjects from both groups were good marathoners with times under two hours, 45 minutes.

When the two groups ran on the treadmill at the same speed, the major difference was that the blacks were able to perform at a much higher percentage of their maximum oxygen capacity. The results, published in the *European Journal of Applied Physiology*, showed that the whites could run only at 81 percent of their max $VO_2$. The blacks could reach 89 percent.

This same characteristic has previously been noted in several great white marathoners, including Derek Clayton and Frank Shorter. Clayton and Shorter didn't have a particularly high max $VO_2$, but they were able to run for longer periods of time at a very high percentage of their max. This enable them to beat other marathoners who actually had higher max $VO_2$ values.

Among white runners, a Clayton or Shorter is a physiologic rarity. Among black South Africans, however, such capacity may be commonplace. Even though the blacks in Noakes' lab were working very hard, their muscles produced little lactic acid and other products of muscle fatigue. How can they do this?

Noakes speculates that the blacks have a muscle fiber quality, as yet unnamed in scientific circles, that he calls "high fatigue resistance." It's pretty much the opposite of what the Canadian researchers found in their 90 second test of West Africans.

Despite their country's longtime ban from international competition, black distance runners from South Africa rank first and second on the all-time list for half-marathons (with identical times of one hour and eleven seconds) and hold two of the top ten positions in the marathon (with times of two hours, eight minutes and four seconds and two hours, eight minutes and fifteen seconds).

Outside the laboratory, Tim Noakes has found that African distance runners train at extremely high intensities, much higher than those observed in most white distance runners. "But what we have here is a chicken or egg situation," says Noakes. "Can they train harder because they have a genetic gift of high fatigue resistance, or can they train harder because they have trained hard to train harder?"

## KENYA: NATURE MEETS NURTURE

Sweden's renowned exercise physiologist Bengt Saltin, director of the Karolinska Institute in Stockholm, has spent most of his professional career investigating the extraordinary endurance performance of Nordic skiers, multiday bicyclists, orienteers, and distance runners. Since all distance-running roads lead to Kenya, Saltin decided to travel there two years ago to observe the phenomenon firsthand. He also took a half-dozen national-class Swedish runners with him. Later, he brought several groups of Kenyans back to Stockholm to test them in his lab.

In competitions in Kenya, at and near St. Patrick's High School, which has produced so many world-class runners, the Swedish 800-meter to 10,000-meter specialists were soundly beaten by hundreds of 15- to 17-year-old Kenyan boys. Indeed, Saltin estimated that this small region of Kenya in the Rift Valley had at least 500 high schoolers who could outrace the Swedes at 2,000 meters.

Back in Stockholm, Saltin uncovered many small differences between the Kenyan and Swedish runners. The results, not yet published in any scientific journal, seemed most extraordinary in the quadriceps muscle area. Here, the Kenyans had more blood-carrying capillaries surrounding the muscle fibers and more mitochondria within the fibers (the mitochondria are the energy-producing "engine" of the muscle).

Saltin also noted that the Kenyans' muscle fibers were smaller than those of the Swedes. Not small enough to limit performance--except perhaps the high-power production needed for sprinting--but small enough to bring the mitochondria closer to the surrounding capillaries. This "closeness" presumably enhances oxygen diffusion from the densely packed capillaries into the mitochondria.

When the oxygen gets there, it is burned with incredible efficiency. After hard workouts and races, Saltin noted, Kenyans show little ammonia buildup (from protein combustion) in the muscles--far less than Swedes and other runners. They seem to have more of the muscle enzymes that burn fat and "spare" glycogen and protein. Sparing glycogen, according to a classic tenet of work physiology, is one of the best ways to improve endurance performance. Added together, all these factors give the Kenyans something very close to what Tim Noakes calls "high fatigue resistance."

Saltin believes Kenyan endurance may result from environmental forces. He told *Runners' World* "Fast Lane" columnist Owen Anderson, that the Kenyans' remarkable quadriceps muscles could develop from years of walking and running over hills at high altitude. Saltin has observed similar capillary densities among orienteers who train and race through hilly forests and similar small muscle fibers among Nordic skiers who train at altitudes.

Of course, Peruvians and Tibetans and other people live at altitude and spend all their lives negotiating steep mountain slopes. Yet they don't seem to develop into great distance runners. Why the Kenyans?

The only plausible answer is that Kenyans from the Rift Valley, perhaps more so than any other peoples on Earth, bring together the perfect combination of genetic endowment with environmental and cultural influences. No one can doubt that many Kenyans are born with great natural talents. But much more is at work, as in the following.

Boys and girls from west Kenya grow up in a high-altitude environment of surpassing beauty and good weather conditions. From an early age, they must walk and jog across a hilly terrain to get anywhere. They are raised in a culture that emphasizes both stoicism (adolescent circumcision) and aggression (cattle raiding). Indeed, the British introduced track and field in Kenya as a way to channel tribal raiding parties into more appropriate behavior. Kip Keino and others since him have provided positive role models, and the society is so male-dominant that Kenyan men are quick to accept their superiority (an aspect of Kenyan society that makes things especially tough for Kenyan women). The financial rewards of modern-day track and road racing provide an income Kenyans can achieve in almost no other activity. In short, nearly everything about Kenyan life points to success (for men) in distance running.

At the World Cross-Country Championships, often considered distance running's most competitive annual event, Kenya has won the last seven senior men's titles and the last five junior men's team titles.

While a student at Washington State University, Kenyan Josh Kimeto once heard a teammate complaining of knee pain. Kimeto quickly replied: "Pain is when you're twelve years old and they take you out in the jungle, cut off your foreskin and beat you for three days. That's pain."

## BARCELONA: THE INSIDE TRACK

Any close inspection of international track results yields one incontrovertible fact: black-skinned athletes are winning most races. This phenomenon is likely to grow even more pronounced in the future. Many African athletes and countries have barely begun to show their potential. Yet it would be incredibly myopic to conclude, simply, that blacks are faster than whites. A more accurate albeit admittedly speculative mile.[5]

In the past, discussion of racial-group success in sports has largely involved the relative success of blacks in basketball, football, and baseball and their relative failure in tennis, golf, and swimming. The "country club" aspects of the latter three sports guaranteed that these discussions centered on social and economic status: blacks weren't good at tennis, golf, and swimming because they didn't belong to country clubs. Does an analysis of running add anything new to the discussion?

I think so. Where pure explosive power--that is, sprinting and jumping--is required for excellence in a sport, blacks of West African heritage excel. The more a sport moves away from speed and toward technique and other prerequisites, like eye-hand coordination, the more other racial groups find themselves on a level playing field.

The Kenyans and other East Africans, despite their amazing endurance, will hardly come to dominate world sports. As many of us distance runners have learned the hard way-from a lifetime of reality checks on playgrounds and various courts and fields-endurance counts for next to nothing in most big-time sports.

While sports aren't necessarily fair, we can still take heart in the many exceptions to the rule. The truly outstanding athlete always fights his way to the top, no matter what the odds, inspiring us with his courage and determination. In the movie *White Men Can't Jump* the hero, Billy Hoyle, wins the big game with a slam-dunk shot that had previously eluded him. Billy's climactic shot stands as testimony to the ability of any man, of any race, to rise high, beat the odds, and achieve his goal. The marvel of the human spirit is that it accepts no limits.

Of course, *Jump* is only a movie. The Olympic track races in Barcelona are for real.

## NOTES

This chapter was previously published as "White Men Can't Run," *Runner's World* (July 1992). Reprinted by permission of *Runner's World Magazine*. Copyrighted 1992, Rodale Press, Inc., all rights reserved.

1.    S. L. Price, in a 1997 *Sports Illustrated* piece, "Is It in the Genes," touched on many of the same arguments and names involed that appear in Burfoot's thesis, namely, that science is beginning to identify certain physical differences that may explain the differing performances between blacks and whites. Yet to underscore the sensitivity of such a position, scientists refuse to make a firm stand on genetics versus nurture.

2.    Edwards reiterated this position in a 1988 NBC television broadcast, "Black Athletes: Fact and Fiction," in which he said performance and style of African Americans are "culturally linked."

3.    Malina is now at Penn State University.

4.    Sports Illustrated returned to the subject of black and white sports performance and participation in a 1997 issue, "What Ever Happened to the White Athlete," 87, no. 23: 30-51.

5.    Wilson Kipketer broke Coe's long-standing 800 meter record in 1997. Kipketer is now a Danish citizen but is of Kenyan ancestry.

# chapter 5

## The Fastest White Man in the World

### John Hoberman

In August 1993 the president of the German Track and Field Federation, Dr. Helmut Digel, made an extraordinary public comment about the demoralized state of white athletes around the world. In the developed countries, he said, "track and field is caught in a deep crisis: the athletes see the superiority of the Africans in the distance races, and many simply give up. No one young person is going to try for the title of "world's fastest white man" ("Die Profis abkoppeln," *Der Spiegal*, August 23, 1994).

In fact, Dr. Digel's portrait of Caucasian athletic inferiority did not portray its real dimensions, since his remarks referred only to the longtime hegemony of East African distance runners and, more recently, the achievements of North Africans like Noureddine Morceli, the invincible Algerian middle-distance specialist, and Khalid Skah, the Moroccan distance star who has himself been defeated by packs of tireless Kenyans. He did not point out that the racial performance gap has spread throughout the running and jumping events in track and field and far beyond. Today the white male sprinter is all but extinct, and even the last remaining white world record has been called into question in a way that emphasizes the race consciousness of modern sport.[1] According to his former coach, Pietro Mennea's 200-meter time of 19.72 seconds owes something to the black African blood that flows through his veins.[2]

Nor have the white sprinters' female counterparts done much better. With the demise of the steroid-assisted East German women, now the Russian Irina Primalova has declared that she will be the fastest woman in the world; and she, too, like many athletes from the impoverished regions of Eastern Europe (and some Africans), may be using illegal drugs to survive in the pitiless new world of professional track and field in the postcommunist age (See "Ich werde die Schnellste Frau der Welt: 13).

France and Great Britain have run all-black sprint-relay teams in international competitions, while other citizen-athletes of African descent, like the flamboyantly African Yannick Noah, have become familiar figures across the face of Europe. In the United States, the highest profile sports are dominated by black athletes at both the college and professional levels. There is not a white star left in the National Basketball Association nor a white running back worth mentioning in the National Football League; the idea of a white cornerback in today's National Football League (NFL) has become virtually unthinkable; a high and increasing percentage of the batting stars in Major League baseball are African Americans. In summary, the dramatic ascent of the black athlete during the twentieth century has been a linear development that will continue into the foreseeable future because there are no cultural or political forces to inhibit it.

Having understated the dimensions of black athletic dominance, Dr. Digel proceeded to overestimate the resolve of many white athletes to remain competitive with their black counterparts. A year after his prediction that white athletes would never consign themselves to an inferior intraracial competition, the Norwegian sprinter Geir Moen, a member of the European elite, told an interviewer that he was looking forward to being the first white man who manages to run 100 meters in less than 10 seconds ("Klar for det sote liv"). One man who will not beat him to it is Andreas Berger of Austria. The world's fastest white sprinter of 1993, with an excellent time of 10.15 seconds, Berger's career as a white hope fell victim to the doping police that summer, even as one tabloid celebrated him as an unappreciated hero ("Wenn der Wengo zweimal Kingelt").

The racial isolation of German sprinters and distance runners is often noted by the sportswriters who cover their attempts to keep up with faster black athletes. Thus, Florian Schwarthoff is presented not only as the solitary white man in one field of hurdlers but as the only German high-hurdler of any stature whatsoever; similarly, the sprinter Marc Blume is introduced as the only white athlete entered in the 100-meter dash at another meet. Dieter Baumann, the great star of German track and field since his gold medal in the 5,000-meter run at the 1992 Barcelona Olympic Games, is often depicted as a beleaguered white hero against a backdrop of the Africans who outnumber (and often outrun) him. To his credit, Baumann has refrained from playing on the intense German fantasies about African physiology that have been so evident over the past two centuries, and he has even tried to defuse the racial issue in his public statements. " I am a white Kenyan," he said just before the 1992 Olympic Games, conveying to his devoted German public a deep respect for Africans they are unlikely to share. In further pursuit of Baumann has exhorted his racial brethren to throw off the chains of their self-inflicted complexes about African athletes. "We Europeans," he said after his victory in Barcelona, "are just as good as them and no less suited for distance running. I don't see myself on the defensive, because the Africans are simply normal opponents." See "Eine Handvoll Großer und mitten drin der Flo," "Jetzt habe ich hier meine Arbeit getan," "Erst beten, dann siegen," "Die Lungen Africas," This stereotype is also widespread among African Americans.

A year later his teammate Stephane Franke expressed his own feelings about the growing fatalism regarding white runners. "What I just can't stand to hear is talk about how the Europeans don't have it in them any more," he said in exasperation ("Und das Nutellabrot kommt nicht mehr auf den Tisch"). Eamonn Coghlan, the Irish runner whose indoor mile mark of 3:49.78 seconds is one of only two middle-distance records still held by white runners, speaks of the profoundly opposed mind-sets of athletes who have been shaped by different cultural worlds. "The African," he said in 1993, "runs with no fear. Runners in the Western world have to create psychological barriers for themselves. [Noureddine] Morceli runs at will, with no inhibitions" (Post 1993: 55).

These issues receive limited coverage in the press, in part, because racial athletic aptitude remains a delicate topic for public discussion in predominantly white societies. In addition, there is widespread resignation about closing the performance gap. We do not know how many white athletes can bring themselves to believe what Dieter Baumann once claimed regarding the physiological parity of the races. Indeed, his own sense of resignation in the face of African superiority has grown stronger in recent years (e.g., see "Die Ehre des Abendlandes retten"). On the European road-racing circuit, which stretches from the Baltic to the Pyrenees, it is clear that relatively large numbers of first-class African runners have had a demoralizing effect on many white competitors. "When you are trying to earn your living on the road it is getting silly," one top British runner said in 1992. "There are 10 or 15 Kenyans everywhere." Spanish athletes have shown open resentment of the African presence, while the Belgian track-and-field federation has responded by establishing a lucrative Cross Challenge that is limited to Belgian runners--in effect, a racially segregated event to provide financial incentives to Belgium's best runners. The strongest white Europeans understand that they need to test themselves against the Africans simply because their own countrymen cannot push them hard enough. But the attitude of second-tier Europeans who try to survive as professionals tends to be less ambitious and more practical ("Taking on the Prize Guys").

Yet it is not white athletes who feel most disadvantaged in multiracial competitions. Racial inferiority complexes are an even more serious problem among Asian athletes and those who train them to compete in the Western sports that monopolize Olympic competition. During the 1988 Seoul Olympic Games, the head of the Sri Lankan gymnastics association argued for a eugenic solution, declaring that Asians would have to breed with Europeans, Americans, or Soviet citizens if they were to have any chance of becoming world-class athletes ("Blacks Catch Up"). For the Chinese, who have mounted a serious drive to become a world sports power, a principal problem is the black athlete and his alleged natural advantages. During preparations for the 1988 Seoul games, one Chinese track coach admitted that Chinese coaches and athletes are not very liberal. "One of our most popular notions is that physiologically black people are more talented than Chinese, so there's no way we can even get close. Belief in physiological inferiority," he said, "had created psychological obstacles to performance" (Gabriel 1988). Some Japanese who participate in competitive sailing are similarly convinced that their performance is impaired by a physiological deficit (Smith 1992).

By 1994 the Chinese sports establishment had put into effect a policy of avoiding sports, such as basketball, boxing, and sprinting, where black athletes are dominant. They decided, instead, to concentrate on other sports, such as distance running, swimming, gymnastics, and diving, to which people with small torsos could better adapt. The rationale for this policy includes a racial biology of athletic aptitude that is both uniquely Chinese and, like some related ideas of Western origin, pseudoscientific. According to Professor Tian Maijiu, vice president of the Beijing Institute of Physical Education, sprinting aptitude is linked to both blood type and body type. "Seventy to ninety percent of blacks, but only thirty percent of Asians," he claims, "have blood type O, and O-type people get excited very easily, and that is why they make very good sprinters. In addition, black people have very good genetics. Compared with them, the people in Asia are very inferior. The buttocks the blacks have in very high position. The whites, a little bit lower. The Asians, even lower. Because of that, muscles [in blacks] are longer, [and have] more power. That forms a very good lever" ("Avoiding Competition against Blacks").

Such ideas are typical of the tabloid-style racial science we will examine later in this book. While the blood-group theory is simple nonsense, the anatomical thesis caricatures reliable anthropometric data about small average racial differences that may or may not be relevant to elite performance. The political and biological significance of these data will be investigated in due course. What matters here are the roles of fantasy and scientific semiliteracy in the construction of ideas about racial difference, and such ideas can focus on less tangible attributes than the position of the buttocks. Chinese ambitions to progress up through the ranks of World Cup soccer, for example, have prompted the national federation to put their most talented young athletes in the hands of highly qualified foreign tutors with whom Chinese officials can feel something resembling a racial affinity. Finding European soccer too awkward, they sent their best and brightest to Brazil, since South Americans are small and agile and have the body proportions and mentality of the Chinese. The banner that stretches across the entrance to their spartan training camp southwest of Sao Paulo reads "Faster, Higher, Stronger," and here the young Asians are learning a whole new somatic style. "The Chinese are fast but still much too stiff, "says their Brazilian trainer, who has hired a samba teacher and an expert in Brazilian martial arts to loosen them up. "If they learn their lessons well, then the Chinese, too, will have acquired the art of Ginga, the Brazilian technique of dribbling the ball around an opponent like a dancer. Their goal is to win at least one game in major international competition by the year 2000" ("Klein und wendig").

The preceding evidence shows that the globalizing of modern sport has brought about a simultaneous globalizing of racial folklore bearing on athletic performance. The standard repertory of stereotype--gazellelike Africans, fiery Latins, tenacious Finns, emotional Italians, impassive Slav--has proven to be remarkably stable throughout the twentieth century. Yet it is also clear, as the Chinese pilgrimage to Brazil suggests, temale runners and swimmers during 1993 and 1994, there is a conspicuous absence of theorizing about racial anatomy and physiology. Many foreign observers have assumed that these performances were made possible by illicit drugs, and subsequent drug testing of Chinese swimmers appeared to confirm that thesis. At the same time, we must keep in mind that cross-cultural suspicions about the origins of record-breaking athletic performances transcend the purely scientific issues and focus inevitably on myths of national character and capacity. Westerners are prepared to accept the idea of Chinese deceit, but we do not associate Asians with supernormal athletic ability. The stellar Olympic performances of Japanese (and native Hawaiian) swimmers prior to the Second World War are remembered by aficionados of the sport, but they did not create an enduring image of racial fortitude. (The image of Japanese males was dramatically improved by their smashing victory in the Russo-Japanese War of 1904-1905. Conversely, positive images of victorious Japanese swimmers at the 1932 Los Angeles Olympic Games may have been erased by American propaganda about subhuman Japanese during the Second World War.) This law of deficient returns can also apply to those who are racially identified as Africans. In 1974 a young black woman from Curacao was the fastest female swimmer in the world, but her performances and those of other swimmers of African descent have hardly made a dent in the universal image of blacks as a race that can barely stay afloat, appearing to confirm the African proverb that water is the enemy of man ("Knochen Sinken").[3]

In short, every racial myth of athletic aptitude or athletic inadequacy, as in the case of big-boned African sinkers or uncoordinated Jews, results from the interplay of what athletes actually do and the powerful racial or ethnic stereotypes that shape our interpretations of their performances.

Responses to fatalism about white athletic decline will be a useful barometer of race relations for the foreseeable future. Months after Geir Moen's disappointing sixth-place finish in the 200-meter race in the 1995 World Championships ("He was the only white man in the final"), the major Oslo paper devoted most of a page to a postmortem--"Blacks Have the Speed and the Strength"--that recapitulated the past 60 years of theorizing for it's readers. Here, too, there was a note of Caucasian impatience. According to this writer, a combination of "astonishment, admiration, and irritation" has created a demand among spectators, athletes, and scientists for an explanation of black dominance. (see "Neste år skal Geir bli god," *Aftenposten*, August 12, 1995; "Sorte har styrken og farten," *Aftenposten*, March 10, 1996).

The rampant commercialization of track and field has also been affected, in that advertisers find themselves wondering how to make black African athletes into marketing vehicles that can appeal to white audiences.[4] "In every race," Dieter Baumann lamented before the 1996 Olympic Games, "I am supposed to defend the honor of the West against each and every African" ("Die Ehre des Abendlandes retten"). Knowledgeable observers, including Baumann himself, recognize the sheer impossibility of such a challenge. "Right now," as one German journalist dryly noted, "there are only the white also-rans who may, perhaps, be able to learn something from the Africans. Whatever that is they will have to find out for themselves" ("Ein Dilemma,"*Süddeutsche Zeitung*, March 29, 1996). In the absence of such salvational knowledge, there remains the hope that Western science will eventually be able to explain the phsyiological secrets of the black body.


## NOTES

This chapter was adapted from "The Fastest White Man in the World," from *Darwin's Athletes* by John Hoberman. Copyright © 1997 by John Hoberman. Reprinted by permission of Houghton Mifflin Company. All rights reserved.

1. See George, *The Virtual Disappearance of the Caucasian Sprinter*, 70-78. It is worth noting that a white, 200-meter runner, Kevin Little, was a member of the American team that competed at the 1995 World Track and Field Championships in Göteborg, an anomaly that may have attracted more media attention in Germany than it did in the United States. "You feel intimidated when you're the only white in the field," Little told an interviewer. See "Außenseiter Little."

2. Mennea's coach was Professor Carlo Vittori. See "Das ist erst der Anfang gewesen. In 1995 an Australian sports magazine, quoting the American track coach Loren Seagrave, invoked Mennea's still-extant world record as evidence that black sprinters do not enjoy a natural physical advantage. See Hurst 1995: 25.

3. See "Ich werde die Schnellste Frau der Welt," 13; "Laufend Gelt verdienen, mit allen Mitteln.

4. See "Von allein läuft nichts"; "Ein Dilemma, *Süddeutsche Zeitung*, March 29, 1996. The same problem with reluctant sponsors has appeared in the only recently integrated world of Brazilian surfing. See "Die ganz große Welle," 256.


## REFERENCES

"Außenseiter Little" *Süddeutsche Zeitung*, August 11, 1995.

"Avoiding Competition against Blacks" *Atlanta Journal/Constution*, April 17, 1994.

"Blacks Race to Catch Up."

"Das ist erst er Anfang gewesen: Dank westlichem Know-how kommt das uberlegene Talent farbiger Futßaller zum Tragen" *Süddeutsche Zeitung*, June 25, 1990.

"Die Ehre des Abendlandes retten" *Der Spiegel*, March 11, 1996, 198, 202, 203.

"Die ganz große Welle" *Der Spiegel*, March 25, 1995.

"Die Lungen Africas" *Zeitmagazin*, July 17, 1992.

"Die Profis abkoppeln" *Der Spiegel*, August 23, 1993.

"Eine Handvoll Großer und mitten drinder Flo" *Süddeutsche Zeitung*, August 16, 1993.

"Erst betan, dann siegan" *Süddeutsche Zeitung*, August 10, 1992.

Gabriel, Tripp. "China Strains for Olympic Glory." *New York Times Magazine*, April 24, 1988.

George, John. The Virtual Disappearance of the White Male Sprinter in the United States: A Speculative Essay." *Sociology of Sport Journal* 11 (1944).

"Ich werde die Schnellste Frau der Welt" *Süddeutsche Zeitung Magazin*, August 6, 1993.

"Jetzt habe ich hier meine Arbeit getan" *Süddeutsche Zeitung*, August 16, 1992.

"Klar for det søte liv" *Aftenposten*, September 14, 1994.

"Klein und wendig" *Der Spiegel*, November 21, 1994.

"Knochen sinken" *Der Spiegel*, April 1, 1974, 131.

"Laufend Gelt verdienen, mit allen Mitteln" *Süddeutsche Zeitung*, August 20, 1993.

"Neste år skal Geir bli god" *Aftenposten*, August 12, 1995.

Post, Marty. "Prince of Times." *Runner's World* (December 1993): 55.

Smith, Patrick. "Letter from Japan" *New Yorker*, April 23, 1992.

"Sorte har styrken og farten" *Aftenposten*, March 10, 1996.

"Taking on the Prize Guys" *The European*, Novemeber 12-15, 1992.

"Und das Nutellabrot Kommt nicht nehr auf den Tisch" *Süddeutsche Zeitung*, September 16, 1993.

"Von allein lauft nichts" *Der Spiegel*, August 14, 1995.

"Wenn der Wengo zweimal Kingel" *Süddeutsche Zeitung*, October 26, 1993.

# *chapter 6*

# Kenyan Runners in a Global System

## *John Bale*

In recent decades major changes have occurred that have increased the global character of the relationships impinging on various domains of human experience (Lash and Urry 1993). Among these domains are sports in general and track and field athletics in particular. The significance of track-and-field in this respect is that it attracts representatives of more nations to its major spectacles than any other sport. It is arguably the most global of sports, with over 200 nations being affiliated with the International Amateur Athletics Federation (IAAF) and, as such, typifies many aspects of the globalization phenomenon. Nations often thought of as being marginal to the global system find themselves occupying central roles through their involvement in sport. This chapter focuses on the ways in which track and field in Kenya is clearly implicated in the globalization process. It is argued that an understanding of the country's post-1950 emergence as one of the major powers in global track and field can be achieved only by taking global dimension into account. Kenya's success in the world of sports cannot be explained by looking at events and environments in Kenya alone.

Kenya's presence on the global athletics scene was first recognized in 1954, though international, if not global, influences were clearly being felt in East Africa well before that (Bale and Sang 1996). British *imperialism* had contributed greatly to the development of track from about 1900 onward. Since the mid-1950s, however, the dominantly British connections with Kenya, while continuing, have been supplemented by impacts from America, Asia, and other nations of Europe. Although the Olympic movement acts as a kind of *neocolonialism*, we can see in the post-1950s the relevance of *modernization* and the policies favored by international organizations to Kenya's track-and-field "development." The neocolonial nature of the intercontinental connections can be argued to have led to a state of "*dependency*" in Kenyan track. These themes of imperialism, dependency, and modernization need not be viewed separately but can be seen as overlapping sets of structures that have contributed to the nature of Kenya's track and field "industry" in the 1990s.

## THE GLOBAL ATHLETIC SYSTEM

It has long been recognized that national sports systems have become "totalized" as nations have increasingly sought glory in events like the Olympic Games. Heinilä (1971) proposed that the success and effectiveness of the individual athlete depended more and more on the resources and effectiveness of the total systems of national sport and less on individual effort independent of the system as a whole. He argued that the total efficiency and the total resources of the national sports system had replaced the efforts of the individual athlete; the athlete was now part of a system. It could be argued that the world of sport had already moved on at the time Heinilä was writing. By the 1960s athletes were increasingly crossing national boundaries, not simply to compete but to train. The upsurge in the number of foreigners obtaining athletic scholarships in American universities during the post-1960s period is a case in point (Bale 1991). Increasingly, the major organizations involved in the international dimensions of athletics were not state agencies. The governance of the IAAF and the International Olympic Committee were increasingly apparent. So were more explicitly commercial global organizations. The international trade in athletic footwear and equipment had been well under way since the 1950s. By the 1980s shoe (and later, athletic clothing) firms such as Adidas, Puma, Reebok, and Nike, which were to become multinational corporations with an international division of labor, were enrolling athletes of any nation as part of their media and publicity campaigns (Bale and Sang 1996).

According to a world systems view, a particular change within one of the nations in the system can be understood only within the context of the system as a whole. Hence, for example, the decline of British long-distance running in the 1980s is not (in Taylor's, words from a quite different context) "merely a British phenomenon, [but] it is part of a wider world-system process" (Taylor 1988). It was related, for example, to the legitimating of professionalism in athletics, to the commercialization of road racing in the US, to the increasing media coverage of "speed-oriented" events as speed and time became prominent cultural fetishes (Penz 1990) and to the emergence of long-distance runners from nations like Kenya that had not previously posed a threat to European hegemony in these events. At the same time, a number of developments not directly concerned with athletics have also influenced the globalization of the sport. Sport has undoubtedly become a form of global culture. This does not mean that it is homogeneous and that local differences in "sport culture" have been totally eliminated. One has only to observe an inter-collegiate track-and field meeting in the US and compare it and its respective "meaning" with one in Britain to appreciate national differences. It is possible, of course, to "read" the Olympics and international sport differently in different countries. It cannot be denied, however, that a number of global processes have impinged on track and field in recent decades. Among these are the intensification of preexisting pressures for the adoption of a common ideology of achievement sport and the necessary standardization of the microspaces of sports arenas. Today the IAAF insists that all running tracks must be exactly the same size and of a standard composition for major competitions to take place and for records to be validated (Bale 1995). Unlike other cultural practices, there are few, if any, countercurrents in track and field; the sport *is* moving in the direction of uniformity, universality, and standardization with little sign of the hybridization that Pieterse (1994) sees in other cultural forms. Other processes of a global nature include the new forms of communications that make intercontinental travel much easier than had been the case in the 1950s. This has been achieved by what is known as "time-space compression" (Harvey 1989). Kenya is today "closer" to the US and Europe in "time-space" than it was 30 years ago. Such compression or convergence of space has enabled Kenyans to participate in *global* sport--both as athletes and as part of a global television audience. The Olympics, along with *Dallas*, is each part of the "the global cultural currency of the late twentieth century" (Lash and Urry 1993). In addition, the international bureaucracy that governs track and field has been able to create global sports events at a scale previously unknown outside the Olympics. These are exemplified by Grand Prix events at which globally contested prizes become the norm, rather than opportunities that occur only once every four years. In order to understand the processes that are taking place in individual nation-states it is important to be aware of events occurring beyond local and national levels.

A track-and-field meet is a *local experience,* but it is part of the *global reality* of achievement sport; the local meet subscribes to global rules and regulations. If it organizes things its own way, it is removing itself from the international standards by which performances are judged. Global reality and local experience are, however, mediated via a *national ideology* (Figure 6.1). This can be illustrated with an example. Consider the case of young Kenyan athletes who accept scholarships to American universities. They are lost to Kenya and are unable to represent their district in local competitions. They are no longer so readily able to act as local models for younger athletes. The power that the colleges are able to exert over the athletes may also prevent them from representing their region or nation. This is the local *experience.* In Kenya, track and field is seen nationally as a "good thing" and in order to maximize "athletic output" it has been quite acceptable for Kenyan athletes to leave their own country and obtain "athletic scholarships" in America. This form of athletic migration is part of the *national ideology.* Such athletes could not make such a transition, however, unless the rules and underlying philosophy of athletics were the same in Kentucky as they are in Kenya--unless, that is, global sport was organized under a centralized bureaucracy that subscribes to the global reality of the *citius-altius-fortius* model of sports and aggressively seeks to convert the nations of the world to its ethos. This example shows that the experience at the local level can be fully understood only through an awareness of the *global reality*. This is not to say, however, that individuals are incapable of working to alter such global structures.

**Figure 6.1**
**Alternative View of Concentric Circles**

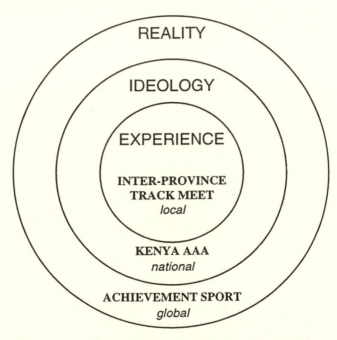

An alternative view of the concentric circles shown in Figure 6.1 is to see them as a central core, a semiperiphery, and a periphery. The core and the periphery can be interpreted as the exploiter and the exploited, respectively, with the semiperiphery forming an ambiguous zone between the two (Taylor 1988). The idea of the core nations of the world exploiting those of the periphery is an attractive idea in a sports context. Would Grand Prix track events be as profitable if Kenyan "sports workers" were absent? A steeplechase race without Kenyans is no longer regarded as attractive as it would have been in the 1950s, when the Europeans dominated the event. But I am now beginning to more than hint at exploitation, and will return to this question and that of athletic underdevelopment in our final chapter. We may also be giving the impression that athletes are passive pawns in the hands of globally organized manipulators. This, too, would be an oversimplification.

Having cleared the conceptual ground, it is now appropriate to explore in more detail the nature of the global impacts on Kenyan track that have occurred since the 1950s. In the remainder of this chapter two sides of the global system within which Kenya finds itself are considered. First, elements of sports culture have "moved in" to Kenya from outside are reviewed; second, the opposite tendencies, the outflows of athletic-related personnel from Kenya, are exemplified.

## FOREIGN SPORTS AID

Western forms of athletic activity were introduced into Kenya as part of he British colonial project. The major "change agents" were the military, the education and prison services, and the colonial district officers (Bale and Sang 1996). Space does not permit a detailed description of their roles, and for illustrative purpose only post-1950s examples will be considered.

In 1964 Kenya achieved independence but remained within the Commonwealth. The imperial links were formally severed, but the severance was superficial. In terms of cultural practice the new Kenyan political elite continued to promote imperial traditions, including achievement-oriented sports. Kenyan leaders, like many others from the "newly independent" nations, "soon enough found that they needed the West and that the idea of total independence was a nationalist fiction" (Said 1993). Far from reinstating Kenyan folk body cultures, which could have been one form of revolutionary cultural strategy, the Western traditions that had been imposed from the 1920s were continued. Jomo Kenyatta, Kenya's first president, was interested in athletics himself, and his daughter Jane was a talented school athlete. He did not fail to miss the political capital to be gained from success in international sport (Monnington 1986). The same can be said of President Moi, an athletics enthusiast who, as vice-president of the Arab and African Sports Association in the 1950s, was among the first African sports officials in Kenya. Such continued Europeanization suggests that sport, being the export of culture, serves to counter the "mental decolonization" that radicals in newly independent countries sometimes urge on their populations. Kenya, like most other African and Asian countries, has been an enthusiastic participant in colonial-imposed sports and, apart from the boycott of the Edinburgh games in 1986, a continuing participant in the Commonwealth Games. This could be interpreted as an example of the victims of imperialism being turned into its supporters.

Sports aid is part of the overall package of foreign aid that has been provided for the advantage of both Kenya and its several donors. It is not possible in space available here to provide an exhaustive list of all forms of foreign aid to the

Kenyan track-and-field scene, but the flavor of the kinds of aid that have been provided can be illustrated by the following examples.

### Great Britain

The first British athletics coaches were sent to Kenya as part of an assistance program during the 1950s. They continued the work of the many British teachers and administrators who had sown the seeds of Kenyan track in the prewar period. Some of Britain's most prominent athletes also visited Kenya at this time. In 1958 an English physical education and athletics coach, John Velzian, accepted the post of physical education instructor and coach at Kagumo Teacher Training College, Nyeri. His main early contribution to athletics was his work with the police from the Kenya Police Training School at Kiganjo. His job was also to tap and harness the athletic talent that was to be found in Kenya's schools. In 1962 at Nyeri, he allegedly "discovered" Kipchoge Keino running the mile on a grass track in four minutes 21.8 seconds (Baker 1987). As well as helping nurture Keino's talent, he went on to assist in the coaching of Ben Kogo, Naftali Temu, Wilson Kiprugut, and Daniel Rudisha. An excellent administrator, Velzian acted as head coach of the Kenyan team and also started a national secondary schools athletic championship. He was to fall out with the Kenyan authorities and was not reassigned any major duties until the 1990s. Although other U.K. coaches were of importance, Velzian who is recognized by many as the major contributor to the emergence of Kenyan athletics since 1960.

The significance of the imported printed word, as much as the foreign coach, should not be ignored. In 1960 a coaching manual titled *Athletics: A Coaching Handbook for Tropical Areas* was published in London (Millar and Crawley 1960). The authors were education officers in Kenya and argued that athletics should form part of the school curriculum from the primary phase onward. With the admitted paucity of technical equipment it was suggested that hurdles could be manufactured from improvised materials and that bamboo poles could be used for pole-vaulting. This was at the time that the synthetic track, the fiberglass vaulting pole, and the aerodynamic javelin were making their appearance in North America and Europe. Although the authors believed that Africans were "natural athletes" an insistence on *technique* made sure that their natural body cultures would be molded in forms cultured by the Occident. Such books as this illustrate how physical education and sports science were, and continue to be (along with a variety of other "academic disciplines"), complicit in the (neo-) colonial project.

## Germany

With the aid of the Federal Republic of Germany, the Ministry of Culture and Social Services and the Kenya AAA have been able to work out a long-term program for upcoming athletes. Within the next 4 to 5 years the results of this scheme should show that with help and guidance of qualified coaches, the athletes will have gained broader knowledge and improved their standards (Abmayr 1983b).

In these words the German coach, Walter Abmayr, summarized the contribution of Germany to Kenyan track and field, though it is not made clear whether "improvement in standards" is meant in an absolute or relative sense. During the early 1980s the (then West) German government was significantly involved in the "development" of Kenyan athletics, as explicated by the quotation. Although it would be over-simplistic to aver that German aid alone caused the "development" of Kenyan athletics, it certainly seems to have been *associated* with an improvement in athletics performances during the decade of the 1980s. Although a number of German agencies were assisting in sport development during the 1960s, they tended to work independently of each other. From the mid-1970s a special branch of the *Deutsche Gesellschaft für-Technische Zusammensarbeit* (GTZ) has dealt with sports aid. The GTZ has mainly involved the provision of top coaches and advisers on both a long-and short-term basis. The most influential of such coaches has undoubtedly been Abmayr, who made a short-term visit in 1972 but returned as national athletics coach from 1980 to1985. Abmayr could be argued to have been the driving force behind Kenyan track in the 1980s. He set up the Kenya Athletic Coaches Association and between 1981 and 1985 was responsible for the training of 260 athletic coaches. In addition Abmayr instituted a particularly Western form of recording of information about Kenyan athletics. Abmayr sought to monitor the performances of athletes at the national scale, establishing an annual publication of the 50 best Kenyan performers in each athletic event. While common in Europe, such national statistical publications are rare in Africa. Ranking lists such as these concretize the notion of the record and an athletic hierarchy and further marginalize nonserious forms of movement culture.

## The United States of America

Sports aid to Kenya from the U.S. has been undertaken mainly by the Peace Corps. In the mid-1950s coaching visits to Kenya were arranged for Bob Mathias, the dual Olympic decathlon champion. In 1957 Jack Davis, the then-world record holder for the high hurdles, and Mal Whitfield, dual Olympic 800 metros champion, undertook short visits. The former was based at Jeanes School, and the Kenyan hurdler, Bartonjo Rotich, acknowledged Davis' help. Like John Velzian, Whitfield was instrumental in assisting Kipchoge Keino. Visits were also arranged for eminent coaches such as Chuck Coker and Donald Canham, track-and-field coach at Michigan University, who undertook coaching clinics throughout the country.

Sports featured so prominently in the work of the Peace Corps that it was dubbed the "sports corps." The director of the Peace Corps was well aware that "athletic programs possess a unique ability to transcend political differences and thus gain access in countries with which official relations are strained or even nonexistent. Peace Corps workers were mainly placed in rural communities where they coached track and field along with basketball and volleyball."

One member of the Peace Corps who was particularly influential in spreading athletics at the grassroots level was John Manners, who taught in a number of secondary schools in the Rift Valley province from 1968 to 1971. Also worth noting was the work of Joanna Vincenti, who was stationed at Kapkenda Girls' School near Eldoret. The interest in athletics that she established has resulted in an ongoing enthusiasm for the sport at the school. Vincenti helped nurture the careers of Susan Sirma, Esther Kiplagat, and Helen Kimaiyo, some of Kenya's best runners in the early 1990s. A further important role in the work of the Peace Corps has been the forging of links between the universities and colleges attended by its members and Kenyan athletes who, through such links, have been able to obtain athletic scholarships. The pro-American stance of the Kenyan government ensured the presence of Peace Corps workers during the "take off" period of Kenyan track and field.

### China

Sports aid from China served as a means of establishing friendly relations with African countries. Since 1980 China has played a significant role in the development of Kenya's sport infrastructure in the form of stadium construction. The Moi International Sports Center at Kasarani in Nairobi is the largest Chinese project undertaken in Kenya. The Chinese contributed 52 percent of the cost of the first phase of the development, a 60,000-seat stadium and a 200-bed hostel, in the form of an interest-free loan. Over 200 Chinese workers were involved in aiding Kenyan workers in the stadium's construction.

The building of such mega-stadiums is seen by Kenyan observers as a contribution to the "development" of athletics in their country. Yet the stadium has not been without its problems. There is a temptation to label it as an example of urban monumentalism in a country where the money could have been better spent-- even in a sports context.

**Missionary School Athletics**

Missions and schools played an important role in the early days of colonial-imposed sport in Kenya (Bale and Sang 1996). Following the move toward independence the need for more secondary schools was recognized, and a number of overseas missionary organizations showed interest in further spreading the Christian doctrine to Kenya through the setting up of schools. Among these was the Cardinal Otunga High School in Kisii, established by the Brothers of Tilburg in the Netherlands, and St. Patrick's High School, Iten, established by the St. Patrick's Brothers from Ireland. These two schools exemplify the efforts of overseas organizations and individuals to mold the form of postindependence Kenyan athletics.

Cardinal Otunga High School grew from the request of Bishop Maurice Otunga for missionaries to work in his diocese. The Dutch brothers had been in Kisii since 1958, working on the development of an intermediate school, but not until 1961 was the secondary school started under the headmastership of Brother Innocent de Kok. Although athletics had been part of the school program, not until 1966 that could it be said to have entered the Kenyan athletics scene. Particularly associated with its athletic emergence was an Irishman, Chris Phelan, who had arrived at the school in 1965. He had a rich and lengthy history in athletics, having been a teacher of sports in Sarawak and Hong Kong (Bale and Sang 1996). Phelan started the Kisii District Secondary Schools Association, a body responsible for organizing school sports at the district level. It was a major influence in encouraging further the spread of athletics in the district. Assisted by other teachers, some good athletes soon emerged from such a regime. In 1971 a cross-country meeting was initiated at the school that came to be known as the Mosocho race, an important event in the calendar of Kenyan cross-country racing. The inaugural winner was John Ngeno, a student from Kabianga High School, who was to become a world-class 10,000-meter. runner and a student athlete at Washington State University in the U.S. The traditions established in the late 1960s and 1970s have contributed to the development of a number of world-class athletes from the school. Among them have been Oanda Kironchi, Thomas Osano, Micah Boniett, Osoro Ondoro, Yobes Ondieki, and Robert Ouko. The tradition of "producing" athletes from Cardinal Otunga has been rivaled only by St. Patrick's High School, an institution that is often termed the cradle of modern Kenyan athletics.

St. Patrick's High School at Iten was started in 1960. The first head teacher, Brother Simon, had a keen interest in sports and coached the school athletics team himself. Under Brother Simon all first-year boys at the school were supposed to take part in athletics. This ensured that those of superior quality could be readily identified, and put through a rigorous program of training that culminated in competitions from July to August. Among those influenced by Brother Simon in the early days of St. Patrick's were Mike Boit and Mike Murei. In the 1970s St.

Patrick's attracted other foreign teachers to build on the traditions of the 1960s. More recently, coaching was undertaken by a new head teacher from County Cork in Ireland, Brother Colm O'Connell, prior to his departure to a local teachers' college where he could find more time for his coaching mission. During this period athletes such as Olympic champion Peter Rono, Kip Cheruiyot, Ibrahim Hussein, Matthew Birir, and Charles Cheruiyot have been added to the existing list of athletic giants whose introduction to the sport was at St. Patrick's. Interestingly, the school has never possessed a running track, and most training is done on cross-country routes, up and down the Eigeyo valley. Yet it has been suggested that the school provides an "ideal situation for a favorable attitude towards sports" with its English traditions, its Christian asceticism, its boarding school ethos, and its moderate climate at high altitude (Mählmann 1989). European national athletic squads have often used the school as a base for training.

In recent years O'Connell has assisted in the development of women's running by coaching Lydia Cheromei (1991 World Junior Cross Country champion), Helen Chepngeno (1994 World Women's champion), and Rose Cheruiyot. It has been alleged, however, that the school has willingly accepted students of low academic caliber if they are good athletes. This form of athletic bias is far from unknown in the U.S. colleges to which many Kenyan athletes have migrated over the last three decades (see later).

## The Role of the IAAF

The world governing body of the sport can be viewed as being analogous to a multinational corporation with its headquarters in the "developed" world. As an'imperializing power" its intention is to colonize the world with more and more converts to serious sports. The erosion of regional cultures is explicit in its ambitions, its aim being to "help remove cultural and traditional barriers to participation in athletics" (Abmayr 1983b). African culture is seen as something to "remove" in order that Western forms of movement culture may take its place. In recent years, through the increased television coverage of meetings and the increased professionalism of all athletics organizations, the IAAF has generated a vast source of revenue that it seeks to invest in various nations of the "Third World." The increased commercialization and neocolonialism of the sport are attributed principally to the energies of Primo Nebiolo, the president of the IAAF.

An aim of the IAAF Operational Plan for the World-Wide Development of Track and Field Athletics typifies the organization's global ambitions. In order to implement its plans, a number of IAAF Regional Development centers have been established, the two in Africa being in Cairo and at the Moi International Sports Complex in suburban Nairobi. At these centers courses for coaches are mounted. Between 1986 and 1989, seven such courses were held at the Nairobi center

(Wangeman and Glad 1990). These were intended for coaches in Kenya and other English-language nations in Africa. The IAAF has also assisted Kenya in financing athletes' journeys to take part in competitions outside Kenya. Within Kenya itself, the German coach, Walter Abmayr, established with IAAF resources a development plan involving a hierarchy of coaches from national to local levels. This ranges from the national head coach and four national coaches for each of the main event groups, to coaches who assist in promoting athletics at the local level.

## KENYANS ABROAD

As part of the "new global cultural economy" a large number of "moving groups and persons" are an essential feature. To "the landscape of persons who constitute the shifting world in which we live" Arjun Appadurai (1990) has applied the term "ethnoscapes." Such international movement was exemplified during the early and later twentieth century with the migration to Kenya of missionaries, teachers, administrators, and coaches from Europe. But these have been outnumbered by the substantial overseas migration of Kenyan athletic personnel. Kenyan athletes form part of a sporting "ethnoscape" made up of athletes crisscrossing global space as they ply their athletic trades.

Such migration has assumed two main forms. The first is travel in order to take part in competitions such as international meetings, the Olympics, or Commonwealth Games, following which the athlete returns to Kenya. This was the traditional model in which there was no ambiguity about the athlete's domicile or allegiance. The second involves overseas travel in order to take up sojourn (temporary or permanent) in another country. Sojourn implies a longer period of residence than simply traveling and residing abroad for the duration of the athletic event. This dualism is not quite as simple as it appears, however. Because most Grand Prix meetings are in Europe, it is more convenient for the "journey to compete" to be but part of a temporary sojourn in a European country. In some cases, such residence abroad may last several months or longer. For convenience, however, we explore each of these two general categories in turn.

### Widening Geographic Margins

By the mid-1960s Kenyan athletic performances had become increasingly visible at a global scale. Kenyan athletes were welcomed at events such as the Olympics, the Commonwealth Games, and the African Championships, festivals that involved a stay in a foreign country for a few weeks while representing their countries. Likewise they participated at invitational events in North America or Europe. In 1962, for example, as the wave of Kenyan athletics success was just beginning to surge, the best performances by world-class Kenyan athletes were registered not only in Nairobi and Nakuru but also in DaresSalaam and Kampala, in Belfast and Berlin, and in Perth and Prague. By the mid-1970s the Kenyan elite were undertaking tours of Europe involving a large number of races at a wide variety of places in a relatively short time span. Intensive Scandinavian tours became popular, partly because of the legendary running environment but also because of the availability of illicit payments for performing at a time when track and field was not yet openly professional. Figure 6.2 shows the itinerary of the great Kenyan steeplechaser Ben Jipcho, which involved jetting between Helsinki, Stockholm, Oslo, and several smaller places during a six-week period in the summer of 1973. Since then the significance for the Kenyan elite of participation mainly within Africa and the Commonwealth has declined further. Figure 6.3 shows the global locations where African-class Kenyan runners achieved their best performances during 1993. Although Nairobi remained an important focus, venues for Kenyan athletic performances spanned four continents. A comparable map for all of the throwing events, however, would show that all the best performances were made in Kenya. The spatial margins of the journey to compete among African-class Kenyans vary considerably between event groups.

**Figure 6.2**
**Itinerary of Ben Jipcho**

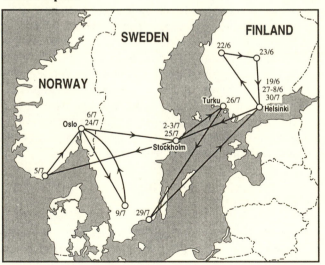

During the 1960s and early 1970s the most successful Kenyan athletes were almost all based in Kenya. Keino was in the police force, Jipcho was a prison officer, and Temu was in the armed forces. These services had a positive policy of recruiting possible internationals and provided them with better than average training facilities (Monnington 1986). From the early 1970s, however, the geography of "producing" --or at least "processing"--(as well as "marketing") of Kenyan athletes change as the geographic margins of the Keyan presence expanded dramatically.

**Figure 6.3**
**Global Locations When Kenyan Runners Achieved in 1993**

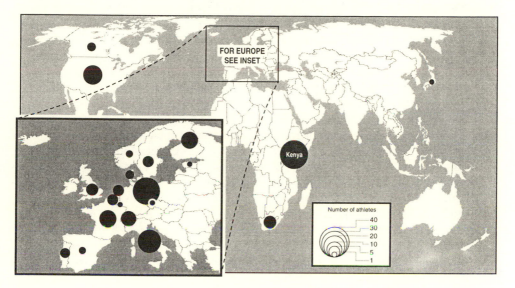

### The Scramble for Africa: American Connections

Sporadic visits of Kenyan athletes to overseas countries, other than those where they competed in events like the Commonwealth and Olympic Games, were not unknown in the 1950s and early 1960s. Some Kenyans were students in British and American universities and happened to compete in track while at college. None of these left a very significant imprint. The major component of the increasing globalization of Kenyan athletics involved the many Kenyan athletes who were attracted to the United States not to represent their country but to improve the prestige of the athletic departments of the nation's universities. These journeys involved more than a flying visit to take part in a single athletic event. They meant temporary residence in a foreign country, often extending over four years or more. The flow of Kenyans to U.S. colleges and universities from the late 1960s and early 1970s was a new dimension in the globalization of Kenyan track, and only it can be fully understood by appreciating the nature and significance of sports in the American higher education system. College and university sport in the United States is of considerable importance in raising and maintaining the visibility of institutions of higher education in the many small towns in which they are located. Athletic scholarships are awarded by quasi-autonomous athletic departments to high-achieving athletes. In the main, these scholarships are awarded to 18-year-old American high school graduates. From the late 1950s, however, many foreign recruits were lured to the U.S. by the promise of support in college while following an athletic "career." Traditionally, the largest number of such foreign track-and-field recruits had come from Canada and Northwest Europe. They often differed from U.S. high school recruits by being seasoned athletes, sometimes internationals in the twilight of their careers (Bale 1991).

Although a few Kenyans arrived in the U. S. in the late 1960s and early 1970s, the explosion in East African recruiting came in the mid-1970s. Kenyans were often cheaper to recruit than Americans. Instead of scouring the nation for the blue-chip recruit, a telephone call or, later, a fax from the track coach to an alumnus in Kenya could get a recruit for almost nothing. This is not to say that U.S. coaches did not go to Kenya. Those who sought Kenyan talent to bring to the U.S. in districts like Nandi or Kisii are regarded by John Hoberman (1992) as the modern counterparts of the nineteenth-century "inquiring travelers" who recorded, and brought back in the form of lantern slides and travelers' tales, the legendary performances of the premodern athletes of "Mother Africa." Whatever way they were recruited, the number of Kenyan collegians grew dramatically. From 1976 onward there were more Kenyans appearing in the National Collegiate Athletic Association championships than athletes from any other foreign country. From 1971 through 1978, 17.2 percent of all men's championship appearances by non-Americans were by Kenyans, compared with a respective figure of 12.5 percent from Canada. Of the 166 Kenyans, 132 or 85 percent were distance runners

(Hollander 1980). This trend continued. As Table 6.1 shows, between 1973 and 1985, Kenya supplied 12.6 per cent of all superior foreign track-and-field athletes in US colleges, Canada accounting for 12.2 percent (Bale 1991).

**Table 6.1**
**Major National Donors of Superior Foreign Track and Field Student Athletes, 1975-1985**

| Country | number | percent |
|---|---|---|
| Kenya | 77 | 12.6 |
| Canada | 74 | 12.2 |
| U.K. | 54 | 8.9 |
| Sweden | 51 | 8.4 |
| Jamaica | 43 | 7.1 |
| Nigeria | 34 | 5.6 |
| Eire | 32 | 5.3 |
| Norway | 25 | 4.1 |
| Ghana | 18 | 3.0 |

*Note:* n = 609.
*Source:* Bale, 1991, p.77.

The kinds of Kenyans the colleges wanted were those with proven skills in events where there was a relative paucity of U.S. high school talent. Hence, as noted earlier, the middle- and long-distance runners were those favored. American colleges did not recruit Kenyan shot-putters or pole vaulters. In 1982, at the peak of the migration of Kenyan athletic talent to the U.S., 24 of the 50 best Kenyan 5,000-meter runners were domiciled in the U.S.; the respective figure for national-class athletes in all field events was 2.44. Of the Kenyan contingent during the period shown in Table 6.1, 86 percent were distance runners. What we see here is an international division of labor--a common feature of globalization. The Caribbean and West Africa provide the sprinters, the Scandinavian countries the throwers, and Kenya the distance runners. The composition of the Canadian and British recruits has been much more diversified. This flow of African recruits included some of the best athletes in the world, including subsequent holders of world records such as

Henry Rono and Samson Kimobwa, and Olympic champions such as Paul Ereng and Peter Rono. Many more Kenyans, sometimes elite runners but often more modest athletes, were attracted to American campuses, the number remaining relatively high until the mid-1980s. These were often *dejure* students but *defacto* full-time athletes.

College destinations of Kenyan athletes were often avoided by native-born American athletes who perceived them as out-of-the way places. The prime example was the University of Texas, El Paso (UTEP), which recruited many foreign athletes to enhance its track-and-field squad. "Small and remote, without any great claim to academic distinction, except in geology, the school found a source of pride and joy in the track team since it rose to prominence in the 1970s" (quoted in Bale 1991), helped greatly by the presence of a large number of foreign "imports." El Paso, situated in what approximated a hot desert environment, was the main destination of Kenyan elite athletes during the 1970s and early 1980s. Other major destinations for superior Kenyan athletes were Washington State and Iowa State Universities (Figure 6.4).

From about 1985 onward, the subsidy of the athletic scholarship became much less significant as the open payment of prize money to athletes became acceptable, something forbidden under the system of intercollegiate sports in the U.S. Track athletes no longer needed to attend an American university to realize their athletic ambitions. Consequently, the number of Kenyans based in the United States began to decline, though a few years in an American college or university are still likely to be attractive to those Kenyan athletes below the elite level or to those who feel like sampling an alternative lifestyle or obtaining an American degree at the same time.

It is difficult to say if the Kenyan athletic experience in the United States has had a major impact on development of Kenyan track and field. Kenyan migrants to the U.S. would have had to be good athletes to be recruited. The basis of their athletic talent and initial "development" lies in Kenya. The American experience for some athletes meant glory followed by disaster. Henry Rono was a world record holder while a student at Washington State University but finished his "career" in the U.S. as a victim of alcohol abuse. Yobes Ondieki became a world-class athlete after he spent four years at Iowa State. Certainly, the flow of Kenyan athletes to the U.S. has had no impact on the "development" of Kenyan field events.

**Figure 6.4
Kenyans at Iowa State University,
1980s.**

## A Kenyan Diaspora

The open professionalism of athletics did not put a halt to the transcontinental migration of Kenyan athletes; it simply redirected it, increasingly to Europe. Of 30 elite Kenyan athletes whose autobiographies were sketched in the 1994 annual of the Association of Track and Field Statisticians, 14 were domiciled in Kenya, while six were living in Europe and six in the U.S. For those below the absolute elite such migration to Europe is often seasonal in nature, a kind of "athletic transhumance" made to coincide with the Grand Prix seasons in track and cross-country running. Others live in Europe and North America to benefit from the lucrative road-racing circuits. A survey undertaken in 1992 revealed that 76 pe cent of a sample of Kenyan runners stated that they were motivated to travel abroad by the proximity of the region to international competition (Bale and Sang 1996). In the world of athletics, Europe has a major advantage over North America in this respect.

In Europe, several groups of Kenyans spend much of their time living in close proximity to each other, close to nodes of regular athletic competition. Other European groups are located in Belgium, Finland, Sweden, Switzerland, Denmark, Italy, Spain, and Germany. In such cases club membership is common. For example, in Italy, Kenyans have joined the Brescia-based Fila team and in Switzerland the LC Zurich club; indeed, clubs may well be the principal recruiters in such countries. There is often a feeling that the presence of Kenyans creates a disincentive to compete for the British runners.

Such seasonal migrants are complemented by a smaller group of longer-term migrants who are, in this respect, more analogous to the American scholarship holders. Kenyan athletic migration to Japan exemplifies this group, and the paradigm example is probably Douglas Wakihuri, a winner of world and Commonwealth marathon championships. Wakihuri had considered attending college in the U.S. but having met Shunichi Kobayashi, a Japanese living in Kenya, he was persuaded that he should write to the Japanese coach Kiyoshi Nakamura. As an 18-year-old, Wakihuri went to Tokyo where he joined the IS and B Track Club, which is sponsored by a spice manufacturing firm. Other Kenyan athletes spending time in Japan have included one of the nation's best women runners, Susan Sirma, and the 1995 World championship marathon runner Eric Wainaina. More recent migrants to Japan have joined the Oki Electronics Club.

Kenyan athletes in Germany were attracted to the Heidelberg area by the contacts built up in Kenya by the German coach Walter Abmayr. The 1988 Olympic 10,000-meter bronze medalist, Kipkemboi Kimeli, was one of the first of such migrants. He was joined by Julius Korir and Benson Kamau, among several others. In Denmark, two Kenyan athletes have opted to represent their adopted country in order to stand a better chance of getting international competition. By doing so, such athletes are able to be sure of international selection without having to face the high-pressure Kenyan trials. The best known is Wilson Kipketer, who was recruited by a Scandinavian coach while at St. Patrick's High School and taken to Denmark at the age of 17. By 1995 he had lived there for five years and obtained Danish qualification shortly before winning the world 800-meter championship in that year (see later).

The diaspora of Kenyan athletes illustrates the twin sociological concepts of globalization--diminishing contrasts and increasing varieties. The global-scale tendency for sports--track and field in particular--to create a common macroculture among some members of each of the world's nations has been noted earlier. At the same time, but on the local scale, we can see in Kenyan talent migration the process of increasing cultural variety. In Ames, Iowa, we find Kenyan student-athletes commingling with those from the American midwest; in Italy and Japan new Kenyan arrivals join clubs with athletes from the host countries. As Kenya becomes Americanized with the import of Nike shoes (and the many other forms of American cultural baggage), so Iowa becomes Africanized with the import of Kenyan athletes. Indeed, Maguire has suggested that migrant athletes are the most visible expressions of not only the globalization of sports but also the increasing diversity of sports culture. But such migration may affect national cultures and national identities (Maguire 1994).

We should point out that relatively few women athletes have been part of the patterns of migration we have been describing in this chapter. This is the result, of course, of their underrepresentation in Kenyan athletics. Whereas in school the ratio of female-to- male participation in track and field is 45:55, from the ages of 17 to 21, when migration would be most likely to occur, the respective ratio is about 15:85 (Abmayr 1983b).

### Culture Shock?

The implications of the kind of migration just described are ambiguous. Any generalizations that can be made about how Kenyan athletes adjust to life overseas will certainly obscure a wide range of individual experiences. For example, when Kiptalem Keter visited Europe for the first time in the 1950s his reception by whites in England was warmer than the contact he was used to with Europeans in his own country (Bale and Sang 1996). Such hospitality may not always be the case, however.

An attempt has been made to establish the feelings of Kenyan and European student-athletes to the sojourn experience in the United States (Bale and Sang 1996). We asked the two samples to score their general feelings on a "feelings thermometer" on which values range from 0 (very cold feeling) to 100 (very warm feeling), with 50 as a neutral response. For 21 Kenyan respondents the modal score was 70, and the mean 77.6. These reflect fairly warm or favorable feelings overall. The European scores were noticeably different, not in direction but in strength. The mode was 100 and the mean 87 for a larger sample of 93 European athletes. How might the less warm--but certainly not cool--feeling felt by Kenyan athletes toward sojourn in the U.S. be explained? It could result from more severe feelings of homesickness, declining athletic performance, exploitation, or discrimination. Is there any evidence to support any of these speculations?

Racial discrimination against African athletes while in American universities has been reported from several sources. It has been noted that African athletes "have been threatened on many occasions with deportation if they do not do as they are told, if they don't race in every meet that comes along" (Ballinger 1981). Our evidence suggests that one-third of Kenyan athletic migrants experience what they perceive as discrimination while in America. Two-thirds do not appear to have any expectations about the extent of discrimination against them before they arrive in the U.S., but once there one-quarter of our sample respondents found more than they expected while none found less than they expected. Apart from the structural racism of American society, U.S. track fans have often felt aggrieved by a limited number of athletic scholarships being given to a large number of foreigners--though this feeling is not reserved for Kenyans. Although discrimination is not enough to make the overall sojourn unpleasant, it is clearly there.

The question of whether Kenyan athletes are exploited while in the U.S. is difficult to establish. On the one hand it is not easy to operationalize the notion of "exploitation" and, even if it were, people may be exploited without being aware of it (i.e., as a result of what is termed "false consciousness"). Yet traces of exploitation are felt by some students. What is unclear is whether exploitation is greater or less in the case of Kenyan student-athletes than it is for any other foreign (black) recruits into the U.S. collegiate setup. A different kind of attitudinal response to Kenyan residence abroad can be illustrated by the case of Wilson Kipketer, as noted earlier, the winner of the 1995 world 800-meter championship in the colors of Denmark. In order to take part in the 1996 Olympics, however, he required seven year residence, the time required to obtain Danish nationality. A survey undertaken by a Danish newspaper soon after Kipketer's 1995 world championship victory revealed that only 31 percent of respondents favored the acceleration of the normal process of naturalization. On the other hand, 51 percent favored the standard procedures taking their course, even if it meant that Kipketer would then be unable to represent them in the Olympics (Bale and Sang 1996). It seemed that Kipketer had been running for Denmark but not *with* Denmark. Perhaps this story reveals how national publics may fail to accurately reflect the more strongly nationalistic ambitions of their sports organizations or (in this case, more likely) the failure to identify with their black "representative".

## CONCLUSION

In conceptualizing any theory of world athletic development a global systems approach is a convincing starting point. This chapter has demonstrated that a variety of global impacts and controls has impinged on Kenyan track and field during the past half century. What is novel is the redirection of the cultural flows that are involved during this period. The early years of this century witnessed sport in Kenya being dominated by inflows of personnel from Britain in the form of missionaries, teachers, and soldiers. Today outflows of human sports capital from Kenya's are more prominent. The increased mobility of athletes throughout the world has resulted in Kenya finding itself in a sort of "new world sports order." This not only involves the redrawing of the world athletic map but, as identities are reconstructed and contested, also raises questions of national identity itself and the inability of national allegiance to describe the geography of the sport.

In his "mapping" of the global condition Roland Robertson (1990) suggests a five-stage path toward the present. This can be adapted to form an outline of what has been described for Kenya:

Phase 1--*the germinal phase,* lasting from the early twentieth century to the early 1920s. During this period the seeds of modern track and field were planted by European imperialists, although Kenyan athletics remained rooted in Kenya.

Phase II--*the incipient phase*, lasting from the 1920s until the 1930s. The gradual bureaucratization of track and field, involving its standardization and recording, meant that the sport was becoming a source of social control, regional bonding, and interregional and potentially international competition.

Phase III--*the struggle for hegemony phase*, from the mid-1930s to the 1950s. For much of this period folk traditions coexisted with modern sports. By the mid-1950s, however, the hegemony of modern sport was completed with the formation of the Kenya AAA.

Phase IV--*the take off phase*, from the 1950s to the 1970s. This period saw Kenya's entering major international competitions, initially in Africa and subsequently in the Empire and Olympic Games. It became known as a significant athletic power, and the international migration of athletes began to take place.

Phase V--*the uncertainty phase*, beginning in the 1970s. Kenya's participation in international competitions became less certain with political boycotts (e.g., Olympics in 1976 and 1980; Commonwealth Games in 1986). Kenyan athletes increasingly migrated overseas to "represent" other units such as colleges and universities in the U.S. or clubs (or even countries) in Europe. Today other athletes face conflicts with the KAAA as they seek to represent themselves. The number of global organizations that seek to claim Kenyan athletes continues to increase. The nation-state (Kenya) may remain the country that Kenyan athletes generally represent (or are seen by the media to represent), yet these athletes, once they reach a certain level, become less and less a part of any Kenyan system (if, given the tribal traditions of Kenya, they ever were). They "work" increasingly within multinational or global systems (shoe companies, the IAAF, the IOC), which may serve to reduce the ability of the nation-state to exert control over them.

This is, of course, a skeletal outline serving to summarize much of what has been discussed. It remains to be seen to what extent such a scheme applies to other nations and other sports.

## NOTE

This chapter is an edited version of Chapter 5, "Kenyan Runners in a Global System," by John Bale and Joe Sang (1996) from *Kenyan Running: Movement Culture, Geography and Global Change,* London: Frank Cass. Reproduced with permission of author and publisher.

## REFERENCES

Abmayr, Walter. "Analysis and Perspectives of the Project in Africa." *Women's Track and Field in Africa* (Report of the first IAAF congress on women's athletics), edited by Darmstadt, Deutscher Leichtatletik Verband. 1983a.

_____. *Track and Field Performances, Kenya, 1982.* Nairobi: Abmayr, 1983a.

Apparduri, Arjun. "Disjuncture and Difference in the Global Cultural Economy." In *Global Culture,* edited by Mike Featherstone. London: Sage, 1990.

Baker, William. "Political Games: The Meaning of International Sport for Independent Africa." In *Sport in Africa: Essays in Social History,* edited by William Baker and James Mangan. New York: Africana,1987.

_____. *The Brawn Drain: Foreign Student-Athletes in American Universities.* Urbana: University of Illinois Press, 1991.

_____. *Landscapes of Modern Sport.* London: Leicester University Press, 1994. Bale, John and Joe Sang. *Kenyan Running: Movement Culture, Geography and Global Change.* London: Frank Cass, 1996

Ballinger, Lyn. *In Your Face! Sports for Love or Money.* Chicago: Vanguard, 1981.

Barff, Robert and James Austen. "It's Gotta Be da Shoes': Domestic Manufacturing, International Subcontracting, and the Production of Athletic Footwear." *Environment and Planning* 25, no. 8 (1993): 1103-14.

Heinilä, Kalevi. "Notes on Inter-Group Conflict in International Sport." In *The Sociology of Sport,* edited by Eric Dunning. London: Frank Cass, 1971.

Harvey, David. *The Condition of Postmodernity.* Oxford: Blackwell, 1989.

Hoberman, John. *Mortal Engines.* New York: Free Press, 1992.

Hollander, Tom. "A Geographical Analysis of Foreign Intercollegiate Track and Field Athletes, Master's Thesis, Eastern Michigan University, 1980.

Lash, Scott, and John Urry. *Economies of Signs and Space.* London: Sage, 1993.

Maguire, Joseph. "Preliminary Observations on Globalization and the Migration of Sports Labor." *Sociological Review* 42, no. 3 (1994): 452-80.

Mählmann, Peter. "Perception of Sport in Kenya." *Journal of East African Research and Development* 19 (1989):119-45.

Millar, J., and D. Crawley. *Athletics: A Coaching Handbook for Tropical Areas*. London: Pitman, 1960.

Penz, Otto. "Sport and Speed." *International Review for the Sociology of Sport* 25, no. 2 (1990): 157-67.

Pieterse, Jan. "Globalization as Hybridization." *International Sociology* 9, no. 2 (1994): 100-84.

Puranaho, Kari, and Pauli Vuolle. *Survey of the Needs of Sports Development Cooperation in Africa*. Jyväskyl: Reports of Physical Culture and Health, 1987.

Robertson, Roland. "Mapping the Global Condition: Globalization as a Central Concept." In *Global Culture*, edited by Mike Featherstone. London: Sage, 1990.

Said, Edward. *Culture and Imperialism*. London: Vintage, 1993.

Smith, Anthony. "Towards a Global Culture?" In *Global Culture*, edited by Mike Featherstone. London: Sage, 1990.

Taylor, Peter. *Political Geography*. London: Longman, 1989.

# PART III

## Sport and Culture Change

*chapter 7*

---

# The Globalist of Them All: The "Everywhere Man" Michael Jordan and American Popular Culture in Postcolonial New Zealand

*Steven Jackson and David Andrews*

## INTRODUCTION

Of the countless contemporary athletes who might be considered to be "global jocks," it would be difficult to find a more legitimate candidate than National Basketball Association (NBA) star Michael Jordan. Indeed, it is no accident that the "global hero of a global show" (Halberstam 1991) has been referred to as "the everywhere man" (McCallum 1991). One only needs to look at the long list of popular books that celebrate and reproduce his iconic status (cf. Equinas 1993; Greene 1992, 1995; Naughton 1992; Smith 1992, 1995) as well as the growing list of academic, (Andrews 1996; Andrews et al. 1996; Armstrong 1996; Cole 1996; Denzin 1996; Dyson 1993; Kellner 1996; McDonald 1995, 1996) to gauge his global impact. Clearly, Jordan's rise to fame and fortune stems from his remarkable athletic achievements, which include five NBA championships with the Chicago Bulls, seven seasons as the NBA's leading scorer, an Olympic gold medal as part of the Dream Team, a brief stint as a semiprofessional baseball player, and an emotional retirement followed by an equally dramatic return to the NBA. However, it is important to recognize that Jordan's global ubiquity is predicated on the technological advancements of satellite television and the commodification of his celebrity. Inasmuch as Jordan emerged as a dominant figure within the NBA in the 1980s, he became one of its key attractions and promoters. The almost symbiotic relationship between Jordan, the NBA and his first major corporate sponsor, Nike, launched an unprecedented career as an athlete, endorser, and what has been described as a commodity-sign (Andrews 1997; Andrews et al. 1996). We outline the conceptual basis of the *commodity-sign* in more detail later in the chapter, but for present purposes we use the term to refer to the fact that, as a "global mediated jock," Michael Jordan embodies a symbolic, commodified meaning. In effect, his commodified image, including the signs and symbols that represent him on his Nike Air Jordan shoes, has become a vehicle for promoting and selling a wide array of consumer products, many of which have little or nothing to do with basketball. Today, in addition to Jordan's deal with Nike, he boasts numerous other commercial relationships, including McDonald's, Gatorade, Oakley, Chevrolet, and Hanes. Most recently, he has launched his own line of Nike clothes and a new cologne.

By and large, Michael Jordan's global presence, not unlike that of the vast array of American multinational corporations with which he is aligned, is taken for granted. Yet, we argue that the very fact that Michael Jordan, an African American basketball player, may be one of the most recognized people in the world and a hero to youths who may never have actually seen him play basketball, warrants serious scholarly analysis. In this chapter we examine two interrelated facets of Michael Jordan, "the everywhere man," as they are located with contemporary debates about the globalization/Americanization of culture. First, we explore the global processes, including the alliance of corporate endorsements that underscored Michael Jordan's emergence as both a celebrity and a commodity. Second, we critically examine the "local" manifestation and meaning of Michael Jordan by focusing on one specific cultural context. Overall, we hope to demonstrate how Michael Jordan, as one particular representation of American popular culture, can serve as both a source of celebration and resistance within New Zealand.

Cultural critics continue to debate the basis and consequences of the globalization phenomenon. More often than not, concerns about globalization address the potential impact of the logic of capitalism as it impacts on the *new world order* by contributing to the economic and cultural colonization of more vulnerable nations. One specific focus of these debates is whether or not the new international economic, national, and cultural alliances, in conjunction with an ever-expanding mediascape, are contributing to a standardized, homogenized, and globally shared culture. The emergent, simulated cultural space and experience, which are largely, but not exclusively, driven by the machinations of American-mediated popular culture, are seemingly demonstrated by the universal presence of commodity-signs such as CNN, Coca-Cola, McDonald's, Nike, Baywatch, the Disney Corporation, the NBA, and the focus of our analysis, Michael Jordan. While it would be a mistake to deny the global ubiquity of this ever-expanding economy of cultural artifacts, it would be equally erroneous to suggest that an increased circulation of commodity-signs inevitably leads to the creation of globally homogeneous or "Americanized" patterns of popular cultural existence (Andrews 1997). Rather, it is important to acknowledge the cultural dialectic at work in relation to globally intrusive texts and practices and their influence upon local identities and experiences. In short, there need to be an acknowledgment of the complexity of the consumption of global commodity-signs and a recognition that the local can be seen as only a "fluid and relational space, constituted only in and through its relation to the global" (Robins 1991: 35). Thus, our aim is to examine how Michael Jordan, the symbolic vanguard of both the National Basketball Association and Nike, Inc., and an explicitly American, yet increasingly global icon, can be located within the popular imagination of postcolonial New Zealand. Specifically, this chapter addresses the following: (1) a historical contextualization of the emergence and global "net"working of Michael Jordan, the NBA and Nike; (2) an examination of the *intertextual* alliances (referring to the fact that meanings move between different contexts and products) between global commodity-signs, such the NBA, Nike, McDonald's, and Coca-Cola, which have contributed to manufacturing Michael Jordan's global presence; (3) an assessment of how Michael Jordan, in and through his relationship with the NBA, Nike, and the ensemble of associated commodity-signs, is consciously, deliberately, and arguably, even inevitably, marketed as an authentic American commodity; and (4) a discussion of the implications about the intersection where the global meets the local, or what we refer to as the *global/local nexus*, of Michael Jordan within postcolonial New Zealand. As we hope to demonstrate, the global/local nexus of "the everywhere man" in New Zealand includes a range of responses, including fascination and celebration, accommodation and negotiation, and suspicion and resistance.

## CONTEXTUALIZING POSTCOLONIAL NEW ZEALAND

Despite its self-proclaimed reputation for being "a great little sporting nation" and its international successes in rugby, netball, and, most recently, the America's Cup, New Zealand would rarely be identified with basketball. Yet, basketball has been played in New Zealand since American soldiers imported the game during the First World War and has gained immense popularity over the past decade, largely as a consequence of television, the emergence of a domestic, national, semiprofessional competition, and star players such as Michael Jordan.

In many ways the popularity of the NBA and individual superstars such as Jordan is symbolic of the transformation of New Zealand as a postcolonial nation. For over a century this small South Pacific nation of 3.7 million people has looked to Britain for almost every aspect of its political, economic, and cultural life but also as a point of resentment and difference. However, owing to global developments, over the last few decades and the last one in particular, New Zealand is beginning to redefine itself with a renewed vision of its place within the Pacific Rim region, increasing solicitation and acceptance of foreign investment, the decline of its welfare state as a consequence of new right politics, and the decision to enact a new electoral system beginning in 1996 (Duncan and Bollard 1992; Haworth 1994). Furthermore, the increasing frequency with which the global encounters the local in New Zealand could be one contributing factor in the new set of emerging social relations of social class, gender, and race/ethnicity. Despite the apparent new wealth of the nation there is an increasing gap between those at the top and those at the bottom of the social class hierarchy. More women are working and pursuing higher education, but they continue to face various forms of discrimination, including unequal access to institutional positions of power and increasing levels of domestic violence. Just over five years after the 150th anniversary of the signing of the Treaty of Waitangi, which established a new political relationship between the British Crown and the indigenous Maori, and at a time when the New Zealand government has offered a $1 billion fiscal envelope to settle land and other claims, race relations are increasingly tense. This is part of the postcolonial context and condition of New Zealand in 1998. It is important to recognize the dynamics of this condition because it locates our discussion of the global/local nexus. However, before we proceed, it is essential that we briefly clarify the concept of postcolonialism simply because its pervasive and indiscriminate use by both popular and critical cultural commentators has been quite problematic. In particular, there is a danger that by envisioning the *postcolonial* as "a uniform and homogeneous experience, the concept inevitably loses its analytical power" (Andrews et al. 1996: 434). As Hall (1996: 245) cautions, "those deploying the concept must attend more carefully to its discriminations and specificities and/or establish more clearly at what level of abstraction the term is operating and how this avoids a spurious universalization." Hence, within the New Zealand context, we argue that there is a need to recognize that the postcolonial experience of the indigenous Maori is different from that of the European white settler society that followed (cf. Spoonley 1995) and that, in turn, the postcolonial formations and experiences of New Zealand are fundamentally different from those of Canada, Australia, India, or South Africa.

In the case of New Zealand the postcolonial condition is characterized by at least two interrelated processes, which can be linked to the country's desire to confirm its maturity as a former British colony while simultaneously attempting to reconcile its own European colonization of the indigenous Maori. First, there is a renewed search for national identity, often embracing what are perceived to be unique traditional cultural practices and symbols and tending to be steeped in nostalgia (Avril Bell 1995; Claudia Bell 1996). Second, there is a resurgence of popular political and cultural consciousness among indigenous and other marginalized voices that seek legitimacy both within and outside the constraints of the existing national formation. Moreover, in light of the fact that identity construction is based on both similarity and difference, it should not be surprising that the process is both inward- and outward-looking. Hence, the postcolonial quest for identity may involve a coexisting nationalist resistance to, and embracement of, "otherness." In postcolonial New Zealand part of this dialectic involves a resistance to, and embracement of, American popular culture, including the NBA and global icons such as Michael Jordan.

## THE HISTORICAL EMERGENCE OF THE NBA AND MICHAEL JORDAN

Given its current global preeminence, it is difficult to imagine a world without the NBA. Yet, the success of the NBA was never guaranteed. In 1977, the newly consolidated NBA was at an all-time low in terms of image and economics, with the league's problems coming to a head during the 1980-1981 season, when only 7 of the NBA's 23 franchises made a profit. With nothing to lose, the league's new commissioner, David Stern, took some drastic steps, which included installing an aggressive antidrug policy, establishing collective bargaining between owners and players, and enforcing a salary cap. In conjunction with these institutional changes there was a timely emergence of a new generation of outstanding players, led by Magic Johnson and Larry Bird, and all of these factors pointed toward the possibility of renewed prosperity for the league. However, on a semiotic and perhaps more significant level, the popular rise of the NBA was engineered through the revolutionary way in which the league's administrators, guided by Commissioner Stern, creatively exploited the expanding channels of the media in order to revitalize the game's image and popularity. The innovative Stern possessed a clear understanding of the fact that American culture had become a "civilization of the image" (Kearney 1989: 1). Hence, Stern's goal was to turn the NBA into a popular commodity-sign. That is, Stern recognized that the NBA could and would sell more than just "a game" by cultivating a broad base of consumption which had become a central feature of contemporary American existence. This was achieved by an aggressive restructuring of the NBA from being an archaic professional sport industry, to becoming a multifaceted marketing and entertainment conglomerate incorporating over 20 divisions, including NBA Properties, NBA Entertainment, NBA International, and NBA Ventures.

Like Disney before it, the NBA became a commodity-sign, an imaged commodity that created, and is, in turn, nurtured by, a cast of simulated characters. David Stern freely admits, indeed, he celebrates, the similarities between the NBA and Disney. "They have theme parks and we have theme parks. Only we call them arenas. They have [Jordan]. Disney sells apparel; we sell apparel. They make home videos; we make home videos" (Swift 1991: 84).

Yet, it would be negligent to overlook the fact that the NBA's strategy of creating an economy of personalized commodity-signs, which would resuscitate the popular signification of the league, was structured according to the domineering logic and impulses of Reaganite racial politics (cf. Clarke 1991; Dent 1992; Denzin 1991; Giroux 1994; Hooks 1992; Jhally and Lewis 1992; Kellner 1995). Within the 1980s new right politics racial difference was deemed distinctly radical and un-American. This is likely why Larry Bird, defined in terms of "the Great White Hope," and Magic Johnson's endearing and nonthreatening style and demeanor became firmly entrenched into the popular consciousness and into the NBA's wider project. Even more instrumental at this stage was the social construction of Michael Jordan as an all-American icon.

Through the mutually reinforcing narrative strategies employed by Nike, the NBA, and a multitude of other corporate interests (e.g., Coca-Cola, McDonalds), Jordan was constructed as a racially neutered (hence, nonthreatening) black version of a white cultural model who projected an "All-American image. Not Norman Rockwell, but a modern American image. Norman Rockwell values, but a contemporary flair" (Castle 1991: 30). Jordan's racially transcendent image (see Andrews 1996) was All-American precisely because "to be an 'all-American' is, by definition, *not* to be an Asian-American, Pacific-American, American Indian, Latino, Arab-American or African-American" (Marable 1993: 113). In light of this and to an even greater degree than his immediate antecedent, Magic Johnson, Jordan became a commodity-sign devoid of racial integrity that effectively ensured the subversion of racial Otherness (see Willis 1991) but that also--because of his media pervasiveness (he is, after all, referred to as "the everywhere man")--further ensured the celebration of the NBA as a racially acceptable social and cultural space. By the mid-1980s through the early 1990s the NBA redefined itself to such an extent that it could justifiably sell itself as "a basic American pastime, as much a part of mainstream culture as baseball" (Lippert 1991: 10). This was evidenced by the rapid rate of growth in the league's gross revenue as derived from ticket sales, television contracts, corporate sponsorship, and the retailing of licensed merchandise. In quantitative terms the NBA's gross revenue leaped from $110 million at the start of the 1980s, to over $1 billion by the end of the 1993-1994 season and is now a multibillion-dollar corporate entity. Yet, for very pragmatic reasons the NBA was forced to embrace a world and market outside America.

## THE NBA AND JORDAN GO GLOBAL

The NBA seemed to have found or perhaps more accurately, invented the magic formula of sporting corporate success. Yet, to a large extent the NBA became a *victim* of its own success in the American market. By the early 1990s and after almost a decade of incredible expansion, the U.S. market had been saturated by NBA products and became relatively stagnant in terms of the all-important indicator of percentage annual growth as measured by game attendance, television audience, and retail sales figures (Helyar 1994). As Don Sperling, director of NBA Entertainment, stated in 1991, "Domestically, we're tapped. Ratings have peaked. Attendance has peaked. The market here has peaked" (Voisin 1991). Soon after David Stern (cited in Moor, 1992: 1B) warned:

> We don't want to become complacent, so we're going to fix it a little bit even if it isn't broken. In today's economy in the United States and the world, you've got to continually examine the way you do business, the audiences to whom you are trying to appeal, the technology that affects you, the competition. We certainly would like to stay where we are. But there's no way you stay some place good if all you do is try to make sure

you stay entrenched. Unless you're constantly pushing forward, you're going to slide back.

Having outgrown its home market, the NBA realized that sustaining its spiraling patterns of economic growth necessitated actively cultivating overseas markets. In Stern's words, "There are 250 million potential NBA fans in the U.S., and there are 5 billion outside the U.S. We like those numbers" (cited in Comte 1993: 42) Hence, pushing forward for the NBA meant deliberately evolving into a transnational, global corporation. As Stern warned, "Global development is a certainty--with or without us" (Heisler 1991: C1). Consequently, the NBA has become the [Trans] NBA, a transnational corporation emerging within the new spaces of postindustrial American capitalism, spaces that disregard constraints of national, regional, or imperial borders to such an extent that the only term available to describe them at the moment is "global." Although globalization per se is not necessarily a new phenomenon, what makes the rise and expansion of the NBA and other American corporations different is the context in which their commodity-signs have emerged. Arguably, the unique context of post-World War II American advancement of technological, capital, and media development has contributed to an Americo-centric flavor to the production, circulation, and consumption of global commodities (Andrews 1997). We briefly referred to the concept of the commodity-sign in our introduction, and at this point we wish to expand upon our understanding of the term by drawing upon the insights of Stuart Hall (1991: 27) who characterizes commodity-sign culture as being

> dominated by the image which crosses and re-crosses linguistic frontiers much more rapidly and more easily and which speaks across languages in a much more immediate way. It is dominated by all the ways in which visual and graphic arts have entered directly into the reconstitution of popular life, of entertainment and of leisure. It is dominated by television and by film, and by the image, imagery, and styles of mass advertising.

As Kellner indicates, America's commodity-sign culture is "exported to the entire world" and invades "cultures all over the world, producing new forms of the *global popular"* (1995). The extent to which the circulation of universal American commodity-signs has resulted in the convergence of global markets, lifestyles, and identities continues to be the focus of contentious debate. However, it is hard to deny the fact that celebrated American commodity-signs, including the NBA, have a vivid global presence. As Alms (1994: 1D) commented: "U.S. sports is well positioned globally. From movies to music, American entertainment dominates the world. It's partly a matter of performers' talent, but there's also a large role for marketing savvy. It's not an accident that Mickey Mouse and Madonna are worldwide icons." Consequently, the question that needs to be addressed is the role played by marketing in the process that saw the NBA become "the world's hottest sports product" (Weir 1993: 1A). In other words, how did the NBA and its key symbolic personification, Michael Jordan, go global?

In order to manufacture the transnational presence that it coveted, the league formed an overseas division, NBA International. Peopled with specialists in business, marketing, and international relations, the NBA International's brief was to mobilize relevant media and commodity flows in order to cultivate the league's visibility overseas and thereby hopefully increase the revenue derived from the global consumption of televised games and licensed products (Boeck 1990). NBA International is structured and organized around regional offices, situated in Geneva, Barcelona, Melbourne, Hong Kong, Mexico City, and Miami, through which television and licensed merchandise deals are negotiated. In terms of television contracts, the majority have been signed with national networks in individual countries, such as the 54-game deal recently signed with Television Azteca in Mexico. The NBA has also signed a number of strategically important regional deals with satellite and cable distributors such as Star, ESPN International, and SkySport. In total, the 1997 NBA finals were broadcast to 205 different countries (Valentine 1997).

However, although NBA events and games played overseas have become a fixture of the league's promotional calendar, according to those charged with its development, at no point was there any intention of setting up NBA franchises on foreign soil. Given the entry of the NBA's two Canadian franchises, the Toronto Raptors and Vancouver Grizzlies, perhaps their plans have changed slightly, though this expansion may simply be viewed as a natural extension of the North American market. Nevertheless, the NBA's strategy still appears to be premised on the power of the media to instantaneously circulate images and commodities beyond regional and national boundaries. Thus, Stern intimated in the early 1990s, "We're really going to be going global. We're not just in the sports business. It's media entertainment, licensing, brand names, home videos and a broad base of other businesses" (Alphen 1992: F3). Dave Checketts, president of the New York Knicks, expressed the league's global intentions more forthrightly, "I think we're just going to keep going (*expanding overseas*). Not for the purpose of selling teams, but to enhance licensing and TV packages" (Moore 1992: 1B). Hence, rather than colonizing the globe through franchise location, the NBA's *simulated* expansion was predicated on the media (in terms of images) and economic (in terms of commodities) dissolution of regional and national boundaries. This provided global citizens with ready access to the mutually reinforcing flows of globally advancing programming and products that s[t]imulated a global demand for the NBA's economy of explicitly American commodity-signs. In other words, NBA International mobilized global channels of televisual communication and product distribution in order to re-create the league, its franchises, and players as being "everywhere [*but nowhere*] at once" (Robins 1991: 28).

The television coverage sold by NBA International has been touted as offering an avenue for integrated, cross-national promotional campaigns. Global consumer-products companies are torn between a variety of ways to reach consumers. We're offering them one vehicle that does it all, that reaches a young and growing market base and that lends its own brand equity to theirs" (Grimm

1992: 20). In light of this a number of America's corporate icons have sought to enhance and refine their localized American identities within the global market by joining forces with the NBA and the likes of Michael Jordan.

Not only does the NBA benefit in terms of increased visibility and commodity-sign definition from the intertextual associations garnered through official sponsorship deals, but its promotional strategies both in the United States and abroad are also aided and abetted by the advertising machinations of numerous basketball footwear and apparel companies, the most significant operators being Converse, Reebok, and Nike. During the latter half of the 1980s Nike developed its own economy of universal basketball personalities, as nurtured through globally circulated commercials. From Nike's viewpoint, Keith Peters, the company's director of public relations, admitted the company "almost probably" profited from the NBA's global presence (Peters 1994). More directly, Josh Rosenfeld declared, "That's the great advantage the NBA has, we have shoe companies. They go out and market our players and our league for us. Nike marketed Michael Jordan for us" (1994). In more recent times Reebok has carried out the same function for the NBA with its aggressive global marketing of Shaquille O'Neal.

As the largest source of overseas revenue, representing worldwide gross retail sales of almost $300 million during the 1993-1994 season ("Licences" 1994), the spread of NBA-licensed merchandise has had a significant impact upon the substantiation and reinforcement of the league's economy of popular American commodity-signs to the global popular consciousness. The NBA is intertextually reinforced through the circulation of products such as caps, T-shirts, jackets, and a myriad of other items, all of which display one or more of the league's popular symbols and hence act as material promotional tools for the league. "Through the ties which have developed between advertising, commercial media, and mass entertainment, the intertext of product promotion has become absorbed into an even wider promotional complex founded on the commodification, and transformation into advertising, of (produced) culture itself" (Wernick 1991: 95).

The question of whether the global consumer is obsessed by the trappings of Americana per se or whether the global mass market is merely dominated by American commodity-signs has largely been overlooked. Instead, there exists a widespread assumption that particular cultural products, personalities, and experiences are universally popular simply because they signify America, and their consumption represents little more than a ritualistic celebration of America. Josh Rosenfeld, the NBA's director of international public relations, expressed precisely this strain of Americocentric cultural conceit in this forthright assertion: "People in other countries like the N.B.A. because they want the American look and the American image. And that's what they get with the N.B.A. Americana, a piece of America" (1994).

Unlike many other multinational corporations that engage in an operational strategy known as global localization in an attempt to blend into the local culture and effectively become a part of the indigenous ethnoscape, the NBA explicitly promotes itself as a signifier of cultural difference. Through its exaggerated

American identity the league is able to appeal to the local consumers, many-but not all-of whom are explicitly looking for commodity-signs that embody difference and Otherness. As Simon Barnes noted, "American-ness remains the prime selling angle for any American product: fizzy drinks, burgers, a sport, a Chicago Bulls cap to wear bill-backwards" (Barnes 1994). Consequently, the NBA's inverted rendition of global localization revolves around *not* becoming an accepted armature of the local culture but remaining and retaining a sense of the cultural difference upon which much of the league's popularity is grounded. Far from downplaying the Otherness of the NBA, the league consciously develops the *authentic* NBA experience as an authentic American experience, which is necessarily fundamentally different from the indigenous practices and experiences of the locale in question. As Rick Welts (cited in Alms, 1994: 1D) reiterated, "We are by definition an American sport. We are not going to be French in France" (or, in this case, Kiwi in New Zealand). In actuality the NBA's global presence and signification, as with its rise to prominence within the American market, have been realized through the attendant circulation of an expansive economy of mutually reinforcing commodity-signs. Yet it is important to recognize that the uniqueness of intertextually constructed commodity-signed cultures demands that, although increasingly constituted in and through global flows, local commodity-sign consumption and, hence, popular identity construction are necessarily contingent upon conjunctural specificities. Hence, not only does America signify different things in different sociocultural settings, but the precise signification and appropriation of the explicitly American NBA and Michael Jordan are equally context-specific.

## MICHAEL JORDAN AND THE GLOBAL/LOCAL NEXUS OF NEW ZEALAND

So, what is the "local" nexus of the NBA, Michael Jordan, and Americana in New Zealand? Without a doubt American cultural signs in the form of New Zealand-owned franchises have appeared, including McDonalds, Pizza Hut, Coca-Cola, and also the less obvious, but equally influential, foreign economic investment and ownership of traditional, state-owned and -regulated industries such as Telecom, NZ Rail, and TV3. As a result, nationalist, and certain cultural protectionist critics in New Zealand, adopting anti-imperialist stances, have condemned the influx of foreign, especially American and Asian, investment and commodities. Discourses dramatizing the threat of Americanization are rife, and this is particularly true in relation to the media. There are increasing concerns being expressed about the lack of local content and the amount of violence in imported U.S. television programming (Lealand 1991). Critiques have even been levied at American advertisements (Wilcox 1996). For example, Reebok's recent Shawn Kemp "kamikaze" campaign, which graphically portrays the NBA star competing one-on-one against a simulated evil video game opponent, was recently banned from New Zealand television by the censors because of excessive and unnecessary violence (Jackson 1997). In part, this reflects New Zealand broadcasting's more stringent (although unclear and often contradictory) codes of practice, but it might also be interpreted as a form of resistance against threatening images of America constructed through sport, technology, commodities, racial "otherness," and violence.

More specifically in relation to our focus, it is striking to observe the extent to which Michael Jordan and his corporate alliances are being increasingly articulated to these discourses. For example, consider the following quote from Ian Robson (Chief Executive Officer [CEO] of the Auckland Warriors, a new rugby league franchise and arguably the first professional sport team in New Zealand), during a roundtable discussion of the potential impact of media mogul Rupert Murdoch on the future of rugby, which highlights one perspective on the supposed "threat" of Michael Jordan, the NBA, and Americanization:

> As traditional a sport rugby is in this country and could I suggest that rugby league is building its own tradition as well, we're in a time now where for the young lads behind us, the most admired recognised and acknowledged sporting hero is not a New Zealander, he's a black American by the name of Michael Jordan and if we, as sporting adminis-trators don't use the resources that men like Murdoch are now placing before us in a positive sense to reestablish and create heroes, create role models I think that's the real challenge. Basketball in this country is the sleeping giant of all sports and if we sit back and don't meet and confront change we stand still at our own peril. (Robson 1995)

Perhaps Robson's and others' suspicions are not completely unfounded. A few brief, empirical examples are provided as some of the evidence of America's presence in New Zealand as articulated in and through the NBA and Michael Jordan. First, a recent (although admittedly pre-Jonah Lomu) study of sport heroes among teenagers in New Zealand indicated that Michael Jordan was, by far, the number one choice (although there was a gender difference) and the favorite television program was *Shortland Street*, a locally produced soap opera (Melnick and Jackson 1996). Second, in an interesting twist on our study of sport heroes, double New Zealand international Jeff Wilson, who was himself cited by some of our subjects, recently revealed his own sport hero. When asked who he'd like to be for one hour of any day, as well as the sportsperson he most admired and would most like to meet, he answered: "Michael Jordan" (Johnstone 1995: B2). Strikingly, Wilson and Jordan share a number of common features: both have competed at an elite level in two sports (Jordan in basketball and baseball, Wilson in rugby and cricket), both have (or have had) contracts with Nike and Coca-Cola (Jordan now endorses Gatorade), and both are part of an ever-expanding world wide web of self-reinforcing commodity-signs.

Third, we had the opportunity to discuss the popular cultural impact of Michael Jordan and the NBA with three young males in New Zealand, aged 7, 8, and 11. We were intrigued by their desire for NBA clothing, but what really astounded us were the depth and intensity of their interest in NBA collector's cards. They possessed not only a genuine business savvy in relation to the exchange and market value of their collections but also a broad knowledge base with respect to the players themselves, including personal anecdotes and performance statistics. Although these youths certainly held an interest in other players, particularly Shaq O'Neill, the return of Michael Jordan this year restored his center-stage position. For example, after drawing attention to his shiny new shoes, we questioned 7-year-old Simon about why he chose Nike, especially given his love of Shaq and his Orlando Magic baseball cap. In an admittedly leading question, we asked him if it was because of Michael Jordan's return, and he said yes. Subsequently, when asked what shoes he would have bought if Jordan had not returned, he said, "Reebok," and when asked why, he simply said: "Shaq." The interviews with the kids highlight an important point. In many respects the fascination of these Kiwi kids' with the NBA and Michael Jordan parallels that of youth in many other countries. Perhaps that only serves to reinforce the "global" point. However, the really fascinating thing about these kids is that they had never actually seen an NBA game; indeed, due to transmission and reception barriers they can't even subscribe to SKY television (the main source of NBA coverage) in the suburb where they live! Hence, while direct media coverage of a particular sport is important in cultivating a mass market of consumers, the available advertisements that employ particular cultural practices such as basketball and high-profile global icons such as Michael Jordan to sell their commodities are equally important in establishing a discourse that popularizes their mutually reinforcing intertextuality.

Fourth, as a follow-up to our interviews with Kiwi youth, a recent visit to Card Crazy, the local collector and trading shop, indicated that Michael Jordan remains the number one selling card, well ahead of Jonah Lomu, New Zealand's own new international rugby sensation. Indeed, when asked about how Michael Jordan cards were selling, the representative on duty simply said, "Is anyone else playing basketball?" While Michael Jordan remains the top-selling collector's card, one might have at least expected that Jonah Lomu would be having some impact on the domestic market. However, the card sales of more local rugby heroes such Otago provincial and All Black player Josh Kronfeld appear more popular. The whole notion of sport hero celebrity, global marketing power, and global/local nexus is currently emerging as an interesting point of discussion within both New Zealand and Australia. For example, in an article entitled "Jordan's Jonah May Be Lomu," Australian Rugby Union executive Ian Ferrier, referring to emerging All Black sensation Jonah Lomu, was quoted as saying that "Lomu is potentially the greatest merchandising animal in the world" (*Sunday Star Times*, October 10, 1995, B5) and that he would "knock Michael Jordan off his merchandising pedestal in the southern hemisphere" (South 1995: B2). Furthermore, Ferrier indicated that he found it "offensive that Michael Jordan, an American, was the highest profile sports star in Australia" (*Sunday Star Times,* October 10, 1995, B5). These comments reveal both a resentment of America and also an attempt to promote the new professional and media icon-oriented global rugby. Only time will tell whether, in fact, Jonah Lomu or some future rugby star will replace Michael Jordan, but the odds may be against them. Given existing American influences, including Nike's penetration of both rugby union and rugby league, and with new corporate and international arrangements materializing, there are already indications that Jordan (and others) may be used to launch the new super leagues. We have already witnessed the ARL's use of Tina Turner to promote rugby league as "simply the best" and Australian Rules football's employment of international sport stars such as Carl Lewis and John McEnroe (among others, including athletes from basketball, soccer, athletics, and boxing) to promote its game through the "I'd like to see that campaign." These examples testify to the significance of the global/local nexus of the increasingly mediated world of global sport. Companies such as Nike can negotiate the commodity-sign value of global icons like Michael Jordan in order to market their products internationally but simultaneously infiltrate and assist in the promotion of local indigenous games (such as Australian Rules Football), whose survival and success are anticipated to contribute to a larger market share.

Fifth and finally, it may be worthwhile to simply acknowledge some of the diverse ways in which Michael Jordan can be consumed within postcolonial New Zealand. For example, New Zealanders are among the world's highest Internet users, allowing them to access such World Wide Web sites as Bob Allison's award-winning home page, featuring Michael Jordan giving a whole new meaning to the term "net" working. Likewise, we can recount a recent exposure to Michael Jordan, albeit an indirect one. Earlier this year while watching CNN on a recently acquired SKY television subscription (effectively doubling the choice of channels to six!), we happened to catch Larry King's 10th anniversary episode, which featured not only highlights from the past 10 years but also congratulatory messages from famous guests and celebrities. One well-wisher was Oprah Winfrey. She described how, on a recent trip to Africa, she was amazed at the number of locals who knew Larry King but not Michael Jordan. Winfrey expressed her surprise and clearly implied that King, too, should be amazed that he was better known than Michael Jordan. This short sequence opens itself to a wide range of critical interpretations concerning the media, race, and self-reinforcing global icons, but it also provides a simple illustration of how Michael Jordan (the "everywhere man") is used as a benchmark by which the global popular itself is measured.

## CONCLUSION

So, does the fact that young New Zealanders idolize Michael Jordan or other American sport heroes and collect their cards despite the fact that they may never have seen them play the sport that made them famous or the fact that New Zealand youth play basketball wearing Nike shoes and clothing lend credence to the Americanization thesis? An understanding of the globalization/Americanization question may be as simple or as complex as the answer to this question.

To even begin to answer this question, several issues need to be considered. First, as Lealand (1994:34) notes, a product may signify "American, but it could be made in Korea, distributed from Taiwan, with profits returning to Germany." Second, several scholars have recognized that when attacks against Americanization emerge, and when protectionist flags of local and national cultures begin to fly, we need to ask what is being defended and in whose interests (cf. Forgacs 1993; Jackson 1994). Ultimately, it must be acknowledged that local and national cultures are not homogeneous, consensual wholes; they are fractured, segmented, and loosely bonded relations of power cutting across social class, gender, and race/ethnicity among other divisions.

Third, while it would be unwise to assume that these "peripherally located consumers" (to use Lash and Urry's 1994 conceptualizing) were fully cognizant with the dominant meanings associated with the NBA and Michael Jordan, it would be equally erroneous to deny that these consumers were not, to some degree, aware that the very style of the caps and/or the symbols stitched on them represented an expression of cultural difference; in this particular case, they signified America. However, the mere consumption of American commodity-signs cannot be equated with the Americanization of local cultures. Whether or not the *American* sign-value of a pair of Michael Jordan Nike Air shoes, a Chicago Bulls cap, or any other NBA-affiliated commodity-sign is prized or wholly inconsequential to its use-value, the mere tacit recognition of national cultural difference is significant to local consumers--both core and peripheral--of the global popular. Only through recognizing difference, in this case a notion of the American cultural Other, does it become possible to distinguish--through varying degrees of opposition--the cultural Self. Although his argument demands careful scrutiny, Geoff Lealand (1994:34) relates this notion of difference and otherness to the New Zealand context, stating that:

> American popular culture continues to be foreign because it is not New Zealand culture. Therein lies the source of its potency and attraction. Maori and Polynesian youth dress themselves in the garb of American basketball stars not necessarily because they want to be little Americans. They seek a more vivid, fantastical world that is beyond the constraints of their age, family, and neighborhood The may be increasing the profits of global marketing interests, but their real loyalty is to a global tribal network.

In this way, it could be argued that the accelerated circulation of *American* commodity-signs in the postwar era has not only produced a circulation of global cultural products and practices, but has led to the rearticulation of national and local cultural identities. Hence, rather than contributing to the dissolution of local identities through the establishment of a homogeneous global culture, the NBA, Michael Jordan, Nike and so on represent arms of a globally expansive media complex that, although a product of pervasive global processes, may nonetheless be responsible for energizing multiple popular and local cultures that in Grossberg's (1992) terms, have a (non) necessary relationship to dominant, but increasingly unstable national cultures.

When products, images, and services are exported to Other societies from some mythical, simulated (American) homeland, to some extent they inalienably become indigenized and consumed according to the conjunctural specificities of the national culture in which consumption is taking place. This reaffirms Appadurai's (1990) assertion that the global cultural economy is a derivative of "the growing disjunctures between ethnoscapes, technoscapes, finanscapes, mediascapes and ideoscapes."

As Michael Jordan's basketball career draws to a close, he remains one of the most successful athletes in history. However, beyond his sporting achievements we have argued that Jordan has become an international celebrity and a global commodity-sign. As such, he not only represents the NBA and the Chicago Bulls, but is a powerful symbol of American popular culture, and a vehicle for understanding the complexities of postindustrial economies, postmodern culture, and the status of America's influence on the world order. We have examined Michael Jordan's location within one specific context, New Zealand. However, only time and further analysis will inform us of the global meanings, politics, and effects on those who heed the calling to "be like Mike."

## REFERENCES

Allison, Peter. "Big Macs and Baseball Caps: The Americanisation of Auckland." *Metro* 24 (1991): 124-30.

Alms, R. "Globe Trotters: NBA Takes a World View of Marketing." *Dallas Morning News*, November 1, 1994, 1D.

Alphen, T. "NBA Czar Forecasts Big Exports For Sports." *Toronto Star*, January 22, 1992, F3.

Andrews, David. "Deconstructing Michael Jordan: Reconstructing Post-Industrial America." *Sociology of Sport Journal* 13 (1966): 315-318.

_____. *Deconstructing Michael Jordan: Popular Culture, Politics and Postmodern America*. Diss., University of Illinois, Urbana-Champaign, 1993.

_____. "The (Trans)National Basketball Association: American Commodity-Sign Culture and Global-Local Conjuncturalism." In *Politics and Cultural Studies between the Global and the Local*, edited by A. Cvetovitvh and D. Kellner. Boulder, CO: Westview Press, 1997.

Andrews, David, Ben Carrington, Steven Jackson, and Zbyniew Mazur, "Jordanscapes: A Preliminary Analysis of the Global Popular." *Sociology of Sport Journal* 13 (1996): 428-57.

Appadurai, Arjun. "Disjuncture and Difference in the Global Cultural Economy." *Theory, Culture and Society* 7 (1990): 295-310.

Armstrong, Edward. "The Commodified 23, or, Michael Jordan as Text." *Sociology of Sport Journal* 13 (1996): 325-343.

Atkinson, Joe. "The Americanisation of One Network News." *Australian Journal of American Studies* 13(1994): 1-26.

Barnes, Simon. "The Cream on Sport's American Pie Starts Turning Sour." *The Times*, October 21, 1994.

Becht, Richard. *A New Breed Rising*. New Zealand: Harper Collins New Zealand, 1994.

Bell, Avril. "An Endangered Species: Local Programming in the New Zealand Television Market." *Media, Culture and Society* 17 (1995):181-200.

Bell, Avril, and Gregor. "National Identities: From the General to the Pacific." *Sites* 30 (1995): 1-8.

Bell, Claudia. *Inventing New Zealand: Everyday Myths of Pakeha Identity*. Auckland: Penguin, 1996.

Boeck, G. "NBA Expands Its Horizons," *U.S.A. Today*, October 10, 1990, 2C.

Clarke, John. *New Times and Old Enemies: Essays on Cultural Studies and America*. London: HarperCollins, 1991.

Cole, Cheryl. "American P.L.A.Y., Consensus, and Punishment." *Sociology of Sport Journal* 13 (1996): 366-397.

Cole, Cheryl, and David Andrews. "Look--It's NBA Showtime!: Visions of Race in the Popular Imaginary." In *Cultural Studies: A Research Volume*, edited by N. Denzin, vol. 1. Greenwich, CT: JAI Press, 1996.

Comte, E. "How High Can David Stern Jump?" *Forbes* (June 7, 1993): 42.

Deeks, John, and Nick Perry. *Controlling Interests: Business, the State and Society in New Zealand*. Auckland: Auckland University Press, 1992.

Dent, G. *Black Popular Culture*. Seattle: Bay Press, 1992.

Denzin, Norman. *Images of Postmodern Society: Social Theory and Contemporary Cinema*. London: Sage, 1991.

_____. "More Rare Air: Michael Jordan on Michael Jordan." *Sociology of Sport Journal* 13 (1996): 319-324.

Duncan, I., and A. Bollard,. *Corporatization and Privatization: Lessons from New Zealand*. Auckland: Oxford University Press, 1992.

Du Plessis, Rosemary. *Feminist Voices: Women's Studies Texts for Aotearoa/New Zealand*. Auckland: Oxford University Press, 1992.

Dyson, Michael. "Be like Mike: Michael Jordan and the Pedagogy of Desire." *Cultural Studies* 7, no.1 (1993): 64—72.

Equinas, R. *Michael and Me: Our Gambling Addiction My Cry for Help*. San Diego, CA.: Athletic Guidance Center, 1993.

Featherstone, Mike. *Global Culture: Nationalism, Globalization and Modernity*. London: Sage, 1990.

Forgacs, D. "Americanisation: The Italian Case 1938-1954." *Borderlines* 1, no. 2 (1993): 157-69.

Giroux, Henry. *Disturbing Pleasures: Learning Popular Culture*. New York: Routledge, 1994.

"Gratuitous Violence" Otago Daily Times, editorial, October 24, 1992, 8.

Greene, Bob. *Hang Time: Days and Dreams with Michael Jordan*. New York: Doubleday, 1992.

_____. *Rebound: The Odyssey of Michael Jordan*. New York: Viking, 1995.

Greif, S. W. "Introduction: The Interweaving Themes of New Zealand Immigration." In *Immigration and National Identity in New Zealand*. Palmerston North: Dunmore Press, 1995.

Grimm, M. "The Marketers of the Year: David Stern." *Brandweek* (November 16, 1992): 20.

Grossberg, Lawrence. "Cultural Studies, Modern Logics, and Theories of Globalization." In *Back to Reality? Social Experience and Cultural Studies*, edited by A. McRobbie. Manchester: Manchester University Press, 1978.

Halberstam, David. "A Hero for the Wired World: In the In Satellite Age, Michael Jordan Has Become the Global Hero of a Global Show." *Sports Illustrated* (December 23, 1991):76-81.

Hall, Stuart. "The Local and the Gobal: Globalization and Ethnicity." In *Culture, Globalization and the World-System*, edited by A. D. King. London: Macmillan, 1991.

Hall, S. et al. *Policing the Crisis: Mugging, the State, and Law and Orders*. New York: Holmes and Meier Publishers, 1978.

Haworth, N. "Neo-Liberalism, Economic Internationalisation and the Contemporary State. In New Zealand." In *Leap into the Dark: The Changing Role of the State in New Zealand since 1984*, edited by A.Sharp. Auckland: Auckland University Press, 1994.

Heisler, M. "Uncommon Marketing" *Los Angeles Times*, October 18, 1991, C1.

Helyar, J. "The Inflated Riches of the NBA Are Pulling at the League's Seams." *Wall Street Journal*, November 1, 1994 A1, A4.

Hooks, B. "Representing Whiteness in the Black Imagination." In *Cultural Studies*, edited by L. Grossberg, C. Nelson and P. Treichler. London: Routledge, 1992.

Hutchison, Ian, and Geogg Lealand. "Introduction: A New Mediascape." *Continuum: The Australian Journal of Media and Culture* 10, no. 1 (1996):7-11.

Hutchison, V. "The Planetary Pakeha." In *Pakeha: The Quest for Identity in NewZealand*, edited by M. King. Auckland: Penguin Books, 1991.

Jackson, Steven. "Gretzky, Crisis and Canadian Identity in 1988: Rearticulating the Americanization of Culture Debate." *Sociology of Sport Journal* 11 (1994): 428-446.

_____. "Sport, Violence and Advertising: A Case Study of Global/Local Disjuncture in New Zealand." Paper presented at the North American Society for the Sociology of Sport Conference, November 5-8, Toronto, Canada, 1997.

_____. "Excavating the (Trans) National Basketball Association: Locating the Global/ Local Nexus of America's World and the World's America." *Australasian Journal of American Studies* 15 (1996): 57-64.

_____. *Mapping the Meaning of Michael Jordan: A Survey of New Zealand University Undergraduate Students*. New Zealand School of Physical Education, University of Otago, May 1994.

James, Colin. *New Territory: The Transformation of New Zealand 1984-1992*. Wellington: Bridget Williams Books, 1992.

James, C., and A. McRobie. *Turning Point: The 1993 Election and Beyond*. Wellington: Bridget Williams Books, 1993.

Jhally, S., and J. Lewis. *Enlightened Racism: The Cosby Show, Audiences, and the Myth of the American Dream*. Boulder, CO: Westview, 1992.

Johnstone, D. "Wilson Ready to Prove White Men Can Jump." *Sunday Star Times*, June 11,1995, B2.

"Jordan's Jonah May be Lomu," *Sunday Star Times*, October 10, 1995, B5.

Kearney, R. *The Wake of Imagination: Toward a Postmodern Culture*. Minneapolis: University of Minnesota Press, 1989.

Kellner, Douglas. *Media Culture: Cultural Studies, Identity and Politics Between the Modern and the Postmodern*. London: Routledge, 1995.

_____. "Sports, Media Culture and Race--Some Reflections on Michael Jordan."*Sociology of Sport Journal* 13 (1996): 458-467.

Kelsey, J. *Rolling Back the State: Privatisation of Power in Aotearoa/New Zealand*. Wellington: Bridget Williams Books, 1993.

_____. *Some Reflections on Globalisation, Sovereignty and the State—A WorldModel for Structural Adjustment?* Auckland: Pluto Press, 1996.

Lash, S,. and J. Urry. *Economies of Signs and Space*. London: Verso, 1994.

Lealand,Geoff. *A Foreign Egg in our Nest? American Popular Culture in New Zealand*. Wellington: Victoria University Press, 1988.

_____. "Selling the Airwaves: Deregulation, Local Content and Television Audiences in New Zealand." *Media Information Australia* 62 (1991): 68-73.

_____. "American Popular Culture and Emerging Nationalism in New Zealand." *National Forum: The Phi Kappa Phi Journal* 74, no. 4 (1994): 34-37.

"Licences to Thrive." *Daily News Record*, July 11, 1994, 10.

Lippert, B. "NBA Ads Make Game of Hoops as American as" *Adweek* (April 8, 1991): 10.

Marable, M. "Beyond Racial Identity Politics: Towards a Liberal Theory for Multicultural Democracy." *Race and Class* 35 (1993): 113-130.

McCallum, J. "The Everywhere Man." *Sports Illustrated* (December 23, 1991): 64-69.

McDonald, Mary. "Clean Air: Representing Michael Jordan in the Reagan-Bush Era. Diss.,University of Iowa, Iowa City, 1995.

_____. "Michael Jordan's Family Values: Marketing, Meaning and Post-Reagan America." *Sociology of Sport Journal* 13 (1996): 344-65.

Melechi, A. "The Transatlantic Gaze Masculinities, Youth and the American Imaginary." In *Men, Masculinity, and the Media*, edited by S. Craig. Newbury Park, CA: Sage,1992.

Melnick, Merrill, and Steven Jackson. "Globalization, the Mass Media and Reference IdolSelection: The Case of New Zealand Adolescents." Paper presented at the annualmeeting of the North American Society for the Sociology of Sport, Birmingham, Alabama, November 13-16, 1996.

Moffett, David. Chief Executive of the N.Z.R.F.U. quoted during an episode of *Assignment: Profitable Goals* (TV-One, Television New Zealand). Kerryanne EvansReporting, April 22, 1996.

Moore, D. "A New World for the NBA in the 90's." *Dallas Morning News*, November 6,1992, 1B.

Naughton, J. *Taking to the Air: The Rise of Michael Jordan*. New York: Warner Book,1992.

Palmer, G. W. *New Zealand's Constitution in Crisis: Reforming our Political System*. Dunedin: John McIndoe, 1992.

Perry, Nick. *The Dominion of Signs: Television, Advertising and Other New Zealand Fictions*. Auckland: Auckland University Press, 1994.

Peters, K. Personal communication, December 19, 1994.

Phillips, Jock. *A Man's Country?* Auckland: Penguin, 1987.

Ritchie, J., and J. Ritchie. *Violence in New Zealand*. Wellington: Allen and Unwin, 1990.

Robertson, R. *Globalization: Social Theory and Global Culture*. London: Sage, 1992.

Robins, Kevin. "Tradition and Translation: National Culture in Its Global Context." In*Enterprise and Heritage: Cross-Currents of National Culture*, edited by J. Corner andR. Harvey. London: Routledge, 1991.

Robson, Ian. Quoted during special rugby edition of *Fraser*. Television One, Television New Zealand, Mark Champion producer, June 26, 1995.

Rosenfeld, Josh. Personal communication, December 22, 1994.

Smith, S. *The Jordan Rules: The Inside Story of a Turbulent Season with Michael Jordan and the Chicago Bulls*. New York: Simon and Schuster, 1992.

_____. *The Strange Odyssey of Michael Jordan--From Courtside to Home Plateand Back Again*. New York: HarperCollins, 1995.

South, Bob. "Jordan's Stardom Light Years Ahead," *Sunday Star Times*, September 17,1995, B2.

Spicer, B., M. Powell, and D. Emanuel. *The Remaking of Television New Zealand 1984-1992*. Auckland: Auckland University Press, 1996.

Spoonley, Paul. Critical Issues in Society: Racism and Ethnicity. 2d ed. Auckland: OxfordUniversity Press, 1993.

_____. "The Political Economy of Racism." In *Studies in New Zealand Social Problems*, edited by P. F. Green. Palmerstown North: The Dumore Press, 1994.

_____. "The Challenges of Post-Colonialism." *Sites* 30 (1995): 48-68.

"Sport Shoe Ban Stuns Reebok" *The Dominion* June 20, 1995, 7.

Strasser, J. B., and L. Becklund. *Swoosh: The Unauthorized Story of Nike and the Men Who Played There.* New York: Harper Collins, 1991.

"Super League Kick Off Could Be Up in the Air." *Sunday Star Times*, September 24, 1995,B20.

Swift, E. M. "From Caviar to Corned Beef." *Sports Illustrated* (June 3, 1991): 78-4.

"TVNZ Axes Power Rangers." *Otago Daily Times*, August 25, 1994, 1.

"TVNZ Criticised for Violent Movie." *Otago Daily Times*, July 2, 1993, 1-2.

"TVNZ Rejected 48 Violent Programmes." *Otago Daily Times*, March 23, 1994, 31.

Valentine, John. "Show Me the Money! The Evolution of Revenue Accumulation in Professional Sport." Paper presented at the North American Society for the Sociology of Sport Conference, November 5-8, Toronto, Canada, 1997.

"Violence Rebuke." Editorial, *Otago Daily Times*, July 5, 193, 8.

Voisin, A. "NBA Takes Active Role in Dealing with AIDS Issue." *Atlanta Journal and Constitution*, December 3, 1991, F1.

Walker, R. "Immigration Policy and the Political Economy of New Zealand." In Immigration and National Identity in New Zealand edited by S. W. Grief. Palmerston North: Dunmore Press, 1995.

Weaver, K. "The Television and Violence Debate in New Zealand: Some Problems of Context." *Continuum: The Australian Journal of Media and Culture* 10 (1966): 64-75.

White, Richard. *Inventing Australia: Images and Identity 1688-1980.* Sydney: Allen andUnwin, 1981.

Wilcox. L. "Saatchi Rap: The 'Worlding of America' and Racist Ideology in New Zealand." *Continuum: The Australian Journal of Media and Culture* 10 (1996): 121-135.

## chapter 8

# Nelson Mandela, the Number 6 Jersey, and the 1995 Rugby World Cup: Sport as a Transcendent Unifying Force, or a Transparent Illustration of Bicultural Opportunism

*Scott Crawford*

## HISTORICAL INTRODUCTION

In 1652 Dutch pioneers established the Cape Town settlement. In 1795 the British invaded the Cape area and by 1833 had abolished slavery. A migration of dissident Dutch farmers known as Boers began the "Great Trek" eastward in the same year and, in so doing, set in motion the clear concept of an Afrikaner, separate nation that would be based not on racial integration but rather on racial superiority.

South Africa's history took a dramatic economic turn for the better with diamond discoveries in 1869 at Kimberley and gold discoveries in 1886. An examination of the life of Sir Cecil John Rhodes (1853-1902), the British industrialist and imperialist, helps to explain a colonial and South African mind-set where notions of social Darwinism and the view of the indigenous peoples as being childlike and primitive set the scene for a racially divided/compartmentalized society. Rhodes founded the De Beers Mining Company in 1880, and his British South Africa Company (1889) created a virtual monopoly over South African mining. Rhodes was prime minister of Cape Colony from 1890 to 1896. It should be pointed out that the Rhodes scholarships, supported by his vast personal fortune, did not exclude applications based on racial diversity.

In 1910 the Union of South Africa (what is known today as South Africa) was established. Virtually from the outset the native people and people of color were marginalized. By 1913, 70 percent of South African blacks found themselves restricted to 7.5 percent of the land area. The year 1948 saw Prime Minister D. F. Malan enacting apartheid laws. These draconian and highly racist state laws did much, much more than create a "separate but equal" division between white and black South Africans. Apartheid, for example, made it a criminal offense to take part in a "mixed marriage." Blacks were excluded from whites-only churches, universities, beaches, parks, buses, communities, and, of course, sporting clubs/associations. The race laws, as they came to be known, made it mandatory that all South Africans of color carried, at all times, a collection of documents--very similar to a passport--that would be shown to law enforcement agencies to show that they were "colored." Just as the United States (late 1940s and early 1950s) was beginning to look anew at its "separate but equal" policy on race in America, and the National Association for the Advancement of Colored People (NAACP) started to flex the "muscles" that eventually saw the emergence of political activists such as Medgar Evers and Martin Luther King, here was a civilized country, South Africa, implementing a nationwide system that implicitly relied on division, oppression, and ostracism.

## RUGBY IN SOUTH AFRICA

Rugby was introduced to South Africa in 1862, in the same decade rugby was first played at New Zealand boys' schools, by Canon George Ogilvie when he emigrated from Britain. With the exception of rugby, which Afrikaners adopted, most sports were English in their following as in their origin. However, there was a growing resentment against Britain within the Boer population, as Afrikaner nationalism was growing. Rugby then became uniquely associated with a way of life and with values to which the Afrikaner population was firmly committed.

South African sport did not generally cross the "color line" until the 1920s. Sport, one of the strongest expressions of leisure and rank in white society, became one of the dividing lines between the races in South Africa and a symbol of white status. It was not by chance that from the beginning the first clubs and federations were exclusively white. Reflecting this, the black clubs catered, with rare exceptions, to an exclusively colored, Indian, or African membership.

The colored population of the Cape had taken to colony rugby almost at once. In comparison, the black Africans working in Cape Town had little social contact with whites, and few of them adopted the game. At the beginning of the twentieth century the South African Coloured Rugby Football Board ran all colored rugby until the 1950s and administered African rugby until the 1930s. The Coloured Rugby Board's policy throughout the period was open with respect to race, and, in areas where no African clubs existed, black African players continued to play on its teams.

There were several reasons the Afrikaners adopted rugby so early and so enthusiastically. First, the period in which Boer nationalism took shape corresponded almost exactly with the period during which rugby appeared and spread across the country. Second, economic factors contributed. Of the two team sports available to them, football (soccer) and rugby, rugby had the advantage in that it could be played more easily on rough, unleveled, rural ground. Rugby also had symbolic significance: "Rugby is a sport ideally suited to ideological investment and the Afrikaners, who considered themselves to be a civilizing elite, a pioneer people conquering barbarism, recognized an image of their ideology in its symbols" (Archer and Bouillon 1982: 66).

The concept of "Afrikanerdom" advocated an unequivocal policy of racism. White and black were to remain in their allotted states of master and servant. It is not surprising, then, that South African rugby developed into a sport that was intrinsically "white." "Rugby was a game for pureness, for the elite it is 'the game of a social group,' the expression of a certain form of civilization" (Archer and Bouillon 1982: 69).

Some appreciation of the global impact of the 1948 South African apartheid legislation can be seen by a decision taken by the New Zealand Rugby Football Union (NZRFU). The NZRFU, realizing that apartheid would prevent New Zealand Maori players (selected to play for the New Zealand national team known as the All Blacks) from being admitted to play rugby for the All Blacks on a South African tour, had two choices. One choice, seemingly a straightforward and simple moral and ethical decision, would have been for the NZRFU to decline to tour South Africa. The actual decision, then and now, raises profound questions on the importance attached to preserving Springbok (the name of the South African national team)-All Black rugby exchanges.

In August 1948, the NZRFU announced that "players to be selected to tour South Africa cannot be other than wholly European." In other words, Maori (indigenous New Zealanders of Polynesian origin) players could not be considered because the South African apartheid and race laws would not permit them to enter the country. The incident exploded the myth of New Zealand as some Southern Pacific multicultural paradise. Simply stated, New Zealand Maoris were being discriminated against because of the colossal, overriding significance attached to the opportunity of New Zealand's taking on the South African national team at rugby. While the NZRFU "regretted" the situation, the acting leader of the opposition party, K. J. Holyoake, was, indeed, speaking for many New Zealanders when he said that "the honour and prestige of the whole of New Zealand are in the team's hands."

New Zealand rugby players have accepted the omnipotence of the NZRFU almost without question. In the history of New Zealand rugby teams playing in South Africa there has not been one clear example of resistance where a player said, "Apartheid is in operation; therefore, I quit." The one exception was the national team captain Graham Mourie, who declined to play against the South African tourists in 1981.

As a result of South Africa's apartheid laws various international sporting bodies and associations gradually, over time, began to boycott athletic contacts with South Africa. South Africa was excluded both from both the Olympic arena and from participating in the Commonwealth Games. International sports persons, both in individual and in team sports, came to realize that to visit South Africa and to play sports against South Africans gave a degree of credibility to a racist form of government. The sports boycott movement was energized and given greater political clout in the 1970s as United Nations resolutions called for a no-sports-contact-policy with South Africa. The Olympic Project for Human Rights was set in motion at San Jose State College in 1967 by African American sociologist Harry Edwards. This organization wanted a 1968 Olympic boycott, the return of Muhammed Ali's boxing titles, and the maintenance of a hard-line, exclusionary position vis-a-vis apartheid in South Africa and sporting contacts with that country. However, Arthur Ashe, the 1975 Wimbledon champion, became the first stellar athlete to come out and unequivocally decry any sporting links with South Africa.

Just one year later (1976) the All Blacks accepted an invitation to tour South Africa and play against the Springboks. Despite the protest withdrawal of several African countries from the 1976 Olympics and major riots and disturbances within South Africa, the tour went on.

## SPRINGBOK-ALL BLACK RUGBY EXCHANGES

The sociocultural impact of the Springbok's tours of New Zealand (1981) is still being studied by analysts. Clearly, there was a pro-rugby corps that seemed unable to perceive the wider ramifications of the attendant social upheaval. One match report of the final New Zealand versus South Africa test match concluded that "the referee sounded no-side to end a most dramatic and tense international" (Chester and McMillan 1983: 93). During the rugby match, antiapartheid protest culminated in a small plane's buzzing the field and dropping flour bombs on the spectators and scoring a direct hit with one missile on a New Zealand player in midfield. As a gesture of South African claims that sports provided opportunities for nonwhites, the Springboks included a colored player, Errol Tobias, on the team. This was, in their eyes, a symbol of integration. For some people it smacked much more of tokenism. Vincent Crapanzano (1985: 189) succinctly comments, "All of the Coloured and Blacks with whom I talked thought Tobias was a sellout."

In 1985 Geoff Chapple published *1981: The Tour*, a shattering and savage description of the events of the 1981 tour. What the book graphically illustrates is that New Zealanders were confronted with a series of social disturbances, including an account of the New Zealand police using their batons to strike down antiapartheid marchers. Although the majority may have clung to a tattered philosophy that "sport and politics should be mutually exclusive," the harsh reality of battered heads and flailing batons showed that rugby had become the fulcrum of profound social upheaval.

In conjunction with the launching of Chapple's book, the *New Zealand Times* compiled five book reviews. This collection of reviews is one of the most complete and wide-ranging accounts on the 1981 tour. The reviews were by Mike Steel; a *New Zealand Times* reporter, Trevor Richards, head of the Halt All Racist Tours organization; Bob Walton, the senior police officer in charge of "law and order" for the 1981 tour; Tom Johnston, a NZRFU councilor; and Sir Robert

Muldoon, then the country's prime minister. Their reviews reflect very different attitudes and values.

Retired police commissioner Bob Walton wrote, "Actually there was never any doubt in my mind that the tour had to continue. The alternative created unacceptable consequences for the future . If police failed to meet the challenge, what next. If the laws are not acceptable to the majority there is the ballot box."

Tom Johnston, NZRFU councilor, commented:

> It (the book) glories the anti-tour movement in an unabashedly partisan manner and wallows in moral self-righteous and self-professed intellectual superiority. In my contact with anti-tour people over the years I have been appalled by their fanaticism, their arrogant moral superiority and their conceited attitude of monopolizing intelligence. These themes manifest themselves throughout the text. Conversely, over the years rugby administrators charged only with the responsibility of administering their sport in the interests of participant members. The fact remains that the responsibility for political decisions lies solely with governments.

Sir Robert Muldoon, the country's prime minister:

> The pity of it all is the separation of football and apartheid--and this was a multi-racial Springbok team--from all the other problems and tragedies of Africa. Nearly as bad is the attitude which pervades the book that the police are not the custodians of our freedom under the law, the hallmark of a civilized community, but thugs, oppressors and villains. Fortunately exaggeration and selective observation by the author destroys the credibility of this theme for anyone but the most biased reader.

## THE 1985 TOUR

The 1981 tour of New Zealand by the South African rugby team effectively polarized New Zealand society. New Zealanders were categorized as "pro-" or "anti" tour. The manner and the scale of this 1981 polarization were so profound that it formed the "starting-off point" for the various campaigning groups in 1985 as plans went forward to send the national team to South Africa. Both in 1981 and in 1985 the polarization of New Zealand society tended to follow political and socioeconomic divisions. Lawyers, doctors, authors, professors, businessmen, and university students were prominent in making public statements condemning the tour. The National Party, both in 1981 and in 1985, was in favor of rugby links with South Africa; the Labor Party was not. One writer described the social division thus: "Middle class men opted for batons, indicating a willingness to charge the riot police--working class men [opted] for rugby boots" (Dann 1982). The tour and the antitour movements of 1981 and 1985 demonstrated a social class split and exacerbated class differences and hostility in New Zealand.

Empirical data to chart the changing mood of New Zealanders toward rugby links with South Africa are difficult to come by. Consider, however, the town of Palmerston North in New Zealand's North Island. In 1965, 10,000 citizens of Palmerston North welcomed the touring South Africans with a street procession and parade. In 1981, when the South African rugby team visited Palmerston North, the field was surrounded with a barbed-wire fence, and outside the ground 3,000 protesters fought with police riot squads. Nevertheless, inside the ground a packed attendance of 25,000 showed that for most New Zealanders "the game's the thing." A *New Zealand Herald* poll of New Zealanders on December 22, 1984, indicated 44 percent opposing a tour and 42 percent favoring it. It seemed as if the ghost of the 1981 tour would be resurrected.

The 1985 social divisions of New Zealand saw the NZRFU, the majority of the police, sections of the National Party, and most of the blue-collar working class in favor of an All Black tour to South Africa. On the other side were the antiapartheid organizations, the churches, those attached to New Zealand's liberal tradition, radical Maori groups, and a great majority of the middle class.

The ongoing debate over rugby contact with South Africa has revealed complex differences among Maoris that have nothing to do with strategies and tactics. "Cultural resurgence implied a reaction against the official view of identity, tradition, radical Maori society as a single cultural unit, and a renewed emphasis on tribal identity, traditions, and protocol" (Dunstall 1982). Maori groups were unable to produce a policy statement regarding the tours of 1981 and 1985. Common factors were disagreement, tribal solidarity, and conflict between the moderate, conservative New Zealand Maori Council and young, left-wing Maori activists.

Brian Lochore, the coach of the 1985 national team, emphasized the prevailing characteristic of rugby exchanges between New Zealand and South Africa:

> I have good friends, black and white, in South Africa and I have no anger in my approach to individuals there. But determination will come to the fore if the tour takes place and it is a determination which would have to be matched by the players. It will take determination and a feeling of national pride beyond anything players have known and expressed before to win a series in South Africa. (Veysey 1984: 23)

Bob Fox, the editor of the *New Zealand Times*, previewed the proposed 1985 tour to South Africa as follows:

> On one side, the protesters argue that treatment of the black in South Africa is a denial of human rights; on the other side the rugby-man argues that his civil rights are being denied by those who would stop the tour. I have the feeling that there is now [1985] a considerably larger group of people who wish the tour would not proceed. These are the ordinary people, the silent majority if you like, who saw the massacre of 1981 when this country was laid open by dissent. We bled. (Fox 1985: 6)

What did South Africans feel about the tour? Obviously, rugby followers were eager to see an All Blacks tour. Unofficially, such a series of test matches would have determined the world championship side, thus lending legitimacy to apartheid. Dr. Dannie Craven, the president of the South African Rugby Board, was interviewed for a program called "Sunday" screened by Television New Zealand on February 24, 1985. He was asked such questions as: "Are you aware of the depth of feeling in New Zealand?" and "Should not the New Zealand Rugby Football Union have some regard for New Zealand society as a whole?" Dr. Craven said that South Africans were in the right, that the New Zealanders were in the wrong, that rugby was the only thing that matters, and that football is more important than other issues, "and we, the administrators, can't be held responsible." Dr. Craven's zealous devotion to rugby for over half a century made him, as it made thousands of South African and New Zealand rugby followers, unable to see the overall picture, the much greater significance of the evils of apartheid. The program revealed that people had taken up their 1981 stance and that the country was again split down the middle.

Wilbur Smith, the best-selling South African novelist, reflected the Reagans' administration's policy of "constructive engagement." The NZRFU had traditionally supported this view of maintaining sporting links, often called the "building of bridges," to maintain lines of communication, while it was opposed to apartheid. Wilbur Smith spoke passionately about keeping open the lines of communication between New Zealand and South Africa:

> The South African has the same tradition of pioneer spirit as the New Zealander and the way to harden his attitudes, and to put ammunition in the hands of the people of ill-will who want to continue the existing system of government, is to shout and scream threats or break off communication. Because then the people of ill-will can turn to the young people and say, "The rest of the world hates you" and the only way to go is into the "laager"--the defensive circle used by the early settlers (Nerney 1985: 11).

Nineteenth- century legislation preventing non-European immigration to New Zealand, the systematic erosion of the Maori culture, the exploitative nature of the Treaty of Waintangi, and, in the sphere of rugby, the acceptance by the NZRFU (for nearly 50 years) of the nonacceptability of Maoris to tour as All Blacks in South Africa make "racism" and "bigotry" key words in contemporary analyses of New Zealand society. Maoris unequivocally got a chance to become stellar rugby players. However, it should be noted that the Maoris are greatly underrepresented in universities and professions in New Zealand and are overrepresented in morbidity, mortality, and crime (Older 1984).

For white South Africans rugby is the national sport. "Both South African and foreign observers have been struck by the quasi-mystical identification of the white community with the fortunes of its rugby players" (Archer and Bouillon 1982: 4). Afrikaners have clothed rugby in the ideology of the state. Rugby is synonymous with competition and rivalry. In historical era of South Africans isolation from the rest of the world, the Springbok team symbolized a political ethic--"the affirmation and strengthening of the racial community, a guarantee of its supremacy" (Archer and Bouillon 1982: 4).

It should be stressed that significant numbers of New Zealanders were supportive of the tour plans. The pro-tour group Society for the Promotion of Individuals Responsibility expressed its view through national spokesman Pat Hunt. He pointed out that numbers of letters had been written to the NZRFU urging it to agree to the tour (*Otago Daily Times*, February 4, 1985).

By March 24, 1985 when the NZRFU officially announced its decision to tour South Africa, there was in operation a nationwide protest movement. Principals and rugby masters from schools in Canterbury and Auckland wrote stinging letters to the NZRFU. The New Zealand media played an important role in extensive coverage of the events in South Africa, highlighting the riots, strikes, and measures used by South African police to control these events. Coalitions of active groups met weekly in Dunedin and Wellington to plan their strategies, and was two "pop" songs were written to show opposition to the tour. One was called "Don't Go," and the other was "You've Gotta Move (Move, Move) Cecil." This was a plea to the Chairman of the NZRFU, Cecil Blazey, that he step down from the office. At the Blue College (police training headquarters), intensive riot training went on to prepare for possible future disorders. The race relations conciliator, Hiwi Tauroa, stated that the tour should not take place, as did the Federation of Labor and the National Council of Churches. At the end of April, the then prime minister, Lange, said the NZRFU's decision was to its eternal shame. In May 1985 the NZRFU asked the High Court to strike out a writ of summons for a declaration and injunction against the union chairman and councillors' decision to send the All Blacks to South Africa. Two Auckland lawyers, Patrick Finnigan and Philip Reardon, both enthusiastic rugby supporters, challenged the validity of the union's decision. On July 9 these lawyers sought an interim injunction to prevent the departure of the All Black team to South Africa. The counsel for lawyers, Ted Thomas, said that the interim injunction was being sought "because the hearing now before the court is not expected to end before the All Blacks scheduled departure for the Republic of South Africa" (*Otago Daily Times*, July 15, 1985).

On Saturday, July 13, the High Court at Wellington granted the interim injunction to restrain the NZRFU, from proceeding with the tour until substantiative action had been determined. On July 17, the NZRFU on the eve of departure, abandoned plans for the All Black tour of South Africa. It should be reiterated that such a decision reinforced sharp divisions of opinion. The leader of the National Party and a qualified lawyer, Jim McClay, said he was "astonished" at the decision and that "it amounts to judicial interference with the freedom of New Zealanders who have committed no crime or illegal act to leave the country" (*Otago Daily Times,* July 15, 1985). Ron Don, a NZRFU councillor, described the interim injunction as being "absolutely incredible" and asked, "Why is rugby the only sport being discriminated against?" (*Otago Daily Times*, July 15, 1985). The national team captain, Andy Dalton, commented that the injunction was a "psychological blow to players selected to tour and a great disappointment" (*Otago Daily Times,* July 15, 1985).

Writing in 1988 in the *Journal of Sport and Social Issues,* this writer commented on New Zealand-South Africa rugby exchanges:

> The battle for Maori inclusion in an All Black side to South Africa was won in1970. In 1985 the New Zealand legal structure showed, in a most remarkable fashion, how the system could be tapped to bring about socially desired outcomes. Future scenarios for projected All Black-Springbok rugby games, while they would gladden the heart of a Dr. Craven, will never be able to shake off the violence of 1981 and the agitation of 1985. Rugby is, after all, only a game, whatever it may encapsulate and symbolize in terms of ideology, ethic and ethos. The bottom line is the necessity to see apartheid ended. The 1985 decision by the New Zealand judicial system showed that the game is subject tothe basic laws of the land. International law possesses the political clout to make certain that what Tom Brown called "the game of glory and hard knocks," must take cognisance of basic human rights.' (Crawford 1988: 117)

Rugby has dominated the cultural and social life of South Africa for nearly a century. The championship rugby trophies of South Africa are more akin to modern Holy Grails than athletic memorabilia. In South Africa the early settlers saw themselves in situations where toughness, resilience, stamina, and fortitude were more than pioneering virtues; they were critical elements to survival. Deeds, not words; actions, not feelings; and battle, not surrender were the roots to security. The environment was one where the game of rugby and its values became consecrated as a way of life. The tragedy has been that other, much more important values such as justice, equality, and fairness were totally disregarded.

For many South Africans token gestures were their response to attacks on apartheid. A mid-1980s interview highlights a tenor of condescension tinged with arrogance. "There are still divisions in the post office and sports stadiums, but rugby is now mixed. Tobias plays for Springboks, and we are proud of him" (Crapanzano 1985: 321). In other words, Afrikaner society was a conundrum. Sports administrators espoused the concept of racially integrated rugby in a society rigidly divided between black and white.

The issue of rugby relations between New Zealand and South Africa (during the apartheid era) was never satisfactorily resolved. In 1986, a group of New Zealand rugby players ignored the "no sporting contact" edict of the NZRFU and, calling themselves the "Cavaliers," slipped secretly out of New Zealand and played a series of unofficial rugby test matches in South Africa. On their return, these "outlaw" players were faced with one international game suspension by the NZRFU. Such an ineffectual response by the NZRFU called into question the degree of their commitment to the notion of "no sporting ties" with South Africa until the dismemberment of apartheid had been completed.

## APARTHEID'S DECLINE

For a most useful overall description of the sporting scene in South Africa during the apartheid era March L. Krotee's 1988 *Sociology of Sport* essay "Apartheid and Sport: South Africa Revisited" is highly recommended. Krotee felt that, despite a 30-year campaign to isolate South Africa from the realm of international sport to pressure and create "internal change" his view was not an optimistic one regarding the "continued bondage of South Africa's apartheid masters." Krotee noted in his conclusion "that the South African government has no intention whatsoever of abandoning apartheid" (Krotee 1988: 133).

Arguably, the pace of the collapse of apartheid surprised the majority of informed observers. By 1990 and under the premiership of F. W. de Klerk, apartheid was systematically dismantled and dismembered. The famous South African political dissident Nelson Mandela was released from the confines of house arrest. He had been sentenced to life in prison in 1963 and served 18 years as a prisoner in a jail on Robben Island. In 1992 South Africa was welcomed back to the Olympic arena, and the de Klerk/Mandela team received the Nobel Peace Prize the following year. In 1994 Mandela was elected president of a multiracial South Africa.

## THE 1995 RUGBY WORLD CUP

At the inaugural 1987 Rugby World Cup South Africa was not allowed to participate because of its apartheid policy. Leading up to 1995 World Cup held in South Africa there were those who, while cheered by the prospect of the renaissance of South Africa, understandably reviewed the dark days of apartheid rugby. John Taylor played for Loughborough Colleges, London Welsh, Wales, and the British Lions in the late 1960s and early 1970s. He is now a leading rugby commentator as both a television announcer and a London Fleet Street sports journalist. In 1995 he covered the World Cup. He spared no punches in a cover article for the *World Cup* magazine. He described the decision by the International Rugby Board in 1989 to send a World Invitation XV to South Africa to celebrate the centenary of the South African Rugby Board as "an appalling decision." Taylor saw 1989 South African politicians as a "totally amoral bunch who cared about nothing beyond a rugby game." Taylor, despite being heartened by Mandela's release on February 11, 1990, was unconvinced that South Africa was philosophically ready for radical change. In August 1992 Taylor was at Ellis Park, South Africa, to commentate on the Springboks/All Blacks game. Despite a clear opposition voice by the African National Congress, the game's opening ceremony highlighted the playing of "Die Stem," the Afrikaner anthem. This would be the equivalent of flying the Confederate flag at a modern-day Grambling College football game or inviting a Ku Klux Klan representative to an NAACP convention. Nevertheless, it is significant to note that on his return to South Africa in 1995 (free elections had been declared in the spring of 1994) Taylor spoke of a country "enjoying a post-election honeymoon" and a "spirit of harmony and understanding [that] had to be experienced to be believed" (Taylor 1995: 9-12).

Certainly, the 1995 World Cup turned into a glorious celebration for a multiracial and united South Africa. The final saw the home country, South Africa, winning a titanic match over New Zealand by a score of 15-12.

In terms of a unique primary source that demands analysis, the actual television film of the game is both remarkable and extraordinary. In the preliminaries there is the sight of a crowd of 60,000 neither segregated nor compartmentalized along racial lines. However, it should be stressed that the vast number of the spectators was white. The popular mass sport for Africans of color has been, and always will be, soccer. Nevertheless, the "new deal" for South Africa was dramatically underscored by a series of symbols and symbolic gestures. Nelson Mandela was dressed in a green and gold rugby jersey with the Springbok logo on his chest. It has to be stressed that it was this Springbok jersey that many black South Africans had historically seen as a talisman of the Afrikaner ancient regime. An additional feature of Mandela's rugby jersey was that it bore the number 6, the same number as that worn by the blond, white Afrikaner Springbok captain Francois Pienaar. Prior to the game Pienaar introduced Mandela to the players of both sides. Arguably, the "crowning glory" of this subplot, if you will, is the sight of Mandela shaking the hands of the one black Springbok, a 25 year policeman called Chester Williams. He then shakes hands with several of the Maori players from the New Zealand team. The scene is a powerful tableau in which, at least symbolically, a racist and divisive past seems shunted off into the wings of this special and compelling South African drama.

One record of the occasion notes, that "June 24 [1995] will stand in South Africa history as a day on which a yearning for national unity helped make their whole country Number One in the world" (*Mandela's Boks* 1995: 81).

*Sports Illustrated,* apart from the Olympics, the soccer World Cup, and occasions at which there is American representation, seldom spotlights overseas sporting exchanges. For example, there was no *Sports Illustrated* coverage of the previous World Cups of 1987 and 1991. However, the magazine had E. M. Swift cover the 1995 championship game, and his eloquent essay captures the magical sense of national togetherness that surrounded the Springboks' triumph. Swift writes of "whites and nonwhites . . . united by a sport" (1995: 33). Swift also highlighted the political astuteness of Mandela, who realized that the Springboks and the World Cup offered him a powerful political podium to promote a sense of national unity. In May 1995 Mandela visited the Springbok training camp, shook hands with the players, wore a Springbok cap, and told the players, "The whole nation is behind you." Swift reveals that this was no empty political rhetoric. One poll taken during one of the Springboks' early matches showed that 44% of the 9 million residents of Soweto, the black township on the fringe of Johannesburg, said that they watched the game. In a speech to a mainly black audience during the World Cup tournament

Mandela said that, "this cap [the Springbok one] does honor to our boys. I ask you to stand by them tomorrow because they are our kind."

Swift concluded his piece with these words:

> Given the right time and place, sport is capable of starting such a process [national unity] in a society. It is only a start, of course. The hard work always lies ahead, after the crowds have dispersed and the headlines have ceased. South Africa's racial and economic woes are not behind it. Far from it. But thanks to the common ground supplied by a rugby pitch, those problems appear less imposing than they did a month ago. (Swift 1995: 33)

Despite Swift's optimism the painful legacy of apartheid is neither easily dismissed nor forgotten. Following the conclusion of World War II there were, according to sports historian Douglas Booth, the growth and acceptance of extensive interracial sport on a global level. "South Africa was the exception. For some decades white South Africans preferred 'to suffer the humiliation of exclusion' from world sport 'rather than accommodate an even symbolic abandonment of their colour privileges and master role'" (Booth 1993: 13).

Somewhat surprisingly, relatively few research essays have been done by South Africans on the complex historical process that elevated Springbok rugby to a national civil religion. One exception is Albert Grundlingh and his paper entitled "Playing for Power." Grundlingh explores the linkages between rugby, Afrikaner nationalism, and masculinity. In his essay Grundlingh quotes Danie Craven upon the occasion of the 75th anniversary of the South African Rugby Board in 1964: "South Africa, this is your celebration, your festival, for the game belongs to you . . . . [the game of rugby] welded you together as nothing else in our history; and it has been this game which has provided you with a feeling of belongingness, of a oneness which so few people ever feel" (Grundlingh 1994: 417).

John Nauright and David Black, in a rugby examination that they published in a volume subtitled *Historical and Contemporary Perspectives*, also underscore the sociocultural importance of South African rugby during the apartheid era. "Afrikaner whites transformed British concepts of rugby imbuing it with qualities like ruggedness, endurance, forcefulness and determination. Games between English-speaking and Afrikaner teams became symbolic wars; however, they reinforced the notion of white male exclusivity by excluding all others from playing" (Nauright and Black 1995: 71).

By the 1980s there was a growing sense of South Africans' beginning to have more positive attitudes toward integrated sport. Nevertheless, these favorable attitudes were directed toward national/international sport, not sport at the club or school level. In the *Social Significance of Sport* the authors draw from a 1984 study carried out by G.J.L. Scholtz and J. L. Oliver which originally appeared in a 1984 issue of the *International Review for the Sociology of Sport:* "In 1983, among whites, the acceptance of integrated sport had actually declined since 1980-81. At the school level, 55% of the white respondents, compared with more than 87% of the other three groups [Indian, colored, black], favored nonracial school sport. These results suggest that within South Africa there is still much resistance to integrated sport, especially at the levels where most respondents would likely participate (McPherson, Curtis, and Loy 1989: 108).

While Nelson Mandela seemed energized by the Springbok success at the 1995 World Cup, it is important to note that both the institutional administrational structure of Springbok rugby and the Springboks themselves showed themselves to be fully aware of the important opportunity to draw a nation together. For example, the decision by the Springbok squad to visit Robben Island (Mandela's prison home for 18 years) and stand inside his prison cell garnered international attention and testified to an emerging new vision of a multicultural South Africa. Then there was the selection of Morne du Plessis as the Springbok manager in January 1995. Plessis was no political moderate. However, he realized that for change to be effective in South African society all South Africans had to get involved. He was a prime mover of grassroots rugby development in the Western Cape, a region where some degree of rugby integration had been successful. Leading up to the World Cup du Plessis supervised the national squad as they conducted coaching clinics in various black townships. In a *Times* (Great Britain) newspaper interview du Plessis commented, "I'm concerned that rugby is still perceived as a white man's sport. The World Cup can do a lot to take the game to the people. I just hope the team does well and the spark ignites, especially in the black community" (Gilmore 1995: 21).

## WORLD CUP POSTSCRIPT

The new South African flag is a bold, modernistic collection of colored stripes built around a motif of green/gold (countryside), blue (sky), and black/white (people). There is no remnant or trappings of the pre-1994 flag.

The Republic of South Africa (a landmass twice the size of Texas) has a population of 45,095,459. The ethnic groups are 75 percent black, 14 percent white, 9 percent colored, and 3 percent Indian. The South African Institute of Race Relations projects that, in the year 2010, white South Africa's total population will reach 59.7 million; the percentage of whites will come close to a single digit. What can one speculate on the state of Springbok rugby as the twenty-first millennium approaches?

*Sunday Times* (Great Britain) journalist Hugh McIlvanney, writing on the eve of the World Cup final in June 1995, posed a number of key questions. McIlvanney wondered if the "colour and celebratory fervour" of the World Cup would quickly fade. He, although profoundly moved by Mandela's "immense personality to regard it [the World Cup] as a significant happening" for Africans of color, wondered if Mandela's optimism would triumph, "set against rugby's eager and total submersion in the poisoned ethos of the apartheid years." Nevertheless, McIlvanney was cheered by two developments. The first was a £3 million building program set in motion by the South African Rugby Football Union. This scheme, to renovate and install 20 new sports grounds, promised to impact on the opportunities and provisions for sports participation by black town dwellers in South Africa. The second feature was the resolve of the 11-man executive committee of the South African Rugby Football Union (SARFU) use a policy of affirmative action to bring about a greater colored presence in future provincial and age-group rugby selections. Edward Griffiths, the SARFU chairman, noted that if South Africa continued to pick white teams, rugby would "stagnate" and it would "eventually lead to the death of the game" (McIlvanney 1995: 27).

Douglas Booth, already used as a source in this chapter, completed his doctoral degree on the sports boycott of South Africa. His voice and insights on rugby, apartheid, and African society are considerable. In 1995 Booth penned a stinging attack on Dannie Craven (president of the South African Rugby Board from 1956 until his death in 1993). Craven, for example, despite welcoming President F. W. de Klerk's political reforms, added, "I am pleased Mr. de Klerk did not say there would be equal votes. In a country like ours that would be fatal; we would have to have qualified votes" (Booth 1993: 9). Booth described Craven, arguably the single most important South African rugby administrator of the twentieth century, as an "incorrigible racist" (Booth 1995: 10). In a recent South African studies monograph, that testifies to the complex and convoluted nature of the interpenetration of rugby and apartheid/postapartheid society, Booth finds much evidence to support his major thesis that sport as a vehicle of social cohesion is but a myth (Booth 1993: 66).

One of South Africa's most brilliant novelists is J. M. Coetzee. Writing in 1978, he observed that "the political importance of rugby in South Africa . . . cannot be overemphasized" (Coetzee 1978: 18). In his 1997 autobiography Coetzee outlined his growing childhood awareness of apartheid and his bafflement of the nuanced behaviors that accompanied apartheid. "After he has left [Golding, a colored visitor] there is a debate about what to do with the teacup. The custom, it appears, is that after a person of colour has drunk from a cup the cup must be smashed. He is surprised that his mother's family, which believes in nothing else, believes in this. However, in the end his mother simply washes the cup with bleach (Coetzee 1997: 157).

In 1999 there will be a general election to find a successor to Nelson Mandela. In early 1998 Thabo Mbeki, the deputy president, succeeded Mandela as head of the African National Congress, which, in the 1994 general election, polled 62.7 percent of votes. The future of the "rainbow country" in terms of sporting integration and national solidarity--ethnic as well as economic--is uncertain. A December 1997 *Economist* analysis, despite touting Mandela as a leader "whose courage and moral stature set him above reproach," was headlined with the cryptic title "The End of the Miracle?" Sport was ignored as issues of race relations, education, economy, and social conditions were examined. Violent crime is at an epidemic level in South Africa--it is seven times higher than in the United States. The price of gold, a onetime staple star of the country's natural resources, reached $290 an ounce, the lowest price in 18 years. The *Economist* piece ended thus, "South Africa's future may well be unspectacular--neither miraculous nor catastrophic, more an ungainly muddling through. When you remember the legacy that apartheid bequeathed to the ANC, and the turmoil which so many predicted, that would be no small achievement" (*End* 1997: 19).

In 1997 the Springboks welcomed the British Lions (a combination of English, Scottish, Welsh, and Irish players) to South African soil. In a closely contested test match series the Springboks were surprisingly defeated. As the year waned, the Springboks toured Great Britain and showed their mettle and tremendous physical power in a drubbing of Scotland the--winning margin was more than 50 points--at the Murrayfield Stadium, Edinburgh. Chester Williams, however, continued to be the *only* colored player in the Springboks/Lions 1997 roster. The *Times* of London, as it reported on the successes of the British Lions against the Springboks in mid-1997, noted, "They [the Springboks] have lost the patronage of Nelson Mandela who, mindful of the government investigation into South African rugby finances, and one suspects silently disapproving of the lack of progress towards developing and integrating the races of his country, has not attended a match so far" (Hughes 1997: 28).

Another setback for South African rugby in 1997 was the dismissal of Springbok coach Andre Markgraaf when it was revealed on tape recordings that he used the term "Kaffir," a racial slur. This happened just at a period when the SAFRU was publicizing its national development program in which 16 athletes of color were being groomed for a hoped for, eventual admission to Springbok- level rugby. In terms of the game's popular appeal journalist Barney Spender wrote that, "rugby has made great strides in the black communities thanks in part to the radio coverage that has taken off since the World Cup. The response has been so good that the South African Broadcasting Company will provide commentary on the international [Springbok versus British Lions] in all 11 [South African] official languages" (Spender 1997).

Moreover, much has been made of the emergence of colored players such as Breyton Paulse and Jeffrey Stevens, who were in the early 1997 10-man squad that lost to Fiji in the final of the World Cup Sevens in Hong Kong. In late 1996 Paulse toured with the full South African team. It is significant to assess the official South African government response to the question of the racial composition of contemporary South African rugby. In January 1998 the embassy of South Africa faxed a 10-page summary of the situation to this writer, and the tenor of the materials seemed positive yet full of what seemed to be an honest appraisal of the extent of the problem. It was pointed out that there continue to be pressing needs for adequate rugby facilities in colored/disadvantaged areas. There was a recognition that colored rugby clubs would never have the appeal of the Kaizer Chiefs, the Orlando Pirates, and the Manning Rangers--soccer clubs! Natal player development head Hans Scriba was quoted as saying, "We estimate that it will take between five and 12 years from the start of our program for many of these (schoolboy) players to come through and make a real impact at provincial senior level" (Mangoaela 1998).

Despite this positive publicity, Springbok rugby continues to be a virtually all-white sport in a country where whites constitute only 14 percent of the population. Such imbalances give credence to both critics and cynics who saw Mandela's presence at the 1995 World Cup as playful posturing, or the guile and slickness of a political opportunist achieving a public relations conjuring trick but signally failing to initiate long-term racial cohesiveness or radical, social restructuring.

For this writer, however, Mandela's presence and persona at the 1995 World Cup were a spellbinding moment, a fragment of transcendent time in which a country with a bitter history of racism, bigotry, and oppression displayed bright hopes and youthful optimism. Rugby provided a unique arena in which South Africa "buried its divided past" (*End* 1997: 17). Despite continuing ethnic divisions and a plethora of social ills, there is a compelling sense that South Africa does have the derring-do to bring about a multicultural state and succeed. The concept of the South African Truth and Reconciliation commission epitomizes a country, especially moral leaders, who take innovative measures. The commission is committed to a free, nonracial South Africa in which blacks and whites can live in harmony. This Commission (under the leadership of Archbishop Desmond Tutu, winner of the 1984 Nobel Peace Prize) has invited confessions in exchange for amnesty for those who committed crimes under apartheid. Tutu's memorable vision of a rebuilt South Africa is, as with Mandela's embrace of Springbok rugby in 1995, much more than a public sleight of hand. It is a testament to processes shaped toward healing and integration.

"To pursue the path of healing for our nation [Tutu said] we need to remember what we have endured. But we must not simply pass on the violence of that experience through the pursuit of punishment. We seek to do justice to the suffering without perpetuating the hatred aroused. We think of this as restorative justice" (Greer 1998: 6).

Stephen Jones, in his account of the 1995 World Cup final between South Africa and New Zealand, concluded with these words, "Last night [Lomu, an All Black with a Pacific Island ethnic origin] was in a corner at the post-match dinner, strumming guitars and singing songs with Chester Williams [the solitary black Springbok], the South African left wing" (Jones 1995: 19).

Such an occasion of international exchange would have been unthinkable during apartheid. The fact that people of color were able to communicate and celebrate at a South African rugby engagement is a perfect corollary to the epiphany of Nelson Mandela and Francois Pienaar, with arms thrust skyward, as they exulted in a world championship for *their* "rainbow" country.

## REFERENCES

Archer, R., and A. Bouillon. *The South African Game: Sport and Racism.* London: Zed Press, 1982.

"A Blight on Rugby: Letter to the Editor." *Journal of Physical Education New Zealand* 28, 3 (1995): 9-10.

Booth, D. "The Consecration of Sport: Idealism in Social Science Theory." *International Journal of Sport History* 10, No. 1 (1993): 1-19.

Chapple, G. *1981: The Tour*. Wellington: A. H. and A. W. Reed, 1985.

Chester, R. H. and N.A.C. McMillan. *Centenary--100 Years of All Black Rugby*. Auckland: Moa, 1984.

Coetzee, J. M. "Four Notes on Rugby." *Speak* (July/ August 1978): 18-20.

_____. *Boyhood: Scenes from Provincial Life*. New York: Viking, 1997.

Crapazano, V. *Waiting--The Whites of South Africa*. New York: Random House, 1985.

Crawford, S.A.G.M. 1988. "Rugby in Contemporary New Zealand." *Journal of Sport andSocial Issues* 12, No. 2 (1988): 108-121.

Dann, C. "The Game Is Over." *Broadsheet* (March 1982): 27.

Dunstall, G. "The Social Pattern." In *The Oxford History of New Zealand*, edited by W.H.Oliver and B. R. Williams. Wellington: Oxford University Press, 1982.

"The End of the Miracle?" *Economist* 345, no. 8047 (1997): 17-19.

Gilmore, I. "Players Man Who Inspires Loyal Respect." *Times*, May 22, 1995: 21.

Greer, C. "Without Memory, There Is No Healing." *Parade* ( January 11, 1998): 4-6.

Grundlingh, A. 1994. "Playing for Power? Rugby, Afrikaner Nationalism and Masculinity in South Africa, c. 1900-1970." *International Journal of the History of Sport* 11, no.3 (1994): 408-430.

Hughes, R. "Tale of Blood, Sweat and Tears." *Times* ( June 30, 1997): 28.

Jones, S. "World Cup Report." *Sunday Times*, June 25, 1995: 19.

Krotee, M. L. "Apartheid and Sport: South Africa Revisited." *Sociology of Sport Journal*5, no. 2 (1988):125-135.

"Mandela's Boks." *Economist* 336, no. 7921 (1995): 81.

Mangoaela, N. Various materials received from Public Affairs, Embassy of South Africa, Washington, D.C., January 22, 1988.

McIlvanney, H. "The World Cup." *Sunday Times* June 25, 1995: 27.

McPherson, B. D., J. E. Curtis, and J. W. Loy. *The Social Significance of Sport*. Champaign, IL: Human Kinetics, 1989.

Nauright, J. and D. Black. "New Zealand and International Sport: The Case of AllBlack-Springbok Rugby, Sanctions and Protest against Apartheid." In *Sport, Powerand Society in New Zealand: Historical and Contemporary Perspectives*, edited by J.Nauright. Sydney: Australian Society for Sports History, 1995.

Nerney, F. "Hunter of Stories." *New Zealand Listener* 109, no. 2347 (1985): 9.

Older, J. "Reducing Racial Imbalance in New Zealand Universities and Professions." *The Australian and New Zealand Journal of Sociology* 20, no. 2 (1984): 243-256. *Otago Daily Times*, February 4 and July 15, 1997.

"The South African Council on Sport and the Political Antinomies of the Sports Boycott." *Journal of South African Studies* 23, no. 1 (1997): 51-56.

Spender, B. "Nation United." *Times* , May 19, 1997.

Swift, E. M. "Bok to the Future." *Sports Illustrated* 83, no. 1 (1995): 33.

Taylor, J. "The Day We Thought We'd Never See." *Rugby World Cup Magazine* (1995):9-12.

Veysey, A. "Lochore Sees Relevance to South Africa Tour." *New Zealand Times*,November 4, 1984.

# chapter 9

## Baseball, Cricket, and Social Change: Jackie Robinson and Frank Worrell

*Michael Malec and Hillary McD. Beckles*

The philosopher Jacques Barzun (1954: 159) once said, "Whoever wants to know the heart and mind of the America had better learn baseball, the rules, the realities of the game." By this he meant, in part, that we can understand a culture by observing its games, and because baseball is "the American pastime," a knowledge of this particular game could help explain the culture. C.L.R. James (1993: xxi), a scholar from the West Indies, once wrote, "What do they know of cricket, who only cricket know?" By this he meant that the game of cricket could be understood as more than just a game; it could be understood as "a metaphor for life" and, when played on the international level, as a "symbolic battle between the nations represented" (Kurlansky 1992: 282). This chapter explores two games, baseball and cricket, and two men who played these games, Jackie Robinson and Frank Worrell, and uses these to illustrate how athletes and their games were instrumental in contributing to large-scale social change in two different cultures.

> The cricket [baseball] field was a stage on which selected individuals played representative roles which were charged with social significance (James 1963: 66).

In ways that were different yet similar, Jackie Robinson, a baseball player from the United States, and Frank Worrell, a cricket player from the West Indies, both played roles that revolutionized their sports and introduced or symbolized significant changes in their societies. This chapter explores the careers of these two men.

On April 15, 1947, Jackie Robinson (1919-1972) took the field to become the first African American in the modern major leagues of baseball. More than 60 years of baseball's formal and informal racial segregation came to an end. A simple game, baseball, broke its "color barrier" a year before the U.S. armed services were fully integrated, 7 years before school segregation was ruled unconstitutional, and nearly 20 years before the significant civil rights legislation of the mid-1960s was passed into law. When Robinson occupied his position on the field, the face of modern American sport was radically changed. At the end of his first season he was named "Rookie of the Year," and two years later, he was his league's "Most Valuable Player." In 1962, he became the first African American admitted to baseball's Hall of Fame.

Robinson's effect on American society went far beyond the playing fields. Intelligent and articulate, passionate and committed, insistent on immediate social change but keenly aware of the need for a long-range plan, Jackie Robinson eventually became a leading spokesman in the battle against a variety of the ugly forms of racial segregation and discrimination in the United States.

The color line in American baseball at the end of World War II seemed as firm and unyielding as did the color lines throughout the United States. In much of the South, blacks and whites were legally barred "from attending the same schools, riding in the same sections of trains and buses, receiving treatment in the same hospitals, and competing in the same athletic contests" (Tygiel 1995: 7). In the North, the laws were less severe, but the everyday folkways were not.

In the West Indies, racism--and the responses to it--took somewhat different forms. Historically, emancipation came to the Anglo-Caribbean in the 1830s, three decades before it came to the United States. The great Caribbean civil rights struggles of the 1930s preceded by three decades similar struggles in the United States. It is highly significant that the population of most of the cricket-playing Caribbean comprised a far larger proportion of African descent than was the case in the United States.

In the West Indies, cricket teams were racially integrated well before Robinson was born. Indeed, there is no figure in West Indies cricket comparable to Jackie Robinson--that is, a figure who is recognized and acclaimed as the man who broke the racial playing barrier. However, the struggles within the West Indies to achieve racial equality in cricket and in society were no less massive, no less historically significant. But in the West Indies, with its majority black populations, the struggle focused not on playing but on leading. Although black West Indians had been playing alongside whites since the turn of the century, no black man had ever captained the West Indies team.[1] (North Americans need to know that the role of captain in cricket is far more important than the roles of captain or manager are in baseball or most team sports. The captain is both a player and a leader, a motivator and decisionmaker, a strategist and tactician.)

At the time when Robinson was integrating baseball, and the United States was slowly moving toward its modern civil rights era, the nations of the British West Indies were moving toward political independence. As they moved toward political equality, it was natural to demand all forms of social equality, including that of the captaincy of the national team. Those who controlled West Indies cricket, however, still maintained the colonial legacy of white superiority. "The whole point was to send black or brown men under a white captain. [This] would emphasize to millions of English people: 'Yes, [blacks] are fine players, but they cannot be responsible for themselves--they must have a white man to lead them'" (James 1993: 233).[2] Thus, in the West Indies, the fact that an integrated team was captained by a white man was a constant reminder, in the face of looming agitation for voting rights and self-rule, that blacks were assumed by whites to be incapable of leadership. Frank Worrell (1924-1967) would be the black West Indian whose athletic career would help to undo much of this colonial legacy.

Throughout Worrell's career as a professional cricketer he engaged and protested the established norms of the status quo as they pertained to ethnic relations, relations between players and officials, and the ideological implication of sport with respect to the rise and maturity of national society. His ascendancy in the postwar years as a distinguished player corresponded with the emergence of organized anticolonial politics and the crises of colonial society. Great black players of the interwar period, such as Learie Constantine (the first West Indian black cricketer to be knighted) and George Headley, had ensured that the cricket culture would become a site for the discourse of decolonization and democratic freedom. Worrell was placed, therefore, within a distinct ideological tradition, and the immediate postwar years would prove seminal. In this sense Worrell was, like Robinson, a product of his time. He was the heir to a political circumstance that saw the attachment of the culture of sports to the emergence of national society, just as Robinson was heir to a social circumstance that led to new norms for racial interaction.

Both Robinson and Worrell were strong-willed, with a passionate distaste for racism and racist institutional practices. But, as agents of social change, both men were seen by their antagonists as arrogant or insubordinate. As a teen, Robinson had a few run-ins with the police, and while in junior college he responded to a racial insult in a way that nearly escalated into a small race riot and left him with a police record. While serving in the army, a racial dispute stemming from his refusal to move to the back of a segregated public bus led to charges of insubordination and a general court-martial; he was subsequently acquitted.

It is well documented how, during his first year as a Dodger, Robinson had to control his passion and had to learn to "turn the other cheek." It was part of his agreement with the team's management that he would always restrain himself, that he would not respond to insult or intimidation, that he would suffer silently the slings and arrows of racism on the field and off. Robinson agreed to behave this way for two reasons. First, it was deemed essential that he conduct himself at all times as a perfect gentleman. His behavior, manners, and demeanor would have to be impeccable so that a racially hostile crowd would have no excuse to find fault with him.[3] Second, it was also agreed that, after the first year, the reins would come off, and Jackie would be free to be himself, free to respond to insults, free to intimidate the intimidators. All of these he did.

From his earliest professional years, Worrell attracted the reputation for being uppity, insubordinate, arrogant, and self-willed. In the context of the

Barbadian society that produced him, a society that saw itself as the Caribbean center of Englishness and as an imperial power within the West Indian empire, these traits had much to do with popular perceptions of his self-determination and his rejection of the ideological world of white supremacy.

For example, as a young cricketer playing for Barbados in regional contests, on a team led and dominated by members of the local white elite, Worrell rejected the policy of separate training for white and black players. Like Robinson, he also criticized the policy of separate travel facilities and accommodations for whites and blacks while on tour. He had so incurred the wrath of the local white business elite that he considered himself unemployed in Barbados. His biography tells the story that as a young man Worrell once walked the length of Bridgetown's Broad Street (the principal commercial area) and was unable to find any gainful employment.

The white community succeeded in promoting a negative image of Worrell through the print media it owned and encouraged the black community to share its opinion. On one occasion Worrell was booed by blacks and whites alike for his decision to leave his native Barbados to find a place where he was welcomed. On a later occasion, as a wider social understanding of his ideological postures developed, he was given hero receptions on his return to the island after short visits overseas.

In 1948, Worrell confronted the white officials of the West Indies Cricket Board of Control over remuneration for the upcoming tour to India. He classified himself as a professional and demanded to be paid £250 to tour. The white players on the team, mostly from planter-merchant families, were amateurs who neither needed nor demanded any salary. When he was denied the fee, Worrell refused to tour, though he was considered the best batsman on the West Indies team. In this regard, Worrell's struggle reminds us of a similar struggle that Curt Flood initiated with baseball's patriarchal "reserve clause"--that part of a standard baseball contract that bound a player for life to a given team. The establishment sought to crush Worrell for his insubordination, but his popularity as a cricketer in islands other than Barbados and among players in England protected him from domestic wrath.

Robinson and Worrell faced other, similar challenges. For example, both had to deal with the prospect of failure. If Robinson failed on the field, all black players would be set back in their quest for participation. If Worrell failed as a captain, it might be decades before another black were awarded that position. Consequently, it was crucial to those who supported both Robinson and Worrell that they chose and nurtured men who had the athletic talent and skill to do what was necessary for success on the playing field. More important, perhaps, baseball and cricket had to select men whose personalities, backgrounds, emotional states, and intelligence would enable them to withstand the challenges that they were about to face.

"Worrell [Robinson] was no accident." (James, quoted in Manley 1988: 147). It was no accident that Worrell was the first black to captain the West Indies team: he was a highly skilled athlete, he was university-educated (University of Manchester), he had a middle-class upbringing that served him well in nonsport social settings, and he had a burning distaste for discrimination in his sport and in his culture. Three of these four traits can be ascribed to Robinson, as well (Robinson, the grandson of a slave, was from a working-class background).

Worrell was no accident, and neither was Robinson. The color line in American baseball at the end of World War II seemed as firm and unyielding as did the color lines throughout the United States. In much of the South, blacks and whites were legally barred "from attending the same schools, riding in the same sections of trains and buses, receiving treatment in the same hospitals, and competing in the same athletic contests" (Tygiel 1995: 7). Robinson excelled in sports in high school, junior college, and college before turning professional. He set a junior college record in the longjump. (The record he broke had been held by Jackie's older brother, Mack. Mack also had won a silver medal in the 200-meter dash at the 1936 Olympics.) Jackie was the first four-letter athlete in the University of California, Los Angeles' (UCLA) history, and it is of some interest that of baseball, basketball, football, and track, the former was probably Jackie's weakest sport! Worrell's career was more singularly focused on one sport, but those who saw him play football (soccer) will attest to his high level of skill in that sport as well.

There is, however, another sense in which Worrell and Robinson were "not accidents." Although one can argue that the tide of history would have eventually produced the first black baseball player and the first black cricket captain, the timing of the tides that specifically produced Robinson and Worrell was not happenstance. Robinson did not appear on the scene and declare his intention to be the first player. Rather, Robinson was identified, scouted, and selected by Branch Rickey, the general manager of the Brooklyn Dodgers and a political conservative. As early as 1942 or 1943, Rickey had developed a six-part plan to bring black players to the Dodgers (Falkner 1995: 104). The parts of his plan included: (1) securing the support of the Dodgers' Directors and stockholders; (2) finding the player who would be the right man on the field; (3) finding the player who would be the right man off the field; (4) ensuring a positive reaction from the press and the public; (5) obtaining the support and understanding of the black community; and (6) securing the cooperation of the other Dodger players. Rickey revealed his plan to the Dodgers' Board of Directors in 1943. He first met Robinson in 1945 and signed him to a professional contract. In 1946, Robinson played in the Dodgers' farm system in Montreal. In 1947, Jackie Robinson made history in the United States.

> "When the local whites started to play cricket, black Barbadians watched and the black middle class began not only to play, but to form clubs. But the white upper classes continued to hold all the economic and political power and social prestige." (James, quoted in Manley 1988: 147)

The histories of baseball in the United States and cricket in the West Indies share many traits. Both sports were initially controlled by whites. While the early history of both games in the nineteenth century is primarily a history of white and middle-class players and white organizations, blacks and the working classes soon embraced both games. The U.S. Civil War era was the period of the "democratization" of baseball, and the post-emancipation era in the West Indies had a similar effect on cricket. Ownership of both games was in the hands of wealthy whites, and this has remained so to the present day. But although ownership is a form of privilege, other positions of privilege and control, in both sports, did not remain exclusively white in the latter half of the twentieth century.

By the early 1950s it was understood by the black West Indian majority that Worrell was the obvious and logical choice as captain of the West Indies team. Yet, less qualified whites were given the task. Public opinion outside Barbados was outraged, and discussions reached fever levels in Jamaica and Trinidad with respect to the issue of racial injustice, the future of colonial rule, and the popular call for democratic decolonization. The public campaign, led by the distinguished intellectual C.L.R. James, assumed national proportions in Trinidad. James returned to his native Trinidad in 1958 and began to write for the *Nation*, one of the island's leading newspapers. The *Nation* was an organ of a political party, the People's National Movement (PNM). James' writings were strongly political and were aligned with the rise of Eric Williams (who was to become the first prime minister of Trinidad and Tobago) and the PNM. "The connections between cricket, culture, and politics in the West Indies are evident in any discussion of Williams and the PNM" (Stoddart 1995: 246). The issue was clear: the ascendancy of a black man--Worrell--to leadership of the regional cricket team would signal the end of white supremacy in the governance of the West Indies and the conceptual abandonment of the colonial project. James knew this, Worrell knew this, and the people of the West Indies knew this, too.

The white community of Barbados and its supportive element within the black middle class never welcomed or accepted Worrell, even while he was captain of the island's team, the star West Indian player, and later captain of the West Indies team.

Robinson and Worrell were similar in that both had their advocates, Rickey and James, respectively. But there was also an important difference: Robinson was selected by a white man more than he was campaigned for by the black population, although many blacks had been working for "a" black player, Rickey selected "the" black player. Worrell was championed by James, but he was more importantly campaigned for by the black masses as both a symbol and "the" individual who deserved the honor.

In 1958, Worrell was offered the job as West Indies captain to engage in a test series against the Indian team in India and the Pakistan team in the West Indies. He refused because he held the view that the white establishment in the West Indies was willing to accept him as captain against only nonwhite teams and not against white teams. He was prepared to accept the leadership against only the Australians or the English. (As an aside, we note that India in the 1930s and Pakistan in the 1940s had captains of color. This perhaps suggests an attitude toward the imperial occupation of India that was different from the attitude toward the West Indies; the legacy of slavery might explain some of these attitude differences.)

Finally, in 1959, the year of his graduation from Manchester, Worrell was appointed captain of the West Indies team for the 1960 tour to Australia and the 1963 tour to England. James noted that once Worrell had done a good job in Australia and had shown the world that black men would manage their own affairs with distinction, he (James) would be off to London to demand constitutional independence for the West Indies islands. "[When] Worrell took over the captaincy of West Indian cricket . . . [he] changed the image of the game in the minds of West Indians and also the expectations . . . with respect to the performance of the captain, team spirit and the behaviour of the West Indian cricket hero" (St. Pierre 1995: 119-120). In 1962, the process of constitutional decolonization began with independence for Jamaica and Trinidad and Tobago. The linkage was clear. Cricket and national society were symbolically represented in the person of Frank Worrell.

Although the West Indies team lost to Australia in the first series led by Worrell, he won the hearts of the Australians and fascinated the English cricketing world not only with his athletic talent but also with his charm, wit, and warm personality. Worrell did not bring instant success to his team, but he laid a foundation on which the West Indies would, over the next decade, build themselves into the world's best cricket team, a distinction that it would hold into the 1990s.

Worrell's achievements in sport can partly be measured by the recognition that was bestowed on him by others outside sport. He was appointed to the Senate in Jamaica; he was appointed dean of Student Services at the University of the West Indies; and he was knighted by Queen Elizabeth in 1964. His face is on the Barbados five-dollar note. No Barbadian had ever received such a constellation of honors (Manley 1988: 169). No West Indian athlete has ever done more to change the face of sport in the Caribbean region and thereby change the entire region's attitudes toward race.

Prior to 1997, Robinson's societal achievements were not rewarded in the same way by his country. (He did appear on a U.S. postage stamp issued in 1982 as part of the "Black Heritage" series.) However, after baseball he did achieve some measure of success in business, was influential on civil rights issues with both Presidents Kennedy and Nixon, and worked as a special assistant to New York governor Nelson Rockefeller. His anniversary year, however, produced numerous tributes to the man who, more than any other athlete, changed the face of modern sport in the United States and thereby greatly contributed to changing the entire society's attitudes toward race.

Both Worrell and Robinson deserve their places of honor in their respective sports. But both men are more fittingly celebrated for the changes that they helped produce in the larger arenas of history and culture. Neither man chose his destiny, but neither shirked his responsibility.

## NOTES

This chapter is revised and expanded from an earlier version.

1. Actually, the great George Headley captained the West Indies team in 1948 for one test match in Barbados because the white captain was ill. Headley was thus, technically, the first black man to captain the West Indies, although it was understood by all that this was a temporary measure with no seminal significance, Headley was probably the greatest West Indian player of his time and therefore the greatest casualty of the concept of white leadership.

2. This view is similar to that expressed by Al Campanis in his infamous remarks, in 1987 that blacks lacked the "necessities" to occupy leadership positions in baseball and other sports.

3. John McPhee (1969: 28-29) tells how the young Arthur Ashe was taught to behave on the court. His teacher was Dr. Robert Johnson, who held certain principles as absolute requirements-in his view-for an assault on a sport as white as tennis. Supreme among these was self-control--"no racquet throwing, no hollering, no indication of discontent with officials' calls." Since players call their own lines in the early rounds of junior tournaments, he insisted that his boys play any opponents' shots that were out of bounds by two inches or less. "We are going into a new world," he told them. "We don't want anybody to be accused of cheating." Dr. Johnson wanted Ashe "to be psychologically prepared for any adversity." just as Rickey wanted Robinson to be prepared.

## REFERENCES

Barzun, Jacques. *God's Country and Mine*. Boston: Little, Brown, 1994.

Beckles, Hilary McD. *An Area of Conquest*. Kingston: Ian Randle, 1994.

Beckles, Hilary McD., and Brian Stoddart. *Liberation Cricket*. Manchester: Manchester University Press, 1995.

Falkner, David. *Great Time Coming*. New York: Simon and Schuster, 1995.

James, C.L.R. *Beyond a Boundary*. Durham, NC: Duke University Press,1993 [1963].

Kurlansky, Mark. *Continent of Nations*. Reading, MA: Addison-Wesley, 1992.

Malec, Michael A., and Hilary McD. Beckles. "Robinson and Worrell: Athletes as Agents of Social Change." *Journal of Sport and Social Issues* 21, no.4 (1996): 412-418.

Manley, Michael. *A History of West Indies Cricket*. London: Andre Deutsch, 1988.

McPhee, John. *Levels of the Game*. New York: Farrar, Strauss, and Giroux, 1969.

Stoddart, Brian. "Caribbean Cricket: The Role of Sport in Emerging Small-Nation Politics." In *Liberation Cricket*, edited by H. Beckles and Brian Stoddart. Manchester: Manchester University Press, 1995.

St. Pierre, Maurice. "West Indian Cricket--Part I: A Socio-Historical Appraisal." In *LiberationCricket*, edited by H. Beckles and Stoddart. Manchester: Manchester University Press, 1995.

Tygiel, Jules. *Baseball's Great Experiment: Jackie Robinson and His Legacy*. New York: Vintage Books, 1995.

# PART IV

## Sport and Cultural Identity

*chapter 10*

---

# Documenting America: Ethnographics of Inner-City Basketball and Logics of Capitalism

## *Cheryl L. Cole and Samantha King*

"In the fourth quarter, when we was putting that showtime down so heavy, the crowd would be sitting in the stands trying to avoid going to the bathroom. Addicts be sittin' there, forget they had habits. When the game was over, people didn't know where they parked their cars. And the most amazing thing was, there were no police. There were never any problems, because people had too much respect for the game" (Pee Wee Kirkland).

We are writing this chapter when *Soul of the Game: Images and Voices of Street Basketball* has just been published (Huet 1997). The book's publication corresponded with the opening of an exhibition by the same name in New York. Most recently, the exhibition came to Chicago's Field Museum. The coffeetable-size book is a 128-page, photographic essay that features urban playground basketball players whose claim to fame is precisely their distance from "the global." The 130 images compiled in *Soul of the Game* were taken by award-winning, Boston-based photographer John Huet. Huet is known for his portraits of athletes and his commercial work for companies like Adidas, Asics, Champion, Fila, Gatorade, Nike, Puma, and Reebok. Given his position in commercial photography, Huet has participated in the production and circulation of what has become one of the most celebrated sites/sights of the black body.

Young, bald-headed, African American men, deftly carved muscles, and lean, sweaty, statuesque bodies dominate the text. The images differ in terms of angles and range; some photographs appear to capture action; others depict seemingly motionless bodies. Photographs of several older, now-retired African American players contribute to a sense of stabilization and coherence between the past and present. The privileged aesthetic--bald heads, topless, slender, shiny, polished, sweaty torsos--is defined within the landscape of asphalt playgrounds. The inner-city mise-en-scene--codified through dilapidated courts, crumbling cement, rusted rims, and chain nets--contributes to the sense that the athletes appear as "they really are." Moreover, the written texts accompanying the images promise to give unknown celebrity players ("legends") names and identities and to trace the playground origins of well known professionals. A mixture of representational strategies--hip-hop and rap poetry; interviews with players; short, descriptive histories; and tritone photographs--evokes codes of autobiography, photographic realism, and humanism. The signs of the inner-city mise-en-scene are codes of authenticity; the physical space (the playground) is a space of invention that explicates and reiterates racial difference. In combination, the images and writings facilitate a sense of discovery of the undiscovered.

Authenticity and ethnographic status are constituted, to a great extent, over and against the more familiar National Basketball Association (NBA). Representations that distance the asphalt game from the NBA's more crassly commercialized, global, theatrical productions enhance and elaborate the conviction that *Soul of the Game* is the point of entry into a privileged subaltern sphere. The assessment of the urban playground as a non-commercialized space recalls the long-celebrated and affective codes of amateurism. Amateurism and its corresponding notion of discipline appear to recapture "the game" and produce players who play for the love of the game rather than financial gain and global fame. A prefatory statement by Richard "Pee Wee" Kirkland, whose legendary status renders his assessments unquestionable, identifies the playground as an original space that predates the NBA:

> The best things you see in pro ball today were invented 25 years ago in the schoolyards of Harlem. And that's still where it's done best. All the moves of tomorrow are being invented by some unknown kid in Philly, Chicago, Atlanta or you name it. Razzle and dazzle, creation and devastation--these are what the street brings to the game. (Huet 1997: 1)

Authenticity and autonomy are insistently inscribed through declarations ranging from the playground game's (the street's) distance from commercialized global sport, to its origin status--the originating space of "moves" popularized and compromised in the hybrid space of the NBA. Stated differently, authenticity and autonomy are representational effects of discourses that simultaneously distance and implicate the urban asphalt game in the NBA's "conditions of existence"--the new global economic. Indeed, in *Soul of the Game*, the freer reign of expression is only one sign of authenticity: the source of the game's ostensible realness is an inner spirit--designated by the concept of soul--possessed and displayed by the individual players. The combination of "street" and "soul," designations of danger and fascination, represents and enforces popular notions of blackness. Just as Paul Gilroy has argued of hip-hop:

> The very qualities in [basketball] that have led to it being identified not as one black culture among many but as the very blackest culture--one that provides the scale on which others can be evaluated--have a complex

relationship to the signs of pleasure and danger that solicit identification
from white affiliates to practitioners. (Gilroy 1994: 56)

Photographic inscriptions of black bodies in *Soul of the Game* provide a
familiar experience in racial looking. Subjects are routinely photographed in
shadow, emerging from darkness, feigning defiant, racially charged looks. The
collection is punctuated by head-only, criminalizing mug shots with familiar front
and side profiles and hooded "gangbangers," scowling and frowning. By extension,
*Soul of the Game* is an element in, and an expression of a, discursive formation in
which fear and fascination are expressed routinely, albeit in varied and contradictory
ways, through the persistent and repeated flow of images across the black bodies of
NBA players. Commodified visual images of players like Michael Jordan contribute
to a "hyperindividualism" that imagines America as progressive, inclusive, and
multicultural. The rank and file are routinely represented, in contrast to ideal-
transcendent figures, in terms related to lack of discipline, excesses, and danger.
Those dangers evoked in and through the images in *Soul of the Game* are immediately relieved by celebrated images of motion, sweat, soul, and purity. This "soul"
privileges the asphalt playground as a critical vantage point for understanding and
reevaluating the more explicitly commercial interests of professional players and
provides a sense of belonging.

In *Looking for the Other*, E. Ann Kaplan (1997) asks, "Does the African
American impoverished male think of himself as belonging to America (to some
construct of the nation as community)? And, if so, does this only deepen his rage at
exploitation and exclusion?" *Soul of the Game* appears to answer Kaplan's
questions. The local playground is celebrated, implicitly and explicitly, as a site of
belonging, a communal space, even a political intervention that facilitates
democratic promises. Indeed, *Soul of the Game* is, in part, a narrative--albeit a
contradictory and complex one--about freedom. The book, like the national culture,
is punctuated by images of unfettered and unshackled bodies suspended in air above,
beside, or below the rim. Such bodies seemingly transcend the weight of history.
While accompanying poetry like "My Freedom Got a Rim" by Poetri sustains the
equation of freedom with basketball, Paul Gilroy (1994) has argued that the pursuit
of freedom is a vanishing element in black vernacular culture. In drawing a
connection between the meaning and possibilities for and of freedom and the
visibility and fetishization of black bodies, Gilroy claims that the longing for
freedom, previously a dominant goal of black culture, has been transposed into a
racial biopolitics of fucking: "a means of bonding, freedom, and life" (1994: 59). It
is in and through this new version of politics that "the person is defined as the body
and in which certain exemplary bodies for example, those of Mike Tyson, Michael
Jordan, Naomi Campbell, and Veronica Webb become instantiations of community"
(1994: 59). Significantly, Gilroy suggests that sport, particularly basketball, occupies
a similar position to that fucking in the new political sphere.

Gilroy is principally concerned with the replacement of political communities with individual bodies: "If it survives, politics becomes an exclusively aesthetic
concern with all the perils that implies, and the racial body, arranged suggestively

with a precision that will be familiar to readers of de Sade, supplies its critical evaluative principle" (Gilroy 1994: 59). Moreover, he suggests that the model of black publicity derived from rituals and musical utility survives, but in a "vestigial and profane form," its "precious dialogical attributes" replaced by "morbid phenomena" like the Americocentric image of the black public sphere as the inner-city basketball court--a space that displaces sound with gestures, a space in which words are second to gestures (1994: 60). The poetry and images in *Soul of the Game* are effects and instruments of power that conflates bodily aesthetics (in particular, the black male bodily aesthetic) and politics. "Carefully Choreographed" by Gregorio Deshawn McDonald captures and reinforces this new "political mood":

> Fades, dreads and bald heads run back and forth across the court sporting high top shoes low-hanging shorts and the competitive nature of all sports: color never matters. Set all differences aside to achieve a common dream. Dr. King died for that message but his ideal lives and breathes as simply as street ballers performing carefully choreographed ballets called plays all across the nation. (Huet 1994: 116)

While Gilroy's analysis focuses on a politics of freedom figured through the body, our interest is in the social and psychic consumption of that politics of freedom in its commodified form. In *Soul of the Game*, street ball is presented as real ball:

> [S]treet ballers test their ability daily to perform these street ballets and they don't need to get paid to play cause you can't put a price tag or a thirty-second infomercial bag on what they do. They like to win the respect of the other nine players on the court and even though they may like wearing a certain brand of shoe if shoes could play basketball don't you think they would have by now? (Huet 1994: 116)

The images--tritone, naturalized frames of the body, the gritty streets, the chain-link fence in combination with black bodies against stark white backgrounds--suggest that these bodies are less spectacular, simulated, trained, constrained, manufactured, and tainted than those on display in popular arenas. Freedom, in this case, is associated not with the freedom of the free market but with being free *of* the market, outside the circuits of capital production and consumption. The irony of this claim is twofold: first, the book is a commodity and product of America's fascination--played out through consumption--with the inner city and African American male bodies; second, the signs of multinationalism are explicitly and implicitly present throughout the text. Most specifically, the representations in *Soul of the Game* repeat the aesthetic associated with the African American male body's entrance into the public through the commercialized realm--that is, through the familiar terms of transformation, transcendence, and corporate logos. Such representations circumvent questions about the multinational corporatization of the NBA, America, and its inner cities.

*Soul of the Game* exists in a long line of representations so saturated with these images that it would be impossible to provide a comprehensive survey. Situated in its broader representational field, *Soul of the Game* exemplifies a contemporary focal point for a growing popular archive of images (the ethnographic urban) that appears as social commentary for consumption. Indeed, "legends" and "soul" are perhaps the latest rendition of these articulations. Perhaps no other media event demonstrates America's desire to know the "urban other" and America's particular fascination with, and consumption of, urban black masculinity more forcefully than *Hoop Dreams*. Although documentaries are typically relegated to the margins of the American film industry and popular media, *Hoop Dreams,* a three-hour, low-budget, independent documentary, drew a phenomenal amount of support and more popular attention than other documentaries this decade. Described as "beautifully made" and "one of the best and most deeply moving American films of 1994," *Hoop Dreams* quickly became a megahit in the United States. Popular critics used the key term "achievement" to affirm the film's "claim to truth"--a truth that ostensibly intervened in previous and more familiar documentations of the inner city, urban problems, and African American inner-city youth.

The release of *Hoop Dreams* coincided with the publication of numerous popular books about the inner city, including Alex Kotlowitz's (1992) *There Are No Children Here*; Daniel Coyle's (1995) *Hardball: A Season in the Projects*; Greg Donaldson's (1994) *The Ville: Cops and Kids in Urban America*; and Darcy Frey's (1994) *The Last Shot: City Streets, Basketball Dreams*. Indeed, the popular reception of *Hoop Dreams* and these books is intricately bound within a historical context in which black bodies and masculinities became highly commodified and marketable. Moreover, this historical context shaped and has been shaped by America's fascination with, and acquired knowledge of, "urban problems," particularly as those problems were rendered visible through coming-of-age narratives of African American male youths. Furthermore, racially coded coming-of-age narratives have accrued political purchase as they have been transmitted to consumers through figures such as Magic Johnson, Isiah Thomas, and Michael Jordan, whose increasing visibility in the public domain remains bound (enabled and limited) to the NBA's economic development and success. NBA superstars were created through, and provided fertile ground for, narratives of limited scope that emphasized recovery, transformation, transcendence, and utopic social visions through discipline. Morality tales of promise and possibility for individuals, families, and nation (the consumption problematic) circulated through the NBA celebrity zone and accrued purchase through the often-invisible, but nonetheless affective, rhetorical figure of the gang member. Black, urban masculinity was visualized (enacted and encoded) through a fundamental distinction between the athlete (primarily figured in the urban basketball player) and the criminal (typically figured through the gang member): the tension generated between the two categories served as the ground for well-rehearsed and familiar 1980s stories continually circulated and fed by the mass media industry for public consumption and spectatorship. While gang members were seen as the embodiment of alien values, athletes were viewed as the embodiment of dominant values. These dominant values were displayed most prominently in assimilationist repetitions of "desires to exit," to "find a way out" of the ghetto. As public consumer spectacle, the sport/gang dyad governed and organized a way of looking, seeing, and recognizing urban America, its problems, and their causes.[1]

Although not immediately apparent, the figures of sport and gangs were "joined" by a third factor--the failed black family. Sport and gangs were epresented not only as channels for what are understood to be the corporeal predispositions of African American youth but as the available substitutes for the "failed black family" (figured through the mythic welfare mother and the mythic, absent, inseminating black male). That is, the "failed black family" (a historical mechanism for displacing the social, economic, and political forces shaping the lives of the urban poor) never simply lurked in the background, lending plausibility to the significance of sport and gangs in the lives of urban youth, but, instead, occupied the same symbolic space: violations of the nuclear family form were a subtext in coming-of-age narratives.[2]

While America's "will to know" and these journalistic portrayals of urban life potentially enter and intervene in America's public debate over federal assistance and urban problems, the analyses of urban youths' conditions and struggles are, according to Massing (1995), typically moved forward at the expense of their parents: an older generation of African Americans is held responsible for the obstacles and struggles that condition the youths' everyday lived experiences. While "real" racially coded coming-of-age stories have increased in popularity, they have failed to introduce alternative or oppositional knowledges into public debates. For us, then, the popularity of such images does not simply convey an innocent cultural enthusiasm; instead, America's contemporary, voracious appetite for such images is an expression of America's social subjectivity--the "nation's state of mind." As we see it, *Hoop Dreams* not only is evidence that the ethnographic urban is a privileged genre but is symptomatic of the ethnographic minutiae of everyday life. As such, *Hoop Dreams* provides a privileged locus for interrogating the obsessive consumption of these images as they combine power, knowledge, and pleasure.[3]

Given the weight of the racist order that the documentary would need to overcome to even simply disturb historically conditioned "ways of seeing" so-called urban problems, racism, whiteness, and America (which we deploy as a signifier for an identity fabricated through imagined origins, community, and character), we examine the national celebratory reception of *Hoop Dreams*. Rather than offering a powerful contrast to previous and more familiar documentations of the inner city, urban problems, and African American inner-city youth, we think that the film encodes and enacts a series of now-familiar themes, events, and figures whose terms actively enable and limit how we imagine violence, power, and our selves in late modern America. We see the film and its popular representations as consistent with a national spirit and imagination inseparable from the prominence accrued by African American basketball players over the last decade. Moreover, we suggest that this prominence needs to be understood within wider global transformations that have devastated, reordered, and revitalized urban areas in ways that are indissolubly linked to the perverse profitability of the transnational corporations. We consider "the urban basketball player," who is implicated in these networks, to be a subject and object of late modern forms of discipline and consumption. In Lauren Berlant's (1993) terms, these "'stars' [are] transformed into trademarks and corporate logos, prosthetic bodies that ideally replace the body of pain with the projected image of safety and satisfaction that commodities represent" (Berlant 1993: 178). As such, these stars (NBA celebrities) are key figures in a reconfigured racism that allows American (middle-class) audiences to recognize themselves as compassionate and ethical subjects in 1990s America. Our primary concern in this chapter is to examine the production of this self-recognition and its implication in the NBA body as a late modern form of discipline and object of public consumption. Investigating "the problematic" of this psychic and social consumption requires that we recognize race as not simply possessive or performative but always contingent and relational.

We contend that America's celebratory reception of *Hoop Dreams* is a celebration of a production whose truth-effect is the self-recognized ethical and compassionate subject. As such, the celebratory reception is intimately bound to a series of exclusions and displacements that inform America's dominant reading of the film. To a great extent, these exclusions and displacements are embodied in the "origin stories" promoted by the mainstream media. By our view, these origin stories are indicative of both America's historical amnesia and its correlate conception of history shaping dominant readings. Moreover, we contend that the film's primary figure of exploitation and social wrongs, "Gene Pingatore," functions as a figure for displacements that allow American middle-class audiences to derive identification and pleasures from the film. In other words, guilt and the audience's implication in exploitative spectatorship and consumption practices are displaced onto Pingatore. We argue that such figures of exploitation and social wrongs work to protect particular understandings of America as they repress the banal violences and monstrosities that shape the everyday lives of already vulnerable populations in urban areas. Stated differently, we read *Hoop Dreams* as an expression of a national imagination and spirit that represses and displaces violence under the guise of care, compassion, social cause, and ethical superiority.

## *HOOP DREAMS*: THE FILM

> *No movie has ever done more to deflate the hot air out of racial stereotyping without making a big deal out of it.*--Mike Clark

*Hoop Dreams* is a three-hour documentary filmed between 1986 and 1991. The film focuses on the experiences of two African American teenagers growing up in racially segregated Chicago neighborhoods. Although only 14, William Gates and Arthur Agee already demonstrate the sort of basketball skills that suggest that they will be recruited to play at the college level and possibly employed to play in the NBA. The film, which begins as they prepare to enter high school and concludes as they begin their college careers, is organized around their high school years. Viewer position and context are immediately established through the opening juxtaposed images: the viewer travels the expressway north toward the Chicago skyline. As the elevated train running parallel to the expressway moves into the frame, a group of young African American men playing basketball on the court below comes into view. The camera follows a player whom we will later recognize as William Gates as he approaches the basket to shoot; the graffiti-laden concrete wall surrounding the court comes into focus. The camera moves around a concrete high-rise, the sign of urban housing projects, to reveal Chicago Stadium as fans enter to attend the 38th annual NBA All-Star game. A picture-perfect steal and dunk by the East's number 23, Michael Jordan, is met by overwhelmingly white, exuberant spectators as they celebrate the physical achievement they have just witnessed.

As the All-Star Game (apparently) continues inside Chicago Stadium, the elevated train moves us to the Cabrini Green Housing Project, where William lives with his mother, Emma, and brother, Curtis. Although housing projects signify danger, the alien, and the antinormative in the national imagination, Cabrini Green is introduced not through signs of decay or danger but through signs of community. Signs of "typical" summertime neighborhood activity surround Cabrini Green: youngsters play in the high spray of an open fire hydrant as a local means of dealing with the heat; men who lean against parked cars and women who mingle on the sidewalk and sit on their front stoops engage in neighborly exchanges; two young boys play basketball on a makeshift court at the corner of the building. As the camera lingers outside the door to someone's home, the sounds of the NBA All-Star game inside suggest that despite, their geographical dispersion, the images are temporally bound. Inside, we see William intensely watching the closing moments of the All-Star game. He steps outside his apartment and onto the playground court, where we watch him, in slow motion, dunk on a netless rim.

> Right now [close-up of William, expressing his aspirations through a wide smile], I want, you know, to play in the NBA like anybody else would want to be. That's something I dream-think about all the time, you know, playin in the NBA.

The camera takes us to the West Garfield Park neighborhood where Arthur lives with his mother, father, sister, and brother. Again, in the intimacy of a home where the NBA All-Star game plays on television (we hear the announcer introducing Isiah Thomas), a smiling Arthur describes his desires and imagined NBA life:

> When I get in the NBA, I'm ah, the first thing I'm gonna do is I gonna see my momma, I'm gonna buy her a house. Probably get my dad...a Cadillac, Oldsmobile, so he can cruise in the game. [Cut to Arthur's mother, Sheila] He dreams about it. He look at those basketball commercials when they be advertising like these Nike shoes and he'll tell, he'll tell his little small brother "Joe, Joe, that's me."

We watch as Arthur is "discovered" by Earl Smith on one of his "expeditions" to a park near Central and Congress Parkway. Smith, an insurance executive and "unofficial scout" for area high schools, instantly recognizes Arthur's talent and arranges for him to attend St. Joseph's summer basketball camp. St. Joseph High School, which remains the featured education-basketball structure in the film, is a predominantly white, private Roman Catholic school in Westchester, a western suburb of Chicago. It maintains its position as one of Chicago's high school basketball powerhouses by recruiting players from across the city.

Based on his basketball skills and performance at the camp, Arthur is recruited to play for St. Joseph High School by Gene Pingatore, the head basketball coach. In a conversation with Arthur and his family, Pingatore not too cautiously promises that Arthur's chances of securing a college scholarship will be enhanced by attending St. Joseph.

Pingatore admits (apparently in conversation with the filmmakers, who remain off-camera) uncertainty about Arthur's potential, given the "playground," which he defines as talent without confidence, he sees in him. However, Pingatore sees it all, which he defines as a "combination of personality, confidence, talent, intelligence," in another new recruit, William Gates. Both Arthur and William are given partial scholarships from St. Joseph and, like Isiah Thomas, will commute three hours daily by train to attend the school. Their first year, William "starts" on the varsity squad, while Arthur wins the freshman team starting point guard position. While both entered reading at a fourth grade level, we routinely see William, whose academic skills improve dramatically his first year, in the classroom. Arthur's academic work does not advance at the same rate: Arthur appears less interested in his high school education and seems to view it as a required detour on his way to the NBA.

Meanwhile, through a series of upbeat, last-minute, high-drama game-day scenes, we learn that William is also excelling on the basketball court and drawing attention from Division I schools and sportswriters who appear on a television talk show and have identified him as the next Isiah Thomas.

A tuition increase at the beginning of their sophomore year creates potential problems for both students. Patricia Wier, president of *Encyclopedia Britannica*, makes a contribution to a scholarship fund that, in combination with other sources, including "Cycle" ( a Cabrini Green organization), covers William's tuition. By midsemester, Arthur is forced to leave St. Joseph's because his parents have been unable to make the required tuition payments and now owe St. Joseph $1,500. This is due, in part, to the cycle of hiring and layoffs that Bo Agee is caught up in throughout the film. Sheila Agee, Arthur, and the coach at Arthur's new (inner-city) school, Marshall High, believe that Arthur's expulsion was due to his failure to live up to coach Gene Pingatore's expectations. Shortly after Arthur starts at Marshall, the narrator tells us that after 20 years of marriage, Arthur's father, Bo, has left the family. Forced to quit her job due to chronic back pain, Sheila Agee eventually receives welfare. She expresses her discomfort with receiving public assistance (apparently aware of, as she implicitly responds to, dominant understanding of "welfare generations") by contrasting her situation to that of her parents, who always worked for a living. The impoverishment cycle continues when Arthur turns 18 (a birthday of particular significance for his mother since, as she explains, many young black men don't live to 18) and is no longer eligible to receive public aid.

Soon after, Arthur's best friend and teammate, Shannon, talks about the importance of his friendship with Arthur and Bo's drug use, violent behavior, and time in jail. As Sheila explains that she has taken out a protection order against Bo, her words fade to music, and the camera sweeps over a collection of legal papers. The camera lingers on black type that allows us to read documentation of Bo's criminal record:

**GUILTY-- BATTERY**
**GUILTY-- BURGLARY**
**SENTENCED TO IMPRISONMENT-- JAIL 37 DAYS**
**SENTENCED TO PROBATION 2 YEARS**

William's freshman and sophomore challenges were narrated around, and confined to, trying to lead his team to the state tournament; however, during his junior year, William injures and then reinjures his knee in an exhausting and intense practice session. Under doctor's instructions, he reluctantly sits out the rest of the season. Indeed, under the stress of his knee surgery and when his basketball career is in jeopardy, Emma Gates reveals her desire and investment in William's professional basketball career. "I really thought Curtis was gonna make it, but he didn't make it, so I just wanted this one to make it." Curtis, a high school standout and player of the decade at Colby Jr. College, developed a reputation for being difficult. Although awarded a scholarship to the University of Central Florida, he dropped out of school because of a conflict with the coach. The clips from Colby do far more than demonstrate Curtis' exceptional talent; they also make inexplicable his refusal to abide by the rules. Now working for a security firm, Curtis describes his life in terms of his disappointment in being just another guy. When he loses his job, he identifies himself as a complete failure. Once injured, the instability of his knee most explicitly organizes William's narrative of uncertainty.

Arthur's narration remains governed by the unpredictability of his basketball and academic skills, along with the unpredictability and potential reversibility of events in his family. While at Marshall, Arthur grows taller, his game improves dramatically, and he becomes a star in Chicago's public school league and the local media. While Arthur succeeds on the basketball court, he continues to struggle with his academic work. During visits to Marshall High, teachers, counselors, and Arthur's coach express concern at his mediocre grades and attitude toward his classroom work. In the meantime, one year after he left, Bo has rejoined the family. Following the reunion of the Agee family, Arthur's mother graduates as a nurse's assistant. Arthur's high school team eventually makes it to the state championships in Champaign, Illinois, where Arthur leads his team to third-place position, the team's best performance since 1960. Since St. Joseph's has yet again failed to make it to the state tournament, Gene Pingatore participates only as a spectator. Arthur is on track for a scholarship to a major university but cannot meet the Scholastic Aptitude Test (SAT) requirements. He receives an athletic scholarship from Mineral Area Junior College in Missouri, where he lives in "Basketball House"--a dormitory located in the middle of a field, far removed from the rest of the campus--along with six of the seven black students at the college.

In the meantime, William and his girlfriend, Catherine, have had a child, Alicia. In two scenes in which the three appear together, William and Catherine discuss the anxiety they experienced on learning of her pregnancy and the arguments caused by William's being unable to attend the birth. He had an important game that day, and Pingatore, William recalls later, was unsympathetic to his family commitments. Despite his recurring knee injury and struggles to attain the minimum SAT score, William performed well at the Nike summer basketball camp and has received an athletic scholarship offer from Marquette University, Milwaukee. The movie ends with William on his way to Marquette but uncertain of his desire to pursue a basketball career. In a written postscript the filmmakers tell us that Arthur graduated from Mineral Area with a C average and went on to study at Arkansas State University, a Division 1 school, where he played starting point guard: "A national basketball magazine judged the team's success to be largely dependent on Arthur's success. In his first start, Arthur hit a 30 foot jump shot at the buzzer to win the game."[4] William, we are told, married Catherine, who moved to Marquette with their daughter. In his junior year, he became increasingly disillusioned with basketball and decided to drop out of school. His family persuaded him otherwise, and the university agreed to let him continue studying without playing basketball.

## AMERICA RESPONDS TO HOOP DREAMS

"Hoop Dreams" is the most powerful movie about sports ever made. This extraordinary documentary about two teenagers who dream of becoming NBA stars is so absorbing and comprehensive and generally profound that it transcends the narrow parameters of the genre. Certainly no other movie--documentary or dramatic feature--in recent memory provides such a vivid account of inner city culture. --Hal Hinson

Since its premiere at the 1994 Sundance Film Festival in Park City, Utah (the premiere showcase for independent films), *Hoop Dreams has* received widespread and enthusiastic endorsement. *Hoop Dreams* won Sundance's "Audience Award" over 16 other documentaries. The film, also an audience favorite at the Toronto Festival, was the first documentary awarded New York Film Festival's distinguished closing position. That showing was met with a 10-minute standing ovation, which filmmaker Steve James portrayed:

"The people at the festival said nothing like this had ever happened before. The audience was just standing there, clapping for the connection

they felt for those families. It was the most amazing experience of my
life" (quoted in Howe 1994: G-4).

Mainstream reviews endlessly applauded *Hoop Dreams* for eluding and
exceeding the boundaries of seductive sport clichés. *Washington Post* film critic Hal
Hinson suggests that "*Hoop Dreams* provides more emotion and human drama than
10 Hollywood movies" (Hinson 1994: F7). Popular critics proclaimed the film "an
American epic" as they identified the two youths on whom the film is based in terms
of "instant celebrity" and its filmmakers as heroes and filmic pioneers. *Hoop
Dreams*, we are repeatedly told, is about something of vastly greater significance
than sport: *Hoop Dreams* is about the real urban America. In the words of Michael
Wilmington (1994a), "We get the true, raw emotion usually buried under the glitz
and hoke of the average Hollywood-ized sports movie. It isn't a slice of life-but a
huge chunk of it" (Wilmington 1994a: 13:5).

Indeed, reviews intimated that the youths' dreams to play professional
basketball set the stage for a larger diagnostics of the inner city. The complex,
realistic, and positive portrait of black inner-city life represented in *Hoop Dreams*
was not, according to most mainstream reviews, typically available to middleclass
America. Mainstream media accounts repeatedly implied that America was prepared
for--apparently even sought--an objective account of the inner city that would
challenge the dominant versions on offer. In a telling comment that punctuates the
affective purchase of the documentary drama, Steve James told the *Chicago
Tribune*, "White people have told us that the only contact they have with inner city
neighborhoods is what they see from their high rise. But seeing a film like this, they
really felt connection" (Wilmington 1994a: 13-20). Despite the stereotypical,
racially coded mythical figures that saturate America's popular, "white high-rise
America" was apparently able to recognize and embrace the "real thing" when they
saw it. Stated differently, mainstream media accounts produced (in collaboration
with *Hoop Dreams* the film) and then represented an American consensus that
designated *Hoop Dreams* the official version of real life in urban America.

Claims to the film's social consciousness are repeated in reviews. Most
obviously, such claims are substantiated through declarations that distinguish the
treatment of the inner city and its residents in *Hoop Dreams* from that in other
Hollywood films. While Patrick McGavin (1994) contends that "the film does not
demonize inner-city life" (McGavin 1994: 26), academic critic Lee Jones (1996)
claims that the film "decenters long held stereotypes about residents who happen to
live in the inner ghetto" (Jones 1996: 8). Such pronouncements and conclusions
reinforced and were consistent with what was identified by director Peter Gilbert as
one of the filmmakers' primary concerns: "One of the things that was very important
to us is that the people in the film are human beings. That they don't fit the
stereotypes of inner city life" (quoted in McGavin 1994: 26).[5]

Through numerous media reviews, *Hoop Dreams* has come to be
understood as an exemplar of realism, social advocacy, and media activism. As we
have discussed, some reviewers identified *Hoop Dreams*' achievement in terms of
its documentation of real inner-city life. Others identified the film's contribution in

terms of its humane representations of poor, urban African Americans. Mainstream reviews lauded the film for its affective dimensions, which were routinely attributed to its realness. Moreover, the filmmakers were commended for providing a much-needed critique of certain aspects of the sport-entertainment system in the United States (which we discuss later in this paper). Overall, *Hoop Dreams* was revered and imbued with the status of a vanguard film that furnished America with a unique educational opportunity--an opportunity that stimulated and satisfied its "will to know." While such knowledge claims are most obviously made possible by the realist pretensions of documentary filmmaking, that aesthetic dimension was complemented with a narrative of integrity culled through a network of recurring themes that drew attention to the good intentions and personal virtues of its three white filmmakers: Steve James, Fred Marx, and Peter Gilbert.

## ORIGIN STORIES OF HISTORY AND CHARACTER

> Most documentary film makers load their cameras, track and shoot their subjects, then move on to the next quarry. But when--as with "Hoop Dreams"--they spend years with their subject, something richer and more elusive than their initial purpose breaks through. Then the movie isn't about catching people in the viewfinder anymore. It's about connecting with them forever.
> --Desson Howe

> Hoop Dreams' history and context are established through an origin story (the popularly constructed history of the film) in which the film is represented as an unplanned and unforeseen social accomplishment. *Hoop Dreams*, we are repeatedly told, developed out of a modest project. Initially, the filmmakers undertook a six-month project to produce a 30-minute, nonprofit educational film short about Chicago's street basketball culture. Their intent was to compare the lives of a former NBA player who had successfully made it through the system (apparently they had Isiah Thomas in mind), a "washed-up" player whose dreams had not materialized, and a talented high school star who aspired to join the professional ranks. The original short film project was funded by Kartemquin Educational Films, noted for "its noble poverty" (Aufderheide 1994: 32).

Kartemquin Educational Films is a Chicago-based production company founded in the 1960s by three University of Chicago alumni. Kartemquin survives by making for-profit films for industry in order to fund the production of its own documentaries. A $2,000 state arts council grant provided a base from which to begin filming the newly conceived project, while Kartemquin continued to sustain the production process by providing donations and office space. In the end, the film cost $600,000 to make and received funding along the way from the Corporation of Public Broadcasting, PBS, and the MacArthur Foundation. According to James, not until the Sundance Film Festival did film distributors begin to show any interest in the film,[6] and the filmmakers signed a contract with Turner Broadcasting. Turner, who own Fine Line Features, the distributor of the documentary, hired Spike Lee as executive producer and director of its made-for-television counterpart. Additionally, Turner had the capacity to cross-promote the film during its airing of NBA games. Thus, the cycle of takeovers and mergers that resulted from Reagan's deregulation policies begins to come into focus. Moreover, Fine Line Features announced that it had "taken the film as a personal cause"-- a cause it advanced with an advertising budget of only $500,000. In the words of its president, Ira Deutchman, Fine Line formulated "the most complex marketing scheme we've ever pulled off" (Collins 1994: B21). The company sought to target a broad audience that included art-house patrons, sports-film fans, teenagers, and inner-city children and their parents. Nike was recruited to endorse television, radio, and billboard advertisements for the movie and subsidize promotional events (the Nike logo appears on print and movie ads). Nike also helped to establish the 800 number for local community group tickets and was also credited with persuading *Sports Illustrated* to pay for the publication and mailing costs of a student/teacher study guide that accompanied the release of the film. Nike, having never before endorsed a film, explained that it "really believed in the message of the film," a message it identified as about hope, spirit, sport, and family (Collins 1994: B21). Dominant accounts that imagine the film being plucked from a sea of independent films doomed for limited release maintain the film's commercial success as purely accidental (thereby maintaining the film and filmmakers' purity) by distancing the film from the capitalist imperatives of mainstream Hollywood production and consumer driven-individualism. Moreover, by locating and restricting stories of the financing and production of the film to the *local* level, the film's implication in the imperatives of global capitalism was erased. This erasure helped establish the authenticity of the film both in terms of its status as an independent, small-scale, local production and in terms of its narrative integrity.

Media collaboration in the production of truth-effects, narrative integrity, and valorized identities is most easily observed in the disproportionate commentary devoted to the "actual making" of the film rather than the narrative of the film itself. We are repeatedly reminded that the filmmakers shot 250 hours of film over a period of four and one-half years, that the film was made on an extremely low budget, and that all three men accumulated huge debts in the process. As Michael Wilmington of the *Chicago Tribune* remarked, "The odds are so stacked against their [Arthur's and William's] success. There's an obvious analogy with the long shot world of independent filmmaking itself" (Wilmington 1994a: 5). Along a related theme, Steve James told *the Washington Post* that the fact that he and his colleagues drove "rust bucket cars" was an important factor in gaining their subjects' trust (Howe 1994: G4). These unifying thematics rely on, and generate, easy slippages between the socioeconomic conditions of the filmmakers and the Agee and Gates families. These slippages trivialize the economic and social devastation defining the conditions of the concentrations of poverty in the post-Fordist inner city and the everyday lives of those who inhabitant such spaces. That reviewers felt able to draw parallels between the socioeconomic situation of two African American youths from Chicago's poor inner city and the economic hardship that defines independent filmmaking is testament to the filmic and popular erasures of the historical forces shaping the lives of the urban poor.

More telling are the repetitions that portray filmmakers James, Marx, and Gilbert as acutely loyal to Arthur, William, and their families, repetitions that are inseparable from those lauding them for the financial and personal sacrifices made in order to complete the film. In what we think are symptomatic repetitions, the filmmakers appear repeatedly through the categories of loyalty and ethical superiority. We are told that, unlike others before them, these filmmakers were persistently loyal despite the difficulties Arthur and William confronted. What the filmmakers take to be, by definition, the subject matter of the film, the predicaments encountered by Arthur and William, are narrated as "tests" of the filmmakers' character. Numerous interviews recount Steve James' depiction of Arthur's astonishment that the filmmakers continued filming him after he was expelled from St. Joseph. Similarly, several reviews draw attention to Emma Gates' initial ambivalence about the film and filmmakers and her subsequent conversion experience: only after the filmmakers made clear that they would not abandon William's story when a knee injury threatened his career, did she come to trust them. "She realized," says Gilbert, "we weren't going to run away because things didn't fit the storybook ideal." When a different kind of trouble threatened Arthur's basketball future, "he was literally surprised when we showed up to film him," Gilbert says. "He told us, 'Why would you want to help me now?' We said, 'It's because we care about you'" (Howe 1994: G-4).

At first glance, such anecdotes may simply appear to be true, real-life, "behind the-scene" stories or background information; yet, such anecdotes reveal America's "political unconscious" (to use Fredrick Jameson's term) as they reshape America's historical consciousness and the public's reception of *Hoop Dreams*. Such repetitions suggest that the narrative is not simply about "trust"; instead, the narrative, which is most often and most explicitly organized around the unexpected material and financial success of the film and, by extension, the filmmakers, appears to be motivated by anxieties about guilt. The origin narrative repeatedly relieves anxieties about guilt by drawing attention to innocence, goodwill, personal virtues, and highly principled and ethical behaviors of the filmmakers. Moreover, the concentrated attention to the philanthropy of the filmmakers reverses the critique that might have ensued through a different and more historical contextualization. For example, *Hoop Dreams'* origin story fails to account for the relationship between the rise of the NBA and its role in revitalizing America's post-Fordist cities. It neglects the correspondence between the making of the African American NBA celebrity and America's war on inner-city youth. Not coincidentally, *Hoop Dreams* was initiated the same year that Michael Jordan *and* crack became national preoccupations. Although eclipsed by the origin story, the conditions of possibility of *Hoop Dreams* (by which we mean the *Hoop Dreams* portfolio, the comprehensive *Hoop Dreams* phenomenon) are embedded in a complex of transnational corporate interests, including the media, the NBA, and manufacturers of sports apparel, that motivate the film and its popularity. The exclusions that govern the promotional *Hoop Dreams'* origin story effectively designate, establish, and stabilize the narrative integrity of the film.

Additionally, the "honorable filmmakers" stories allow the film to be read as a celebration of the promise of political action, social change, and racial harmony based on humanism, individual intervention, and personal interactions. Lauren Berlant helps us understand the American response that positions the filmmakers as the real heroes of *Hoop Dreams*:

> If individual practice in and around the family becomes one nodal point of postmodern national identity, another intimate sphere of public citizenship has been created as sentimental nationality's technological mirror and complement: the mass-mediated national public sphere. While at other moments in US history the mediations of mass culture have been seen as dangers to securing an ethical national life, the collective experiences of national mass culture now constitute a form of intimacy, like the family, whose national value is measured in its subjugation of embodied forms of public life. (Berlant 1996: 400)

In the public response to *Hoop Dreams*, the filmmakers' friendship with the Agees and the Gates comes to represent (for the presumed white, suburban audience invited to identify with the filmmakers) a real solution to America's racial and class tensions, a fantasy that obscures questions about deepseated, systematic violence of racism and economic deprivation. The aesthetic and narrative work by which the film is endowed with integrity and social advocacy both relies on, and is productive of, a notion of sameness in which race (and, by extension, racism) no longer matters. The appeal to sameness, which displaces racism, allows white, middle-class America to view itself as democratic and compassionate even at a time of increased resentment and revenge directed at already vulnerable inner-city populations. But America's ability to derive pleasure from the film, and to celebrate its ethical audience position relies on the film's criticism of sport and, more specifically, the easily identifiable figure of exploitation and wrongdoing, "Gene Pingatore."

## VISUALIZING SOCIAL CRITIQUES: INDIVIDUALS AND MORAL MESSAGES

> Gene Pingatore, the head coach, who never lets the boys forget he launched Isiah Thomas, is the distillation of all the white coaches and recruiters in the film. He talks a good game about caring for the boys' future, but over and over again the film captures his hideously callous behavior. The strongest proof is what happens to Arthur.--Caryn James

In this section of the chapter, we consider the ways in which *Hoop Dreams* indicts and fails to indict the economies of sport. We contend that while *Hoop Dreams* gestures toward criticizing the exploitative treatment and commodification of William, Arthur, and other urban African American youths (an exploitation that we view as endemic to the contemporary sport-entertainment complex), the criticism is ultimately directed to, and displaced onto, the bodies of particular social agents who are visualized as virtuous or vicious. An indictment of the sport-entertainment complex would require examining the economic, political, and cultural forces governing that system (the forces defining the post-Fordist city), a critical examination of the sport-entertainment complex that is an unlikely filmic possibility since the film's origin story and narrative integrity are maintained through these exclusions. Rather than interrogating the sport system, the film displaces and explains racism, greed, and exploitation through individual character. By our view, such displacements work to position viewers ("white, high-rise America") as apparently "discriminating" and "socially conscious" cultural critics who not only easily recognize but are distanced from the everyday violences that shape the lives of the poor in the inner city. Moreover, this dynamic aligns the viewers with "the socially conscious filmmakers": both the filmmakers and audience accrue identity and meaning as they are defined over and against figures of exploitation, defined as those who have been or are involved in exploitative relations with Arthur and William. Such narrative mechanisms *relieve* the audience of the responsibility of critical reflection about their implication in exploitative spectator and consumption practices as well as the everyday conditions that structure the lives of the urban poor. The responsibility of critical reflection is relieved in the sense that it is actively discouraged.

One of the film's more obviously critical moments of the sport system occurs during William's stay at the Nike All-American Camp at Princeton, New Jersey. Also known as the ABCD (Academic Betterment and Career Development), the camp brings together 120 of the nation's top high school players for a weeklong, all-expenses-paid program each summer. The camp, ostensibly designed as an introduction to student-athlete life, reserves mornings for academics and guest lectures and afternoons for games. But the camp is not, as claimed by William DuBois, the camp athletic director, solely an introduction to student-athlete life. Instead, it provides a convenient, centralized location at which university coaches and scouts can assess potential recruits at Nike's expense.

The viewers' arrival at the camp is signaled by an army of white Nike sneakers marching along the cleanly swept paths of the Princeton University campus. The camera cuts to an old, grand, red brick building and then to a large lecture theater filled with young, predominantly African American men decked out in bright red and blue Nike polo shirts. In the front room, Dick Vitale, a well-known sports commentator, performs an energetic, "inspirational" speech in which he tells his audience: "This is America. You can make something of your life."

As we see a close-up of William's face, we hear Spike Lee: "Nobody cares about you. [The camera cuts to Spike Lee, pacing around a lecture theater podium.]

You're black, you're male, all you're supposed to do is deal drugs and mug women. [We see William, looking pensive.] The only reason why you're here, you can make their team win. If their team wins these schools get a lot of money. This whole thing is revolving around money."

Back at the gymnasium, William is excelling on the court. Bo Ellis, the assistant coach at Marquette, claims that if "you look at some of these young boys' bodies they've got NBA bodies already." Bob Gibbons, an independent talent scout, announces, "It's already become a meat market, but I try to do my job, and, you know, serve professional meat." In the next frame, we see Gibbons with another scout discussing the various schools (DePaul, Marquette, Indiana, Michigan) that are interested in William. Soon after, William sustains a muscle injury. Interspersed with shots of an athletic trainer's examining his leg, we see coaches, including O'Neill and Knight, who apparently "look" concerned about the implications of his injury. The coaches' looks are not innocent; instead, the moment is symptomatic of the sort of "racial looking" through which William and the other African American youths are positioned and defined. As a result of a muscle injury, William is unable to compete for the final two days of the camp.

The progression of the scenes leading up to William's trip to Princeton establishes the context that confirms the relevance and worth of the camp experience: two scenes undermine the critical potential of the Nike camp sequence. The first scene takes the form of a "tour" of the neighborhood in which Bo Agee used to buy drugs. As we pass decaying buildings and garbage-strewn patches of wasteland, Bo, our guide, identifies the street corners where he purchased drugs. In combined confession and testimony, he expresses regret for this period in his life and takes responsibility for Arthur's expulsion from St. Joseph's: "I think about it, had I not been on drugs when Arthur went to St. Joseph's just how good it would have been. He wouldn't ha' had to leave. He can just look at my life and say here's good example of what not to do."

Images of Arthur, Shannon, and a friend on a shopping trip punctuate Bo's comments. Jackets embroidered with team logos, a wall lined with sneakers, the Air Jordan silhouette on red shirts and shorts, and other signs of Nike fill the screen, as all three youths admire the display, try on various pairs of shoes, and make purchases. The camera closes in first on Arthur, as he hands $70 over the counter to pay for his goods, and then "the dollars" as they are placed in the register. As Arthur reveals that drug dealers in the neighborhood give promising ball players money to buy athletic gear, we see a series of close-ups: sneaker after sneaker displaying the Nike swoosh in various colors; a shirt decorated with an image of a primitivized and monsterized Michael Jordan; and, finally, the brand name Nike and its signature swoosh emblazoned on shirts. A cut to the army of white Nike sneakers marching on the Princeton path follows the close-up images of Nike consumer goods.

The two scenes condense an array of issues immediately recognizable as "urban problems": drugs, gangs, drug money, family breakdown, sneakers, "sneaker crimes," and insatiable consumer desires. No explanation of the issues is needed, nor is it invited by film: extensive attention directed at these problems in both the scientific and popular realms renders them distinct, obvious, and easily intelligible. Although edited to make "Nike" the link between the camp and the sneakers purchased with drug money, Nike--and its implication in the network of inner-city poverty, deindustrialization, and the global economy--escapes interrogation. The camp and, by extension, Nike accrue their value and meaning in relation to what are presented in the film as alternatives. Despite the offensive attitudes displayed by some of the coaches and the meat market environment at the Nike camp, real possibility, control, and comfort are forged over and against, first, the menial labor that possibly awaits Arthur (the Nike camp sequence is interrupted momentarily by a scene showing Arthur and Shannon working for minimum wage at a Chicago Pizza Hut) and, more forcefully, the despair, disillusion, and dystopic possibility that Arthur might go the way of his father and environment (a prediction made by Arthur's Marshall coach earlier in the film).

Familiar narratives of social problems also overdetermine identities through which characters, regardless of whether they appear in newspaper reports or documentary films, function. In other words, because Bo Agee's identity is already overdetermined by these narratives, his admissions of failure and lack of moral worth, articulated through his claim of responsibility for Arthur's expulsion from St. Joseph's, are immediately understandable. The force of contrast and meaning in this filmic composition is established through the sport/gang dyad that governs the national imagination in general. Combined with critical attention directed to the personalities of individual coaches, audiences are discouraged from thinking about urban violence, drug use, and the late capitalist global economy and consumerism in their complexity. Corporate investments and disinvestments are never broached as potentially crucial issues.[7]

Gene Pingatore *is*, as argued by Caryn James (1994), the distillation of the exploitative relationships we witness, but that distillation, which individuates and distances, is not simply revealed, nor is it easily achieved. Pingatore is positioned early and throughout in the film as the embodiment of social wrongs and exploitation through the considerable time devoted to visual narratives of long, intense practice sessions in which he appears ruthless, impatient, aggressive, and loud. Moreover, Pingatore's unemotional and frank interview style supports this characterization and is particularly jarring when, in a matter-of-fact manner, he explains Arthur's expulsion from St. Joseph as an unfortunate, but unavoidable, financial necessity. His opening conversation with the Agees, coupled with Arthur's dismissal, suggests that Gene Pingatore has feigned care and concern, which makes him an especially despicable character. Interviews with a depressed Sheila Agee, who expresses her anger at the school for expelling him midsemester, and the Marshall High coach, who argues that had Arthur fulfilled his potential, St. Joseph would not have been so swift to force him out, heighten the impact of Pingatore's words. Pingatore appears as uncaring and parasitic in what remains a legitimate and potentially even beneficial sport system. The figure of the coach, who sees young players only as a tool for victory, works to eclipse the broader conditions and policies that deny Arthur as well as other inner-city youths access to a solid public school education and opportunities.

Pingatore's "obviously" questionable character is defined over and against other individuals in the system who appear caring, well intentioned, and loyal. For example, Kevin O'Neill, the Marquette coach with whom William eventually signs, is represented as personable, committed to higher principles, and concerned with William as a person, not simply as a player. While recruiting William, O'Neil displays an unconditional commitment to William when he offers William a four-year scholarship to Marquette that will continue to pay for his education despite prohibitive injuries. In a repetition of the sort of concern and loyalty attributed to the filmmakers, O'Neil displays the sort of loyalty and ethical superiority that both construct white identity and demonstrate the possibilities and promises of the sporting system.

Pingatore's position as the visible and locatable embodiment of guilt and wrongdoing is evident in what, for the audience, are two of the most satisfying scenes in the film. Since Gene Pingatore's parasitic and exploitative tendencies were apparently motivated by his endless desire to "go down state"--that is, to coach his team in the state high school championships--Arthur's trip to Champaign is experienced as particularly pleasurable. Audience satisfaction and pleasure cannot be reduced to Arthur's outstanding play during the championships. Instead, since editing effects have established the sense that we can clearly see where guilt lies, we also sense that we can clearly perceive that justice has been achieved, within allowable bounds, when Arthur, whom Pingatore has most betrayed, has the honor of delivering a stinging moral message to him. Pingatore watches as Arthur realizes Pingatore's dream, leading his team to victory and a third-place finish in the state championship in Champaign's Assembly Hall. While Pingatore did not betray William, at least not to the same degree that he betrayed Arthur, justice, within apparently proper limits, is again served when William delivers *his* moral message to Pingatore. As Pingatore says good-bye to William, William tells Pingatore that he decided to major in communications, so "when you start asking for donations, I'll know the right way to turn you down." Indeed, the effect of these moments suggests that the film has been edited in such a way that one of the biggest challenges presented to William and Arthur is defined in terms of Pingatore. These moments confirm Pingatore's central position in the production and stabilization of audience identity.

## CONCLUSION

How and why have other relations of power and sociality--those, for example, traversing local, national, and global economic institutions--become less central to adjudicating ethical citizenship in the United States?--Lauren Berlant

On the very last page of *Soul of the Game*--placed after the credits, biographies of the contributors, and publishing details--there appears a photograph of a very young African American child, feet firmly planted on the playground floor, eyes and arms pointing skyward at a ball he's apparently just tossed in the air. Overleaf, placed exactly back-to-back with the image of the child, is a waist-up photograph of a young, bare chested African American man spinning a basketball on his middle finger. The conspicuous absence of photographs of children in *Soul of the Game* (there are two prior to this) makes this image particularly prominent and compelling. Berlant's (1996) work, which underscores how attention on youth functions to allow an American audience's self-recognition in terms of compassion, care, and ethical superiority, is helpful in understanding the arrangement of these images. She argues that the celebration of the prepolitical child and other incipient citizens is vital to the American public sphere because the image of the future, a future they convey, works to draw attention away from the more troubling issues of violence and equality in the present.[8] As we see it, *Soul of the Game* is the most recent in a long line of representative strategies that both reflect and incite America's desire to know the "urban other" and the continued significance of the figure of the pre-political in this quest for knowledge. Questions about childhood and the future are also pertinent to our analysis of *Hoop Dreams*. Particularly, Berlant's suggestion that the fantasy of the American Dream, a quintessential fantasy of futurity so absolutely central to the narrative of *Hoop Dreams* and its commercial success, is a central force in the mobilization of violence in the present. For Berlant, the American Dream is a public form of private history that promises public social and economic stability and support for those who work and make families. This promise, she argues, which "connects personal lives to capitalist subjectivity and the cultural forms of national life" (Berlant 1996: 431), allows America to imagine a national people unmarked by public history.

Arthur Agee and William Gates, promising basketball players of fine character, embody the fantastic future that (white) America lives for and through. The frequent references to Isiah Thomas and Michael Jordan remind the audience that William and Arthur's promise lies in their ability to become revenue-producing commodities (of course, the irony is that they already are) who bring pleasure to millions. While both *Soul of the Game* and *Hoop Dreams* celebrate and rely on futurity, the possible futures imagined in and through each text differ. While *Hoop Dreams* imagines Arthur and William as highly marketable celebrities, *Soul of the Game* celebrates its players as unknown celebrities who are seemingly distanced from multinational capital and the NBA. Thus, while the omnipresent Nike/NBA signs in *Hoop Dreams* signify earning potential and the possibility of leaving the ghetto, those omnipresent signs in *Soul of the Game* signify an ostensible freedom found *only* in the ghetto and in a space apparently separate--but, of course, only apparently separate--from the perverse profitability and creative destruction of multinational capitalism.

In spite of the differences between the two narratives, the politics of *Hoop Dreams* and *Soul of the Game* is, to borrow Berlant's words, "vicious, symbolic, optimistic, and banal," embedded in a future that circumvents the terror of the present. This circumvention cannot be understood apart from the conventions of documentary filmmaking (clearly adhered to by the makers of *Hoop Dreams*) and photography (*Soul of the Game*), which deny the limits of the visual register and the significance of location and perspective by rendering them invisible. While *Hoop Dreams'* appeal is routinely cast in terms of its realness, we see that "realness" as symptomatic of a point of view whose limits and exclusion have been naturalized and are therefore not easily recognizable--an effect of familiar and undisturbing knowledges. While the truth-effect of documentary aesthetics exemplified in both *Hoop Dreams* and *Soul of the Game* erases context and location, a familiar visual economy solicits a national appeal and pleasure. This dynamic is integral to the understanding of urban, consumer, racial, and national politics.

In an effort to understand the stakes in the "reality effect" of *Hoop Dreams* and *Soul of the Game*, we want to revisit Steve James' depiction of the 10-minute ovation that met the film's New York Film Festival debut. Again, as James characterized the moment:

> "The people at the festival said nothing like this had ever happened before. The audience was just standing there, clapping for the connection they felt for those families. It was the most amazing experience of my life." (quoted in Howe 1994: G-4)

We agree with Steve James, who assesses the New York ovation as an expression of the connection that the audience felt for those families: the applause, at least on one level, is for the recognition of sameness, shared values and desires. Easy slippages between the conditions of poor, primarily African America, inner-city residents who face inhumane conditions of poverty, public assistance, and employment possibilities, and "white, high-rise America," slippages routinely facilitated through the category of "family," are not necessarily something to be celebrated; instead, by our view, they are indicative of the "knowledges" that govern the audience's understanding of the crisis of the inner city in ways that demonize single parents, welfare, welfare recipients, the under- and unemployed, and African American youths in general. Moreover, these slippages, particularly as they are aligned with, and as they call for, a reconstitution of the family, work in concert with the neoconservative agenda of empowerment--will, self-sufficiency, independence. The affective dimension of the audience's desire to recognize itself in the lives of the urban poor and to celebrate that recognition is deeply problematic and symptomatic of the position from which identity is forged and judgments made, America's quest for sameness, and America's inability to think adequately about difference and inequality. Repeated visual codes and the narrative work not only to displace guilt and implication onto easily identifiable agents such as Pingatore but to reinforce a conservative, normalizing agenda in which the virtuous and vicious are easily distinguished. We do not mean to suggest that these easily identifiable agents are not implicated in exploitative relations; instead, our intent is to direct attention to how such figures of displacement operate in the national popular to relieve guilt and to produce ethically superior subjects. In *Hoop Dreams*, Gene Pingatore helps mainstream audiences reconcile the conflict between inner-city poverty and the sense of themselves as compassionate, virtuous, and morally superior. Moreover, the celebration of the filmmakers and the parallels drawn between their lives and the lives of Arthur and William in America's response to *Hoop Dreams* allow questions of whiteness to be displaced onto Gene Pingatore. In contrast, the ethnographic narrative about photographer John Huet, if articulated, would foreground questions about exploitative spectatorship and commodification. The key difference here lies in Huet's position as a highly regarded, extremely successful, commercial photographer, more obviously bound up in multinational capitalism and culture. Thus, Huet's biography would not only disrupt the possibility for displacement of questions about class and race but potentially undermine *Soul of the Game's* illusory distance from multinational capitalism.

Both *Hoop Dreams* and *Soul of the Game* refuse to trouble the familiar categories that govern knowledges of the inner city; therefore, the exclusions that lend stability to those categories remain invisible and uninterrogated. The figure of the basketball player, defined over and against the criminal (the gang member who governs America's representation of African American men in the mid-1980s to the mid-1990s and who appears explicitly and implicitly in both texts), functions as a means of displacement that reconciles middle-class America's sense of itself as compassionate while it simultaneously calls for, and endorses, increasingly vengeful punitive programs. Again, as projects that translate subjectivity into objectivity, *Hoop Dreams* and *Soul of the Game* tell us less about real urban life and conditions than they do about the nation's state of mind.

## NOTES

1. We analyze the Field Museum exhibition in detail in a forthcoming paper (Cole and King 1998a). This exhibition opened in January 1998 and is housed in what is regarded as one of the world's finest natural history museums. Of particular interest for our analysis is the museum's international reputation for research in evolutionary biology and paleontology and archaeology and ethnography. When we visited the museum, the Soul of the Game collection was located next to an exhibition entitled: Evolution: The Missing Link and surrounded by a variety of "exotic" trees and plants.

2. Vivian Sobchack (1997) uses the phrase "post-American" to describe America's form of social consciousness in a historical moment dominated by multinational capitalism, global communication, and the apparent global dispersion of the "American" project. While Sobchack directs attention to nostalgia, baseball, and mythic times, our project directs attention to a social consciousness that relies on ideal and demonized figures of black masculinity. These figures work to reestablish consensus around foundational themes while displacing the complex economic and psychic violences of global capitalism.

3. An earlier version of our discussion of *Hoop Dreams*, realism, and urban possibilities appears in Cole and King (1998b).

4. For a discussion of the meaning of Michael Jordan's "blackness," see Andrews (1996).

5. Our discussion of the sport/gang dyad is based on Cole's 1995 and 1996 analysis.

6. For an excellent analysis of Reaganism, the War on Drugs, and representations of the inner city and the black family, see Reeves and Campbell (1994). For an analysis that focuses specifically on the war on welfare, see Fraser and Gordan (1994).

7. For a critique of *Hoop Dream*'s mobility narrative see Sandell (1995).

8. For an extremely useful and insightful discussion on modern power, the see-able, the say-able, and the possibility of living ethically and acting politically, see Orlie (1998).

## REFERENCES

Andrews, David. "The Fact of Michael Jordan's Blackness: Excavating a Floating Racial Signifier." *Sociology of Sport Journal* 13, no. 2 (1996: 125-28).

Aufderheide, Pat. "The Dream Team." *The Independent* (October 1994): 32-34.

Berlant, Lauren. "National Brands/National Bodies: Imitation of Life." In *The Phantom Public Sphere*, edited by B. Robbins. Minneapolis: University of Minnesota Press,1993.

_____. "The Face of America and the State of Emergency." In *Disciplinarity and Dissent in Cultural Studies*, edited by C. Nelson and D. P. Gaonkar. New York: Routledge, 1996.

Clark, Mike. "'Hoop Dreams' Reaches for the Rafters and Soars." *USA Today* (October 13,1994): D1.

Cole, Cheryl L. "P.L.A.Y., Nike, and Michael Jordan: National Fantasy and the Racializa-tion of Crime and Punishment." *Working Papers in Sport and Leisure Commerce*, University of Memphis, vol.1, 1995.

_____. "American Jordan: P.L.A.Y., Consensus, and Punishment." *Sociology ofSport Journal* 13, no. 4 (1996): 366-97.

Cole, Cheryl L., and Samantha King. "Inner City Basketball and Ethnographies of Whiteness: The Will to Know/the Will to Punish." Paper presented at the Pacific Sociological Association Meetings, San Francisco, April, 1998a.

_____. "Representing Urban Possibilities: Race, Realism and Basketball." In *Sport and Postmodern Times,* edited by Genevieve Rail . New York: SUNY Press, 1998b.

Collins, Glenn. "Advertising" *New York Times,* November 7, 1994: B-21.

Coyle, Daniel. *Hardball: A Season in the Projects.* New York: Harper Paperbacks, 1995.

Davis, Mike. *City of Quartz: Excavating the Future in Los Angeles.* London: Verso, 1990.

Donaldson, Greg. *The Ville: Cops and Kids in Urban America.* New York: Anchor Books,1994.

Fraser, Nancy, and Linda Gordon. "A Genealogy of Dependency: Tracing a Keyword of theU.S. Welfare State." *Signs: Journal of Women in Culture and Society* 19, no. 2 (1994):309-27.

Gilroy, Paul. "'After the Love Has Gone': Biopolitics and Etho-Poetics in the Black PublicSphere." *Public Culture* 7 (1994): 49-76.

Hinson, Hal. "'Hoop Dreams': A Slam-Dunk Shot of Truth" *Washington Post,* November4, 1994: F1, 7.

Hooks, Bell. "Dreams of Conquest." *Sight and Sound* (April 1995): 22-23.

Howe, Desson. "'Hoop Dreams': An Overtime Victory" *Washington Post,* November 13,1994: G-4.

Huet, John. *Soul of the Game: Images and Voices of Street Basketball.* New York: MelcherMedia/Workman, 1997.

James, Caryn. "Dreaming the Dreams, Realizing the Realities" *New York Times,* October7, 1994: C1, 8.

Jones, Lee. "Hoop Realities." *Jump Cut* 40 (1996): 8-14.

Kaplan, E. Ann. *Looking for the Other: Feminism, Film, and the Imperial Gaze.* New York: Routledge, 1997.

Kasarda, John D. "Inner-city Concentrated Poverty and Neighborhood Distress: 1970-1990." *Housing Policy Debate* 4, no. 3 (1993): 253-302.

Kotlowitz, Alex. *There Are No Children Here.* New York: Anchor Books, 1992.

Massing, Michael. "Ghetto Blasting," *The New Yorker* (January 16, 1995): 32-37.

McGavin, Patrick Z. "From the Street and the Gyms to the Courtroom and Beyond" *New York Times,* October 9, 1994: 26.

Miller, Toby. *Technologies of Truth: Cultural Citizenship and Popular Media.* Minneapo-lis: University of Minnesota Press, 1998.

Orlie, Melissa. *Living Ethically, Acting Politically.* Ithaca, NY: Cornell University Press,1998.

Reeves, Jimmie, and Richard Campbell. *Cracked Coverage: Television News, the Anti-cocaine Crusade, and the Reagan Legacy.* Durham, NC: Duke University Press, 1994.

Riggs, Marlon. *Color Adjustment.* San Francisco: California Newsreel, 1991.

Sandell, Jullian. "Out of the Ghetto and into the Marketplace." *Socialist Review* 95, no. 2(1995): 7-82.

Sobchack, Vivian. "Baseball and the Post-American Cinema, or Life in the Minor Leagues." In *Out of Bounds: Sports, Media and the Politics of Identity*, edited by Aaron Baker and Todd Boyd. Bloomington/Indianapolis: Indiana University Press, 1997.

Telander, Rick. *Heaven Is a Playground.* New York: St. Martin's Press, 1976.

Wilmington, Michael. "When Film Dreams Come True" *Chicago Tribune* October 2,1994a: 5, 20.

_____. "Full Court Pressure: Hoop Dreams Details the Hope Born of Desperation" *Chicago Tribune*, October 21, 1994b 7: C, M.

Wilson, William Julius. *When Work Disappears: The New World of the Urban Poor.* New York: Random House, 1996.

## chapter 11

# Hijacking the Hyphenated Signifier: Donovan Bailey and the Politics of Racial and National Identity in Canada

### Steven Jackson and Klaus Meier

## INTRODUCTION

On June 1, 1997, two dual-Olympic gold medalists confronted each other for the first time in the "One-to-One, Challenge of Champions" race at the Toronto Skydome. The race pitted Canadian Donovan Bailey against American Michael Johnson in a media-hyped race with two million purse (in addition to a $500,000 signing bonus). However, there were much more than bragging rights at stake, particularly for Donovan Bailey. For one thing the race was promoted as determining the "world's fastest man," a title that Donovan Bailey and most Canadians felt he had already earned based on his world-record, gold medal performance in the men's 100-meter final at the 1996 Atlanta Olympics. However, the American media broke with tradition and named their own Michael Johnson, a gold medal winner in both the 200- and 400-meter events, as the world's fastest human. The rationale for the American media's failure to recognize Bailey is unclear. Some suggest it was because Atlanta was only the third Olympics this century in which the Americans had failed to win a medal in the 100-meter event. This, combined with the fact that the favored Americans also lost to the Canadians in the men's 4 X 100-meter relay, a race the United States had won 14 out of the past 18 times, including 11 world records, appeared to have created an air of desperation and a need to confirm a sense of achievement and national pride. For example, commenting on the American loss to the Canadian relay team, *USA Today* sports columnist Tom Weir suggested: "Just as when the Toronto Blue Jays had help from the Dominicans when they won Canada's first World Series, so did its relay have a distinctive Caribbean flavour" (Houston 1996: C9). In short, Weir suggests that the Canadians could win only by importing its athletes. Whatever the reason, the perceived American arrogance and ethnocentrism created enormous resentment in their northern neighbors, the Canadians. As a consequence the Bailey versus Johnson race was invested with considerable emotion and was translated into a duel between Canada and the United States. Expressing a Canadian viewpoint, Brunt (1997: D12) noted, "It would be hard to find more clear-cut evidence that despite globalization, despite North American Free Trade Area, this is still a separate place up on the northern end of the continent."

The buildup to the June 1 race resembled a World Wrestling Federation (see Christie 1997) or Don King boxing extravaganza. Wherever possible, the media played upon the banter between Bailey and Johnson. Bailey claimed that the race would in no way determine the world's fastest man because he already owned the title. In response, Johnson taunted and challenged Bailey to have the courage to race for something more than just the money: "I guess Donovan isn't used to putting things on the line, so he's trying to reap the benefits of competing in the race but not putting the title on the line" (Fish 1997: E16). The tension between the two athletes continued right up until race time, with both athletes publicly airing concerns about the layout of the 150-meter race (a compromise distance between Bailey's 100-meter and Johnson's 200-meter specialties) and lane assignments. Unfortunately, the race did not unfold as expected for either Johnson or Bailey. Despite Las Vegas oddsmakers making Michael Johnson a 3 to 1 favorite, he pulled up with an injury during the race at a point when Bailey was clearly in the lead. In his postrace interview, a highly emotional Donovan Bailey called Johnson "a coward and chicken," a comment for which he later apologized.

For the most part, the Canadian public's response to Bailey's victory and subsequent attack on Michael Johnson was characterized by overzealous nationalism with a particularly anti-American inflection. Among the many e-mails received by the *Globe and Mail* which many view as Canada's "national" newspaper, one said that Bailey "was talking to the American media in their own language He just confirmed for us the world's fastest man is Canadian, taking [the title] back from those who stole it from him" (Christie1997: D12).

Yet, despite the outbreak of nationalism, some were uncomfortable and even embarrassed by Donovan Bailey's and their fellow Canadians', including the media's, boastful celebration. Pugsley (1997: 8), for example, levied a stinging indictment of the Canadian Broadcasting Corporation's (CBC) biased coverage of the one-to-one race: "Whether the highly Canadian bias of Brian Williams and his CBC counterparts was personal or prompted by their producers is unsure. Regardless, never before have Canada's most renown sportscasting personalities shamed an athlete (Johnson) and his country with such devotion to unprofessionalism."

With respect to Bailey's postrace behavior specifically, that is, calling Johnson a "coward and a chicken," one individual suggested; "His lack of class overshadowed the victory" (Christie1997: D12). Another member of the public, expressing the prevailing Canada-U.S. frictions, said that, although they took pride in his achievement, they were "not proud of what he said. He's lowered his standard to the Americans" (Christie 1997: D12). The implicit message in the preceding statement is that Bailey's brash behavior was more akin to what Canadians expect from Americans, and clearly this is not expressed in positive terms. The point was made much more explicitly by Brunt (1997: D12), who noted

> When he crossed the finish line at the SkyDome, Johnson having pulled up lame, it wasn't occasion for one of those rare surges of patriotic emotion from a people not prone to let it all hang out. Not quite Paul Henderson. Not quite Ben before the fall. But close enough to do the trick. And then, with the flags waving, with the anthem playing, Bailey had to go and act, well, so *un-Canadian*. (emphasis added)

Who would have known that one small, hyphenated word: *un-Canadian*, could mean so much. Yet, that one small word represents one aspect of a much larger struggle, a struggle over identity in Canada. For Donovan Bailey, a black, Jamaican-born athlete, it is a struggle to gain acceptance by the Canadian public. Arguably, Bailey's struggle constitutes one aspect of the contemporary politics of Canadian identity and a defining feature of Canadian race relations (Jackson 1998). Hence, if we are to better understand the case of Donovan Bailey, it is essential that we examine the shifting and overlapping terrain of cultural politics of Canadian identity. In Donovan Bailey's case, it is impossible to overlook the influence of Ben Johnson the man, in whose shadow he has been running since he began his sprinting career. Ben Johnson has been described as a "ghost" (Jackson and Meier 1997) and a "phantom" (*Athens to Atlanta: The Olympic Spirit*, 1996) whose legacy continues to haunt all Canadians, in particular black, Jamaican-born, Canadians and those who are athletes.

This chapter explores how both Donovan Bailey and Ben Johnson are constituted by, and constitutive of, the contemporary politics of racial and national identity in Canada. More specifically, we trace the emerging media discourses surrounding these two "Jamaican-born," Canadian sprinters to examine (1) how and why the Ben Johnson affair amounted to a crisis of racial and national identity in Canada in 1988; (2) the discourses that defined and redefined Ben Johnson's racial and national identities before and after the steroid scandal; and (3) evidence of the nature and extent to which Donovan Bailey and other Canadian blacks of Caribbean descent are living in the shadow of Ben Johnson. We begin by describing how and why Ben Johnson became one of Canada's most infamous popular cultural figures.

## BEN JOHNSON AND THE 1988 CRISIS OF CANADIAN IDENTITY

On September 24, 1988, Canadians celebrated the long-awaited victory of Ben Johnson over arch rival American Carl Lewis in the men's 100-meter final of the Seoul Olympics. In the process Johnson had combined several achievements, including establishing a new world record of 9.79 seconds, earning Canada its first gold medal in the event since Percy Williams in 1928, and, perhaps just as significantly, defeating American Carl Lewis. However, Johnson's triumph was a fleeting one because on September 26 it was announced that Ben Johnson had tested positive for the use of anabolic steroids, forcing him to forfeit his gold medal. Dick Pound, Canadian vice president of the IOC, remembers being told the news by his boss, IOC president Juan Antonio Samaranch, at an Olympic sponsors, luncheon. Recollecting the devastating moment, Pound remembers asking a stone-faced Samaranch, "For God's sake has somebody died?" to which Samaranch replied, "Worse. Ben Johnson has tested positive for anabolic steroids" (Corelli and Gains1996: 29).

News of the disqualification sent shock waves throughout the international sporting community. Canadians were sent on an emotional roller coaster character- ized by disbelief, anger, despair, and mourning (Jackson). Eventually, as the initial jolt subsided, and as evidence of Johnson's prolonged steroid use emerged, Canadians seemed to express either sympathy, or anger and resentment (Jackson 1996). The Canadian state, in an attempt to reaffirm its self-idealized innocence within the realm of sport, established the Commission of Inquiry into the Use of Drugs and Banned Practices Intended to Increase Athletic Performance, or, as it is more popularly known, the Dubin Inquiry. In total, Chief Justice Dubin's investigation, which spanned January to October 1989, involved the testimony of 119 witnesses, culminated in 14,817 pages of testimony, and cost Canadian taxpayers $3.6 million (Semotiuk 1994). When it was finally over, it was described by one critic as "an extraordinary pageant of irony, tragedy, and farce" (Burstyn 1990: 45).

It is now more than a decade since Ben Johnson's Olympic disqualification and more than five years since he received a lifetime ban for testing positive for steroids a second time. Nevertheless, despite being referred to as the "nowhere man" (Jackson, Andrews, and Cole 1998) Johnson remains one of the most notorious athletes in both Olympic and Canadian history. Although his recent application for reinstatement into competitive sport has been denied by both a Canadian court and the International Amateur Athletic Federation (IAAF), Johnson and his lawyers are determined to exhaust every possible legal avenue in order to prevent what they view as a case of restraint of trade. Now, as if experiencing selective amnesia, Johnson continues to boast that his 9.79-second race in Seoul makes him the fastest human in history. In his words: "No one has ever run faster, on drugs or not on drugs. Others can say they're the fastest man or whatever, but the people know" (Fish 1997: 6H).

Ben Johnson's legal challenge to make a sporting comeback and his unwavering declaration that he is still the fastest human in history appear to be components of a carefully orchestrated plan to revitalize and reinvent his public persona (Jackson and Meier 1997). Arguably, the Ben Johnson affair marks the genesis of the modern steroid controversy and serves as the reference point by which all subsequent cases have been judged (Jackson 1998). Moreover, the Ben Johnson affair remains a national embarrassment that continues to haunt the Canadian public,

Athletics Canada and Caribbean-born athletes in particular. As such, the ghost of Ben Johnson's legacy, if not Ben Johnson himself, constitutes one aspect of the contemporary politics of Canadian identity and a defining feature of Canadian race relations (Jackson 1998; Jackson and Meier 1997). Even a cursory view of the contemporary media discourses surrounding black athletes, such as Donovan Bailey, reveals the haunting effects of Ben Johnson, both past and present: "Donovan Bailey was unbeatable at the world's, but in Canada he can't outrun the shadow of Ben Johnson" (Farber 1996: 143).

"That night the world champion Canadian sprinter, who has long been overshadowed in his country by a disgraced Ben Johnson, became a star" (Price 1996: 100).

> Ben Johnson has been erased as Olympic champion everywhere but in his own heart he remains a challenge to his country's forgiveness and a phantom who haunts Canada's men of speed (*Athens to Atlanta: The Olympic Spirit*, 1996).

> A country forgot about whatshisname. Those demons are exorcised for good, fading like Bailey's jet stream down the straightway (Young 1996: D3).

An important question that emerges from these narratives is "To what can we attribute the enduring impact of Ben Johnson on contemporary identity politics in Canada?" Our contention is that in order to truly understand the basis of Johnson's legacy, there is a need to understand the *context* from which it emerged. Here, we describe particular features of the conjunctural specificities of Canada in 1988, a year in which Canada was referred to as being in a state of crisis (Jackson 1994). This context, we argue, that facilitated not only Ben Johnson's rise to national hero but also his eventual redefinition as a racial/ethnic "other."

## CONTEXTUALIZING CANADA IN 1988

Ben Johnson's emergence as a national hero in 1988 and his subsequent influence upon the contemporary politics of identity in Canada need to be understood within a complex context of historical, political, economic, and social relations. Several seemingly distinct, yet interrelated, factors may have contributed to a year of heightened anxieties, or what has been described as a "year of crisis of Canadian identity" (Jackson 1994). First and foremost, it is important to acknowledge Canada's historically enduring obsession about its cultural uniqueness. No doubt, Canada's insecurity is invariably linked to its relatively dependent position with respect to its powerful southern neighbor, the United States. In 1988, Canadian apprehensions about the fate of its cultural identity, indeed, its very sovereignty, were intensified by debates linked to the Canada-U.S. Free Trade Agreement (FTA). According to many nationalists, the FTA would inevitably translate American economic domination into political and cultural colonization (cf. Bowker 1988; Davies 1989; Lapierre1987; Scott 1988). Throughout 1988, the Free Trade Agreement served as a focal point of political debate en route to the Canadian federal election held later that year. Arguably, the economic and cultural threat posed by the FTA, whether real or imaginary, contributed to a renewed search for anchors of meaning and symbolic markers of difference in order to confirm Canada's unique culture and identity relative to the United States. On the popular cultural front one sporting hero who figured prominently in Canada's search for identity in 1988 was Ben Johnson, who had become the "nation's No. 1 hero in the wake of the departure of Wayne Gretzky to Los Angeles" (Johnson 1988: 38-39). While the initial Olympic victory was argued to have improved race relations in Canada ("Truth at the Finish Line," 1988), the national response following the steroid scandal was criticized for inhibiting and even setting back any advances in the area of racial equality. Next, we examine the national response to Johnson's rise and fall and the corresponding representation of his identity within the media.

## BEN JOHNSON AND THE POLITICS OF CANADIAN RACIAL AND NATIONAL IDENTITY

Though there were sympathizers as well as those who denied the very significance of the steroid scandal (Brehl 1988; Lauten 1988), within the ongoing media discourses there was overwhelming resentment toward Ben Johnson, revealing both racist and ethnocentric attitudes and practices within Canada. The emergent racism was expressed in several different ways, including a direct suggestion that Johnson leave Canada, a shifting signification of Johnson's racial and national identities, and the use of various racist stereotypes.

Although it could only be described as an extreme position, according to Ben Johnson, he was, in effect, asked to consider leaving Canada in 1993 because of his negative impact on Canada's reputation following his second positive steroid test. Specifically, Johnson recounts the "most disgusting comment I have ever heard" in reference to Pierre Cadieux's, the former Canadian minister of sports, suggestion that he "move back to Jamaica, his birthplace, because he had become a disgrace to Canada" (Blanchard 1996: 23). To reiterate, this appears to be an isolated and extreme position with respect to the range of national responses to Ben Johnson. Far more common were examples of a process of redefining Johnson's identity through the strategic use of racial and national signifiers.

Operating quite subtly at times, the strategic use of racial/ethnic and national signifiers worked to define Ben Johnson's identity within specific contexts. Based on our extensive analysis of media coverage, we assert that the selective employment of these signifiers at particular conjunctures in Johnson's career reveals a means by which the Canadian public could either bask in his reflected glory or, alternatively dissociate from Johnson when he disgraced Canada's reputation. In the latter case, the emergence of what might be called "dissociative discourses" served to define Johnson as a racial/ethnic other, that is, as something "other" than Canadian. A brief overview of the relationship between the highs and lows of Johnson's athletic career and the corresponding variation in the signification of his identity reveal the dynamics of his popular representation, particularly with respect to the media.

For example, at the beginning of his career and as a largely unknown athlete, within the popular press Johnson tended to be referred to as a "Jamaican immigrant" or "Jamaican." As his athletic achievements began to accumulate, he was more frequently defined as a "Jamaican-Canadian." Then, in 1987, after defeating Carl Lewis and setting a new world record at the World Athletic Championships in Rome, Johnson was more consistently referred to as "Canadian." Ben Johnson had become a national hero, and, when he won the gold medal and established yet another new world record at the Seoul Olympics just one year later, he seemed to have won the hearts of all Canadians, inscribing his name in history as Canada's first black sporting superstar. Describing the deeper social significance of Johnson's achievement within Canada's black community specifically, Cecil Foster, himself a Caribbean-Canadian (1996a: D3) recalls: His is one of the most telling and tragic stories of what it means to be black in this country. When Johnson took the tape, all black Canadians were with him. In our petty, insular way, we even celebrated that he kicked the butt of that mouther-man Carl Lewis, who, coincidentally, was not a Caribbean Black. On the battlefield of nations, Canada had been assured of at least one gold medal. Every black person in the country wanted it around his or her neck. That medal was placed around the neck of a Caribbean immigrant who stood proudly in place of the Canadian national anthem and the hoisting of the Canadian flag. A black immigrant had done this for Canada and county this was a moment to be proud. This was the moment to be black in this TV was the fulfilment of the dreams of all those Caribbean and African parents who believed Canada could be home for their children, the pay-off for all those forgotten soldiers who fought for this country and got nothing in return, the reward of perseverance of the descendants of the United Empire Loyalists and the modern immigrants struggling to keep the dream of acceptance and achievement alive. This was proof that if fully integrated in the Canadian system--whether in schools, jobs, boardroom, police and armed forces, in any facet of Canadian life--we could be winners. We could be an integral part of Team Canada. According to Foster, Johnson's victory signaled a turning point in what many blacks viewed as a long struggle for acceptance within Canada. Likewise, Foster suggests that Johnson's Olympic triumph symbolized black Canadian pride, a way forward, a means of being both black and Canadian.

However, within 48 hours the triumph had turned into tragedy, and Ben Johnson's identity was again being redefined through a recycling of the signifiers that had represented him as the "other" prior to his success. *Sports Illustrated* writer Michael Farber specifically identifies the politics of race in Canada and the process of signifying racial and national identity following the Olympic downfall: "There was a disqualification at Seoul, a qualification at home. Johnson was now a

'Jamaican-Canadian.' In losing the gold, he had gained a hyphen, and a silent legacy was established" (Farber 1996:145). Steroid use notwithstanding, Ben Johnson, of course, was the same person. However, as Jackson notes (1998: 28), "his national and racial identities were socially constructed, deconstructed, reconstructed, and reproduced through the media."

Arguably, Johnson's "Canadian" identity, which temporarily displaced the hyphenated racial signifier, that is, "Jamaican-Canadian," was contingent upon translating his personal achievements into national sporting pride (Jackson and Meier 1997). Hyphenation, as a specific type of signifying practice, is particularly powerful with respect to Jamaican-Canadians. As several authors have argued, in the case of "Jamaican-Canadians" the hyphen is both a "national" and a "racial' signifier." In other words, "Jamaican," despite the existence of white Jamaicans and blacks who are not Jamaican, is a euphemism for "black" in Canada (Foster 1996a, b; and Levine 1988a, b). The politics of racial and national in Canada in response to Ben Johnson is perhaps best summed up by Cecil Foster (1996b) in his book *A Place Called Heaven: The Meaning of Being Black in Canada:*

> And we knew that he was paying the price for the so-called double burden of being black: that you can rise to fame as an individual but you crash back to earth as a representative of your race; that several times Johnson had mounted the medal podium as a Canadian hero, but when the medals were stripped from his chest, when the world records were erased he was merely a Jamaican, reduced in the eyes of the mainstream to his most common denominator, his base. ( 74) Arguably, defining Johnson as a Jamaican or Jamaican- Canadian was one way in which he was "reduced to his most common denominator" (Foster 1996b: 74), that is, his race, his blackness.

The use of the "Jamaican" and "hyphenated Jamaican" signifiers was one way in which Johnson's racial and national identity was represented. However, the aftermath of Johnson's disqualification also witnessed the advent of seemingly more blatant racist discourses structured largely within the framework of racial stereotypes. These discourses played an important role in defining his identity and in reinforcing his "otherness." Various racial stereotypes linked to animal imagery (Janofsky 1988; Levin et al. 1988), intelligence (Siegel 1989), and derogatory humor (see Boyd 1988; Farber, 1996) emerged following the Johnson affair at Seoul (see Jackson 1998). Discursive practices involving the use of stereotypes, just like hyphenated signifiers, are important not only because they revealed evidence of racism surrounding Ben Johnson. They are important because of the possibility, indeed, likelihood, that in the aftermath of the steroid scandal, these stereotypes and other racist signifiers are displaced onto other black Jamaican-Canadians. Moreover, the displacement not only impacted on other black track athletes in Canada, but invariably influenced blacks from all walks of life, who were being seen in a new, "displaced" light.

In combination, the use of stereotypes and other racist discourses provide ample evidence of the backlash against Ben Johnson, which serve to both dehumanize him and question the authenticity of his Canadian identity. However, racism is not always as obvious in Canada, as compared to, for example, the United States. Writer Meredith Levine (1988b), for example, has argued that gold medal or no gold medal, scandal or no scandal, Ben Johnson would never have been truly accepted by Canadians simply because he is black. Of course, this would never be made explicit because, as Levine puts it, in Canada racism operates "subtly, covertly and insidiously your enemies do not make themselves known to you" (1988: 8). Likewise, Foster describes the "polite" Canadian version of oppression as "racism with a smile on its face" (1996b: 320). In short, though racism may be expressed in different ways and to different degrees, it does exist in Canada (Bissoondath 1994; Cannon 1995; Foster 1996;, Lazarus 1980; McLellan and Richmond 1994; Richmond 1991; Satzewich, 1992).

The racist responses to Ben Johnson's disqualification in 1988 demonstrate his enduring, haunting presence. By cheating and notably, by getting caught cheating, Johnson had shattered Canada's highly regarded reputation as a nation dedicated to fairness, equality, and sportspersonship. Second, Johnson left a legacy for black Canadians who were suddenly being viewed in a new light, illuminated by an array of displaced racial signifiers (Jackson and Meier 1997). As a consequence, blacks who were poor, unemployed, at odds with the law, or simply walking down the street were subject to being defined within a negative framework. Third and finally, black Caribbean-Canadian sprinters were henceforth forced to run in the shadows of Ben Johnson, the man whose footsteps they were trying to avoid. However, despite their own attempts to dissociate themselves from the "anabolic apparition" (Jackson and Meier 1997), the new generation of black Canadian sprinters was in a precarious position. On one hand, they were expected to be successful, given that Ben Johnson had proven, albeit by illegal means, that Canadians could be world champions. On the other hand, these athletes were under a microscope of suspicion, with Canadians holding their breath and waiting to exhale every time they took a drug test after winning a medal. In sum, there is sufficient evidence to claim that blacks in general and black, Jamaican-born Canadian athletes, such as Donovan Bailey, in particular have been living in the shadow of Ben Johnson for almost a decade.

## A NATION REDEEMED: DONOVAN BAILEY, BEN JOHNSON, AND THE CLEANSING OF CANADA'S SOUL

To begin to understand the nature and degree to which Donovan Bailey (and others) has been living in the shadow of Ben Johnson, it is worth considering some of the parallels between the two men. First and foremost, both are black, Jamaican-born Canadians who immigrated to Canada in their early teens. Johnson arrived from Falmouth in 1976, and Bailey immigrated from Manchester, Jamaica, in 1981. Second, both athletes were relatively late starters in their careers as sprinters. Despite his interest in running, as a teenager Johnson was quite a small individual, and it took some time for coaches to recognize his potential. Bailey was actually a basketball player at Sheridan College prior to establishing his own marketing and consulting company. Not until 1991, at age 23, did Bailey decide that he could beat those he was watching while attending the national track-and-field championships in Montreal (Deacon 1996). The real turning point came in 1994, when Bailey was approached by coach Dan Pfaff at the 1994 World Championships in Stuttgart. Pfaff, then a coach at Louisiana State University, now at the University of Texas, felt that Bailey had the potential to be world champion under the right coaching and training conditions. Shortly thereafter, Bailey moved to the United States to train (Nemeth 1996).

A third similarity between Johnson and Bailey is that both have won World Championships,and an Olympic gold medal (albeit temporarily in Johnson's case) and set new world records. Fourth, both athletes at some point in their career had a major showdown with an American rival. Ben Johnson had a long-standing, antagonistic relationship with Carl Lewis. Donovan Bailey, despite the fact that he faced him directly in only one race, challenged American Michael Johnson. While these and other factors may have contributed to the repeated discursive links between the two athletes, arguably the most conspicuous feature is that they are both black, Jamaican-born Canadian sprinters who bestowed upon the nation its Warholian turn in the international sporting spotlight.

Yet, differences between the two men should not be ignored. For one thing, Bailey is a much more engaging, charismatic individual with relatively more refined verbal and interpersonal skills. There is little doubt that these qualities enhanced his attractiveness to potential sponsors such as Air Canada, Adidas, Maple Leaf Ltd, and many others. In addition, Bailey was a successful businessman prior to his entry into elite athletics, and, in this sense, perhaps he did not need sport to the same extent that Ben Johnson did. However, it is important to note that Ben Johnson has also exhibited some business acumen and is now president of a real estate company called Mountain Glow Enterprises (Blanchard 1996). But perhaps the most significant difference between the men is that Bailey beat the Americans in two Olympic events (100-meter and the 4 X 100 meter relay) without resorting to performance-enhancing drugs. Yet, despite his clean record, Bailey cannot escape his symbolic shadow, Ben Johnson.

A cursory review of the media coverage suggests that in the process of reaching the peak of his career, Bailey has become a vehicle through which Canada has attempted to reclaim its lost innocence in the world of elite sport. For example, there are repeated references to Bailey's potential to "cleanse" and "redeem" Canada's international sporting reputation and to simultaneously "exorcize the ghost of Ben Johnson" (Jackson and Meier 1997). Yet, despite his unsolicited appointment as symbolic saviour, there is a seemingly unspoken, collective suspicion about Bailey's possible drug use. Moreover, what is even more explicit are the Canadian public's persistent questions about Bailey's allegiance to Canada. Specifically, he has been directly confronted with the question of whether he views himself as a Canadian or a Jamaican. In contrast to Ben Johnson, who seemed to simply identify himself as Canadian, Bailey appeared to demonstrate some sense of agency through the management of his identity.

In this chapter, we examine three specific events that we believe demonstrate the enduring Canadian struggle over Donovan Bailey's racial and national identities and, in turn, his own sense of agency in constructing those identities. We introduced our chapter by examining the most recent of these three events, namely, Bailey's controversial reaction following his victory over American Michael Johnson in the 1997 race to determine the "world's fastest man."

As previously noted, although many Canadians celebrated Bailey's victory over Michael Johnson with particular zeal, others felt both uncomfortable and embarrassed by his unsportsmanlike post race display (Christie 1997). Within the context of Canada-United States. relations and the politics of Canadian identity perhaps the most stinging criticism levied against Bailey was when he was referred to as being "un-Canadian" (Brunt 1997: D12) and behaving "like an American" (Christie 1997: D12). This was the latest episode in Donovan Bailey's enduring struggle for acceptance within Canada. As Brunt (1997: D12) put it, Bailey must be asking himself, "I won the race. I didn't cheat. I beat the arrogant Yank. What more do they want?" Thus, irrespective of all of his achievements, Bailey continues to face challenges concerning his national identity.

Though they certainly do not *justify* the reactions of the Canadian public following the 1997 race, we now examine two other key events that led up to the Challenge of Champions that might help *explain* the negative reaction. Initially, we examine the Canadian response to Bailey's *alleged* remarks concerning racism in Canada that were published in *Sports Illustrated* just prior to the 1996 Atlanta Olympics. This is then followed by an analysis of Bailey's public statements immediately following his 1996 Atlanta Olympic gold medal victories.

First, just prior to the commencement of the 1996 Atlanta Olympic Games, Bailey was embroiled in a huge controversy as a result of an interview conducted with Montreal-based *Sports Illustrated* writer Michael Farber. In the interview Bailey was reported as stating: "Canada is as blatantly racist as the United States. I know it exists. People who don't appear to be Canadian--people of color--don't get the same treatment. They associate you with your parents' birthplace or your birthplace. Look at our [sprint] relay. Its an issue" (Farber 1996: 145).

Bailey's remarks were met with shock by some Canadians and with heavy criticism by others. Consider the reaction of Alex Gardiner, Chief Executive Officer, of Athletics Canada who said: "I've know Donovan a few years and this issue has never come up: He's never brought it to our attention. Without presuming to get inside his head, there's all kinds of pressures and probably in the deepest of his emotions he's wondering how he'll be received after the Olympics. But our runners all consider themselves Canadians, and we consider them Canadians, end of sentence (Christie 1996: C12). Not surprisingly, Gardiner takes a cautious and defensive stance that attempts to attribute Bailey's remarks to the pressures of competition. At the same time, though it is not explicitly stated, he reaffirms

Canada's allegiance to its foreign-born, which in this case invariably means black, runners.

Returning to Bailey's original alleged remarks in *Sports Illustrated,* we suggest that if the article would have simply reported that Bailey claimed that there was racism in Canada, it would have gone largely unnoticed. This contention is based on the fact that Bailey, Surin, and other black Canadian athletes have occasionally expressed their personal experiences and frustrations with racism in Canada, though usually with little public reaction or sympathy. However, by *allegedly* claiming that Canadians were as racist "as the Americans," Bailey appeared to be offering the worst possible insult to the Canadian public. In hindsight, it is quite possible that there was an error in Farber's quote, one that he freely admits is conceivable, given that he was using handwritten notes and that he wrote the piece some time after the actual interview ("Could've Erred: SI Writer," 1996: E12). Bailey argued that Farber had omitted the word "*not*" in the passage "Canada is [not] as racist as the United States," and a careful reading of the article certainly seems to support the sprinter's position.

Our third and final key event concerns the candid statements of Donovan Bailey immediately following his 1996 Olympic gold medal performance in the 100 meters. Though he wrapped himself in a Canadian flag during his victory lap, when Bailey was later questioned at the postrace press conference about whether he would consider sharing his victory with Jamaica, he responded: "It's not even Jamaica sharing. I'm Jamaican, man. I'm Jamaican first. You gotta understand that's where I'm from. That's home. That you can never take away from me. I'm a Jamaican-born Canadian sprinter" (Christie 1996: C2). Bailey's response expressed both a confidence in his own dual national identity and also a form of resistance to those Canadians who had questioned his loyalty throughout his career. By consistently acknowledging his Canadian citizenship "and" his Jamaican homeland throughout his career, Bailey appeared to have learned a valuable lesson from Ben Johnson. As he notes: "When Johnson won, he was a Canadian hero. But after he tested positive for steroids, he became a 'Jamaican-born sprinter.' After Silken Laumann screwed up, she was greeted with forgiveness and lucrative sponsorships." That sends a clear message to black athletes: that beneath the patriotic hype, they are still considered foreign" (Christie1996: C2).

Thus, savvy about how particular factions of the Canadian public had redefined Ben into a Jamaican-Canadian following the 1988 disqualification, Bailey empowered himself by deliberately and strategically proclaiming a dual identity. Or, putting it another way, he *hijacked the hegemonic hyphen* in "Jamaican-Canadian" (Jackson and Meier 1997: 7). Klein (1996: H3) refers to this very point in her defense of Bailey: "Perhaps because he knew that Canada would disown him if he failed, he would not let it own him completely in his moment of triumph. Because he would have been Jamaican had he stumbled, Bailey forced Canadians to see him as Jamaican when he won."

What Klein infers, and we concur, is that Bailey was attempting to exert a sense of agency over the nature and extent to which the Canadian public could both own and define his identity. In part, Bailey seems to achieve at least two interrelated objectives with respect to reclaiming his identity. First, he embraces his Jamaican homeland without denying or denouncing his Canadian citizenship. Second, Bailey attempts to position himself such that those Canadians who wish to bask in his reflected glory must come to terms with his "Jamaican" and hence "black" identity. Bailey's success in achieving his objective is difficult to assess. However, as already indicated, any victory he won was certainly temporary, as evidenced by the reactions of some Canadians following his victory in 1997.

To briefly summarize, there is fairly strong evidence to confirm that Donovan Bailey (and others) continues to run in the shadow of Ben Johnson. This not only informs us of the enduring impact of the Johnson steroid scandal but also reveals aspects of the contemporary politics of racial and national identity in Canada. Based our analysis of three key events in the career of Donovan Bailey, we suggest that the struggle over racial and national identity continues in Canada.

## CONCLUSION

Clearly, there is some evidence to suggest that Ben Johnson continues to haunt and overshadow the achievements of Donovan Bailey and other black Canadians. Though some may wish to blame this legacy on Ben Johnson personally for his involvement in two steroid scandals, the problem runs much deeper. As we have tried to demonstrate, the debates and struggles over the social construction of Donovan Bailey's and Ben Johnson's public personas inform us about the politics of racial and national identity in Canada. The emerging discourses reveal evidence of various discriminatory practices, including what we have termed "discursive dissociation," the employment of racial stereotypes, and even the display of blatant racism. In essence, the analysis tells us something about how Canada, despite being the first nation in the world to have an official Multicultural Act, is struggling with how it deals with its racial/ethnic "others."

However, it is important to recognize that Canada, despite its own local cultural specificities, is not alone in its encounters with immigration and the accommodation of new cultures. Indeed, the advent of globalization confronts almost all nations with the problem of reconciling the increasing flow and interdependencies of people, economies, and information while attempting to retain a sense of cultural autonomy and uniqueness on a local, usually defined in terms of the nation-state, level.

Notably, many advocates of sport continue to herald its ability to unite people of different backgrounds and to provide an arena of equality with respect to the performance and achievement of athletes regardless of race, gender, or social class. Like most nations, Canada capitalizes on the opportunity to highlight the achievements of its internationally successful athletes, especially racial/ethnic minorities. The celebration of such sporting achievements and the corresponding public displays of support serve both to show the relative superiority of a nation's social and political system and to prove that all citizens are treated equally. The contemporary Canadian crisis of identity as constitutive of, and constituted by, the identity politics of Donovan Bailey and Ben Johnson supports this contention, at least during the high points of their respective careers.

Given the increasingly international flow of economic and human capital in the "global sports arena" (Bale and Maguire 1994), debates over nationhood, citizenship, and authenticity of national identity are likely to continue to serve as central fixtures of contemporary social theorizing. We conclude by drawing upon the insights of Stuart Hall, who effectively captures the crux of the identity and authenticity debates by advising us that "identities are about questions of using the resources of history, language and culture in the process of becoming rather than being: not 'who we are' or 'where we came from,' so much as what we might become, how we have been represented and how that bears on how we might represent ourselves" (Hall 1996: 4).

## REFERENCES

*Athens to Atlanta: The Olympic Spirit.* (CBC Television). Host: Allen Abel. Producer: Carl Karp July 18, 1996.

Bale, John, and Joseph Maguire. *The Global Sports Arena: Athletic Talent Migration in an Interdependent World.* London: Frank Cass, 1994.

Bissoondath, Neil. *Selling Illusions: The Cult of Multiculturalism in Canada.* Toronto: Penguin Books, 1994.

Blanchard, S. "Running from the World." *New York Times,* July 28, 1996, 23.

Bowker, Marjorie. *On Guard for Thee: An Independent Review of the Free Trade Agreement.* Hull: Voyageur, 1988.

Boyd, D. "Canada Waits for Ben to Say It Ain't So after Steroid Controversy." *Vancouver Sun,* September 27, 1988, A3.

Brehl, J. "Oh Fuddle Duddle! Aren't We Getting a Bit Carried Away?" *Toronto Star,* October 1, 1988, A13.

Brunt, Stephen. "Bailey Fits Modern Hero Model." *Globe and Mail,* June 2, 1997, D12.

Burstyn, Varda. "The Sporting Life." *Saturday Night* 105, no. 2 (1990).

Callinicos, A. *Race and Class.* London: Bookmarks, 1993.

Cannon, M. *The Invisible Empire: Racism in Canada.* Toronto: Random House, 1995.

Chaiton, A., and N. McDonald. *Canadian Schools and Canadian Identity.* Toronto: Gage Educational, 1977.

Christie, James. "Bailey Satellites Do Damage." *Globe and Mail,* July 17, 1996, C2.

_____. "Bailey Apologizes for 'Chicken' Remark." *Globe and Mail,* June 3, 1997, D12.

Corelli, R., and P. Gains, "The Drug Detectives." *Maclean's* 109, no. 30 (1996): 28-29."Could've Erred: SI Writer." *Globe and Mail,* July 18, 1996, E12.

Davies, R. "Signing Away Canada's Soul: Culture, Identity, and the Free Trade Agreement."*Harper's* 278 (1989): 43-47.

Deacon, J. "The Power and the Glory." *Maclean's* 109, no. 30 (1996): 18-19.

Eyton, June. "The Uphill Battle against Bias" [Letter to the Editor]. *The Globe and Mail* October 8, 1988, D7.

Farber, Michael. "Blast from the North." *Sports Illustrated* (July 22, 1996): 142-146.

Fish, Mike. "Other' Johnson Fights Ban." *Atlanta Constitution,* May 31, 1997, 6H.

Foster, Cecil. "Captain Canada: But Will Media Allow Bailey to Escape Johnson's Shadow?" *Toronto Star*, July 30, 1996a D3.

_____. *A Place Called Heaven: The Meaning of Being Black in Canada*. Toronto: HarperCollins 1996b.

Fotheringham, Alan. "The Johnson Saga in Perspective."*Maclean's* 101 (1988): 64.

Gross, George. "The Last Word." *Toronto Sun*, July 17, 1996, p. 12.

Gwyn, Richard. *Nationalism without Walls: The Unbearable Lightness of being Canadian*. Toronto: McClelland and Stewart, 1995.

Hall, Stuart. "Introduction: Who Needs Identity?" In *Questions of Culture and Identity*, edited by S. Hall and P. DuGay. London: Sage, 1996.

Hargreaves, John. "Media Sport." In *The Polity Reader in Cultural Theory*. Cambridge: Polity Press, 1984.

"Heroics Overshadow Cowardly Bombing." [Our Opinion section] *London Free Press*, July 20, 1996, B6.

Ibsen, Henrik. *Ibsen: Four Major Plays*. Translated by Rolf Fjelde. Signet Classic New York: Penguin Books,1970.

Jackson, Steven. "Gretzky, Crisis and Canadian Identity in 1988: Rearticulating the Americanization of Culture Debate." *Sociology of Sport Journal* 11 (1994): 428-446.

_____. "Disjunctural Ethnoscapes: Ben Johnson and the Canadian Crisis of Racial and National Identity." Paper presented at the Crossroads International Cultural Studies Conference, July 1-4, Tampere, Finland, 1996.

_____. "A Twist of Race: Ben Johnson and the Canadian Crisis of Racial and National Identity." *Sociology of Sport Journal* 15 (1998): 21-40.

_____. "Life in the Faust Lane: Ben Johnson, National Affect and the 1988 Crisis of Canadian Identity."

Jackson, Steven, David Andrews, and Cheryl Cole. "Race, Nation, and Authenticity of Identity: Interrogating the "Everywhere" Man (Michael Jordan) and the "Nowhere" Man(Ben Johnson)." *Journal of Immigrants and Minorities*, (in press).

Jackson, Steven, and Klaus Meier. "Exorcizing the Ghost: Donovan Bailey, Ben Johnson and the Politics of Canadian Identity." Paper presented at the North American Society for the Sociology of Sport Conference, November 5-8, Toronto Canada, 1997.

Janofsky, M. "Johnson Loses His Gold to Lewis after a Drug Test." *New York Times*, September 27, 1988, D31.

Johnson, Oscar. "The Games." *Sports Illustrated* (October 10, 1998): 8-40.

Kilbourn, William. "The Peaceable Kingdom Still." *Daedalus* 17 (1988): 1-29.

Klein, N. "Olympic Fictions, Racial Realities and Fair-Weather Friends." Toronto Star, August 2, 1996, H3.

Lapierre, L. *If You Love This Country: Facts and Feelings on Free Trade*. Toronto: McClelland and Stewart , 1987.

Lautens, G. "Johnson Cheated But the Nation Not in Disgrace."*Toronto Star*, September 28, 1988, A4.

Lazarus, D. *A Crack in the Mosaic: Canada's Race Relations in Crisis*. Cornwall, Ontario: Vesta, 1980.

Levin, B. et al. "The Steroid Scandal." *Maclean's* 101, no. 42 (1988): 50-53.

Levine, Meredith. "What If He'd Kept the Gold?" *Globe and Mail*, p. A-7, October 13, 1988a, A7.

_____. "Canadians Secretly Relieved at Johnson's Fall." *New Statesman Society* 1 (1988): 8.

Longman, J. "Bailey and Johnson's Running Feud Is Finally About to Be Settled." *New York Times*, June 1, 1997, 21.

"Loose talk." *US Magazine*, compiled by Holly A. Millea,( September 4, 1989.): 6.

MacAloon, John. "Steroids and the State: Dubin, Melodrama and the Accomplishment of Innocence." *Public Culture* 2 (1990): 41-64.

McLellan, J., and A. H. Richmond. *Multiculturalism in Crisis: A Postmodern Perspective on Canada.* Halifax: Fernwood, 1994.

McMartin, P. "Johnson Loses Medal, Canada Loses Pride." *Vancouver Sun*, September 27, 1988. A-1, A-8, A-9.

Patrick, D. "Canadian Campaigns against Media Calling Johnson Fastest Man." *USA Today*, August 23, 1996, C11.

Price, S. L. "Let the Games Begin Again." *Sports Illustrated* (August 12, 1996): 100.

Pugsley, J. "Running Right into Trouble." *Gazette*, June 6, 1997, 8.

Satzewich, V. Ed. *Deconstructing a Nation: Immigration, Multiculturalism and Racism in '90's Canada.* Halifax, NS,: Fernwood, 1992.

Scott, M. *From Nation to Colony.* Lindsay, Ontario: Tri-M, 1988.

Semotiuk, Darwin. "Restructuring Canada's National Sports System: The Legacy of the Dubin Inquiry." In *Sport in the Global Village*, edited by R. C. Wilcox. Morgantown, WV: Fitness Information Technology, 1994.

Siegel, L. "Ben Johnson Case Questions Validity of IQ Tests." *Toronto Star*, June 20, 1989, A15.

"Truth at the Finish Line." Editorial in *Globe and Mail*, September 28, 1988, A6.

Young, C. "Amid Tackiness, Athletes the Genuine Article." *Toronto Star*, August 5, 1996, D3.

# PART V

## Culture, Sport, and Ritual

# chapter 12

---

# Baseball Magic

## George Gmelch

On each pitching day for the first three months of a winning season, Dennis Grossini, a pitcher on a Detroit Tiger farm team, arose from bed at exactly 10:00 A.M. At 1:00 P.M. he went to the nearest restaurant for two glasses of iced tea and a tuna fish sandwich. Although the afternoon was free, he changed into the sweatshirt and supporter he wore during his last winning game, and one hour before the game he chewed a wad of Beech-Nut chewing tobacco. After each pitch during the game he touched the letters on his uniform and straightened his cap after each ball. Before the start of each inning he replaced the pitcher's rosin bag next to the spot where it was the inning before. After every inning in which he gave up a run, he washed his hands.

When asked which part of the ritual was most important, he said, "You can't really tell what's most important so it all becomes important. I'd be afraid to change anything. As long as I'm winning, I do everything the same."

Trobriand Islanders, according to anthropologist Bronislaw Malinowski, felt the same way about their fishing magic. Among the Trobrianders, fishing took two forms: in the *inner lagoon,* where fish were plentiful, and there was little danger, and on the *open sea,* where fishing was dangerous, and yields varied widely. Malinowski found that magic was not used in lagoon fishing, where men could rely solely on their knowledge and skill. But when fishing on the open sea, Trobrianders used a great deal of magical ritual to ensure safety and increase their catch.

Baseball, America's national pastime, is an arena in which players behave remarkably like Malinowski's Trobriand fishermen. To professional baseball players, baseball is more than just a game. It is an occupation. Since their livelihoods depend on how well they perform, many use magic to try to control the chance and uncertainty built into baseball.

To control uncertainty, for example, Tampa's Wade Boggs eats chicken before every game (that's 162 meals of chicken per year), and he has being doing that for 11 years. Jim Leyritz eats turkey, and Dennis Grossini, tuna fish. White Sox pitcher Jason Bere listens to the same song on his Walkman on the days he is to pitch. San Francisco Giant pitcher Ron Bryant added a new stick of bubble gum to the collection in his bulging back pocket after each game he won. Jim Ohms, my teammate and pitcher on the Daytona Beach Islanders, put another penny in the pouch of his supporter after each win. Clanging against the hard plastic genital cup, the pennies made an audible sound as he ran the bases toward the end of a winning season.

Whether they are professional baseball players, Trobriand fishermen, soldiers, or even students taking final exams, some people turn to magic in situations of chance, when they believe they have limited control over the success of their activities, and the outcome is important. In both technologically advanced societies that pride themselves on a scientific approach to problem solving, and tribal societies, rituals of magic are common. Magic is a human attempt to impose order and certainty on an otherwise uncertain situation. This attempt is irrational in that there is no causal connection between the rituals and instruments of magic and the desired effect. But it is rational in that it creates in the practitioner a sense of confidence and control, which, in turn, help him execute the activity and achieve the desired result. Put simply, what you believe can have an effect on what happens.

I have long had a close relationship with baseball, first as a participant and then as an observer. I devoted much of my youth to the game and played professionally as first baseman for five teams in the Detroit Tiger organization in the 1960s. Shortly after the end of my last baseball season, I took an anthropology course called Magic, Religion, and Witchcraft. As my professor described the magic practiced by a tribe in Papua New Guinea, it occurred to me that what these so-called primitive people did wasn't all that different from what my teammates and I had done to give ourselves luck while playing professional baseball.

In baseball there are three essential activities--pitching, hitting, and fielding. Each varies in the amount of chance and uncertainty associated with it. The pitcher is the player least able to control the outcome of his own efforts. His best pitch may be hit for a home run, while his worst pitch may be hit directly into the hands of a fielder for an out or be swung at and missed for a third strike. He may limit the opposing team to a few hits yet lose the game, or he may give up a dozen hits and still win. One has only to look at the frequency with which pitchers end a season with poor won-lost records but have good earned run averages, or vice versa. For example, in 1990 Dwight Gooden gave up more runs per game than his teammate Sid Fernandez but had a won-lost record nearly twice as good. Gooden won 19 games and lost only 7, while Fernandez won only 9 games, while losing 14. They pitched for the same team--the New York Mets--and therefore had the same fielders behind them. Regardless of how well he performs, on every outing the pitcher depends the proficiency of his teammates, the ineptitude of the opposition, and caprice.

Hitting is also full of risk and uncertainty--Hall of Famer Ted Williams called it the most difficult single task in the world of sports. Consider the forces and time constraints operating against the batter. A fastball travels from the pitcher's mound to the batter's box, just over 60 feet, in under four-tenths of a second. For only 3 feet of the journey, an absurdly short two-hundredths of a second, the ball is in a position where it can be hit. To be hit well, the ball must be neither too close to the batter's body nor too far from the "meat" of his bat. Any distraction, any slip of a muscle or change in stance, can throw a swing off. Once the ball is hit, chance plays a large role in determining whether it will go into a waiting glove, whistle past a fielder's diving stab, or enter the wide-open spaces. In a quirky example of luck, some years ago Giant outfielder Willie Mays "dove for the dirt" to avoid being hit in the head by a fastball. While he was falling, the pitch hit his bat, and the ball went shooting down the left field line. Mays jumped up and ran, turning the play into a double, while the pitcher looked on in disgust.

In fielding, on the other hand, the player has almost complete control over the outcome. Once a ball has been hit in his direction, no one can intervene and ruin his chances of catching it for an out. Infielders have approximately three seconds in which to judge the flight of the ball, field it cleanly, and throw it to first base. Outfielders have almost double that amount of time to track down a fly ball. The average fielding percentage (or success rate) of .975, compared with a hitter's success rate or average batting percentage of .250, reflects the degree of certainty in fielding. Compared with the pitcher or the hitter, the fielder has little to worry about. He knows that in better than 9.7 times out of 10 he will execute his task flawlessly.

In sum, pitching and hitting involve a great deal of chance and are comparable to the Trobriand fishermen's open sea. Fielding, on the other hand, involves little uncertainty and is similar to the Trobrianders' inner lagoon. In keeping with Malinowski's hypothesis about the relationship between magic and uncertainty, we can expect that baseball players will use magic for hitting and pitching but not for fielding. Indeed, I observed a wide assortment of magic-rituals, taboos, and fetishes-associated with both hitting and pitching but never observed the use of any directly connected to fielding. I have known only one player, a shortstop with a weak glove, who practiced any rituals connected with fielding. Let us now turn to the specific kinds of baseball magic used by ballplayers.

## RITUAL

The most common form of baseball magic is personal ritual--a prescribed behavior that players scrupulously observe in an effort to ensure that things go their way. These personal rituals, like those practiced by Trobriand fishermen, are performed in a routine, unemotional manner, much as players do nonmagical things to improve their play such as applying pine tar to their bats to improve the grip, or eye black on their upper cheeks to reduce the sun's glare. Rituals are infinitely varied since a ballplayer may formalize any activity that he considers important or somehow linked to performing well.

Many hitters go through a series of preparatory rituals before stepping into the batter's box. These include tugging on their caps, touching their uniform letters or medallions, crossing themselves, tapping or bouncing the bat on the plate, or swinging the weighted warm-up bat a prescribed number of times. Mike Hargrove, former Cleveland Indian first baseman, had more than a dozen individual elements in his batting ritual, which included grabbing his belt in the middle of his back, pushing down his helmet tight, and pressing the thumb pad on his left hand. After each pitch he would step out of the batter's box and repeat the entire sequence. His rituals were so time-consuming that he was called "the human rain delay."

Rituals may become so important that they override practicality. Catcher Matt Allen, for example, was wearing a long sleeve turtleneck shirt on a cool evening in the New York-Penn League when he had a three-hit game. "I kept wearing the shirt and had a good week," he explained. "Then the weather got hot as hell, 85 degrees and muggy, but I would not take that shirt off. I wore if for another ten days--catching--and people thought I was crazy."

One ritual associated with hitting is tagging a base when leaving and returning to the dugout between innings. Mickey Mantle habitually tagged second base on the way to or from the outfield. Dave Jaeger stepped on third base on his way to the dugout after the third, sixth, and ninth innings of each game. Asked if he ever purposely failed to step on the bag, he replied, "Never! I wouldn't dare. It would destroy my confidence to hit." A hitter who is playing poorly may try different combinations of tagging and not tagging particular bases in an attempt to find a successful combination.

When players are not hitting, some managers may rattle the bat bin, as if the bats are in a stupor and can be aroused by a good shaking. Similarly, I have seen hitters rub their hands along the handles of the bats protruding from the bin, presumably in hopes of picking up some power or luck from those bats that are getting hits for their owners.

Rituals usually grow out of exceptionally good performances. When a player does well, he seldom attributes his success to skill alone. Rather, he reasons that his skills were no better tonight, when he got three hits, than they were last night, when he went hitless. Therefore he attributes the inconsistencies in his performance to an object, a food he ate, not having shaved, a new shirt he bought that day, or just about any behavior different from his normal routine. By repeating that behavior, the player seeks to gain control over his performance. Outfielder John White explained how one of his rituals started:

> I was jogging out to centerfield after the national anthem when I picked up a scrap of paper. I got some good hits that night and I guess I decided that the paper had something to do with it. The next night I picked up a gum wrapper and had another good night at the plate. I've been picking up paper every night since.

Like many hitters, John abandoned this ritual and looked for a new one when he stopped hitting.

Because most pitchers play only once every four days, they perform rituals less frequently than hitters. But their rituals are just as important, perhaps more so. A starting pitcher cannot make up for a poor performance the next day, and having to wait three days to redeem oneself can be miserable. Moreover, the team's performance depends more on the pitcher than on any other player. Considering the pressures to do well, it is not surprising that pitchers' rituals are often more complex than those of hitters.

Most baseball fans observe ritual behavior, such as pitcher's tugging their caps between pitches, touching the rosin bag after each bad pitch, smoothing the dirt on the mound before each new batter or inning, never realizing that these actions may be as important to the pitcher as actually throwing the ball.

Many other rituals take place off the field, out of public view. On the days they are scheduled to start, many pitchers avoid activities that they believe sap their strength and detract from their effectiveness or that they otherwise link with poor performance. Some avoid eating certain foods; some will not shave on the day of a game; some pitchers don't shave as long as they are winning. Early in the 1989 season Oakland's Dave Stewart had six consecutive victories and a beard before he finally lost. Ex-St. Louis Cardinal Al Hrabosky took this taboo to extremes; Samsonlike, he refused to cut his hair or beard during the entire season, which was part of the reason for his nickname, the "Mad Hungarian."

Mike Griffin begins his ritual routine a full day before he pitches, by washing his hair. The next day, although he does not consider himself superstitious, he eats bacon for lunch. When Griffin dresses for the game, he puts on his clothes in the same order, making certain he puts the slightly longer of his two "stirrup" socks on his right leg. "I just wouldn't feel right mentally if I did it the other way around," he explains. He always wears the same shirt under his uniform on the day he pitches. During the game he takes off his cap after each pitch, and between innings he sits in the same place on the dugout bench. He believes his rituals give him a sense of order that reduces his anxiety about pitching.

Some pitchers even involve their wives or girlfriends in their rituals. One wife reported that her husband insisted that she wash her hair each day he was to pitch. In her memoirs, Danielle Torrez reported that one "rule" she learned as a baseball wife was "to support your husband's superstitions, whether you believe in them or not. I joined the player's wives who ate ice cream in the sixth inning or tacos in the fifth, or who attended games in a pink sweater, a tan scarf, or a floppy hat" (1983: 79). About ballplayers generally, Marlin coach Rich Donelly said:

> They're like trained animals. They come out here [ballpark] and everything has to be the same, they don't like anything that knocks them off their routine. Just look at the dugout and you'll see every guy sitting in the same spot every night. It's amazing, everybody is in the same spot. And don't you dare take someone's seat.

## TABOO

The word "taboo" comes from a Polynesian term meaning prohibition. Breaking a taboo or prohibition leads to undesirable consequences or bad luck. Most players observe at least a few taboos. Some are careful never to step on the chalk foul lines or lines of the batter's box. One teammate of mine would never watch a movie on a game day, despite the fact that we played nearly every day from April to September. Another teammate refused to read anything before a game because he believed it weakened his batting eye.

Taboos usually grow out of exceptionally poor performances, which players, in search of a reason or cause, attribute to a particular behavior. During my first season of pro ball I ate pancakes before a game in which I struck out four times. A few weeks later I had another terrible game, again after eating pancakes. The result was a pancake taboo: I never ate pancakes during the season from that day on.

Some Latin players have a taboo against crossing bats, against permitting one bat to rest on top of another. One of my Dominican teammates became agitated when another player tossed a bat from the batting cage, and it landed on top of his bat. Later he explained that the top bat might steal hits from the lower one. In his view, bats contained a finite number of hits, a sort of baseball "image of limited good." For Hall of Famer Honus Wagner, each bat contained only 100 hits and never more. Regardless of the quality of the bat, he would discard it after its 100th hit. One player told me that many of his teammates on the Class A Asheville Tourists would not let pitchers touch or swing their bats, not even to loosen up. Poorly hitting pitchers were said to pollute or weaken the bats.

## FETISHES

Fetishes or charms are material objects believed to embody supernatural power that can aid or protect the owner. Good luck fetishes are standard equipment for some ballplayers. They include a wide assortment of objects, from coins, chains, and crucifixes, to a particular baseball hat. Ordinary objects acquire power by being connected to exceptionally hot batting or pitching streaks, especially ones in which players get all the breaks. The object is often a new possession or something a player finds that coincides with the start of the streak and holds responsible for his good fortune. The player attributes the improvement in his performance to the influence of the new object and comes to regard it as a fetish.

While playing in the Pacific Coast League, Alan Foster forgot his baseball shoes on a road trip and borrowed a pair from a teammate. That night he pitched a no-hitter, which he attributed to the shoes. After he bought them from his teammate, they became a fetish. The prized rock of Expo farmhand Mark LaRosa has a very different origin and use: "I found it on the field in Elmira after I had gotten bombed [pitched poorly]. It's unusual, perfectly round, and it caught my attention. I keep it to remind me of how important it is to concentrate. When I am going well I look at the rock and remember to keep my focus, the rock reminds me of what can happen when I lose my concentration."

For one season Marge Schott, owner of the Cincinnati Reds, insisted that her field manager rub her St. Bernard "Schotzie" for good luck before each game. When the Reds were on the road, Schott would sometimes send a bag of the dog's hair to the field manager's hotel room.

During World War II American soldiers used fetishes in much that same way. Social psychologist Samuel Stouffer and his colleagues found that in the face of great danger and uncertainty, soldiers developed magical practices, particularly the use of protective amulets and good luck charms (crosses, Bibles, rabbits' feet, medals), and jealously guarded articles of clothing they associated with past experiences of escape from danger. Stouffer also found that prebattle preparations were carried out in fixed "ritual" order, much as ballplayers prepare for a game.

Uniform numbers have special significance for some players. Many have a lucky number that they request. Since the choice is usually limited, players may try to get a number that at least contains their lucky number, such as 14, 24, 34, or 44 for the pitcher whose lucky number is four. Oddly enough, there is no consensus about the effect of wearing number 13. Some players will not wear it, others will, and a few like the Yankee's David Cone request it.

The way in which number preferences emerge varies. Occasionally a young player requests the number of a former star, hoping that--in a form of *imitative magic*--it will bring him a similar measure of success. Or he may request a favorite number that he has always associated with good luck. Vida Blue changed his uniform number from 35 to 14, the number he wore as a high school quarterback. When the new number did not produce the better pitching performance he was looking for, he switched back to his old number.

Clothing, both the choice of clothes and the order in which they are put on, combines elements of both ritual and fetish. Some players put on their uniform in a specified order. Expos farmhand Jim Austin always puts on his left sleeve, left pants leg, and left shoe before the right. Most players, however, single out one or two lucky articles or quirks of dress rather than ritualizing all items of clothing. After hitting two home runs in a game, for example, infielder Jim Davenport of the San Francisco Giants discovered that he had missed a buttonhole while dressing for the game. For the remainder of his career he left the same button undone. For Brian Hunter the focus is on his shoes: "I have a pair of high tops and a pair of low tops. Whichever shoes don't get a hit that game, I switch to the other pair." At the time of our interview, he was struggling at the plate and switching shoes almost every day. For Birmingham Baron pitcher Bo Kennedy the *arrangement* of the different pairs of baseball shoes in his locker is critical: "I tell the clubies [clubhouse boys] when you hang stuff in my locker don't touch my shoes. If you bump them move them back. I want the Pony's in front, the turfs to the right, and I want them nice and neat with each pair touching each other. Everyone on the team knows not to mess with my shoes when I pitch."

During streaks--hitting or winning--players may wear the same clothes for each game. Once I changed sweatshirts midway through the game for seven consecutive games to keep a hitting streak going. During a 16-game winning streak, the 1954 New York Giants wore the same clothes in each game and refused to let them be cleaned for fear that their good fortune might be washed away with the dirt. Taking this ritual to the extreme, Leo Durocher, managing the Brooklyn Dodgers to a pennant in 1941, spent three and a half weeks in the same black shoes, gray slacks, blue coat, and knitted blue tie. Conversely, when losing, the opposite may occur. Several of the Oakland A's players, for example, went out and bought new street clothes in an attempt to break a 14-game losing streak.

While most taboos are idiosyncratic, there are a few that all players hold and that do not develop out of individual experience or misfortune. These taboos are learned, some as early as Little League. Mentioning a no-hitter while one is in progress is a widely known example. It is believed that if a pitcher hears the words "no-hitter," the spell will be broken, and the no-hitter lost. This taboo is still observed by many sports broadcasters, who use various linguistic subterfuges to inform their listeners that the pitcher has not given up a hit, never mentioning "no-hitter."

Such superstitions, like most everything else, change over time. Many of the rituals and beliefs of early baseball are no longer remembered. In the 1920s and 1930s sportswriters reported that a player who tripped en route to the field would often retrace his steps and carefully walk over the stumbling block for "insurance." A century ago players spent time off the field and on it looking for items that would bring them luck. For example, to find a hairpin on the street assured a batter of hitting safely in that day's game (today women don't wear hairpins--a good reason the belief has died out). To catch sight of a white horse or a wagonload of barrels was also a good omen. In 1904 the manager of the New York Giants, John McGraw, hired a driver and a team of white horses to drive past the Polo Grounds around the time his players were arriving at the ballpark. He knew that if his players saw white horses, they'd have more confidence, and that could only help them during the game. Belief in the power of white horses survived in a few backwaters until the 1960s. A gray-haired manager of a team I played for in Quebec would drive around the countryside before important games and during the playoffs looking for a white horse. When he was successful, he'd announce it to everyone in the clubhouse before the game.

B. F. Skinner's early research with pigeons sheds some light on how these rituals, taboos, and fetishes get established in the first place. Like human beings, pigeons quickly learn to associate their behavior with rewards or punishment. By rewarding the birds at the appropriate time, Skinner taught them such elaborate games as table tennis, miniature bowling, and how to play simple tunes on a toy piano.

On one occasion he decided to see what would happen if pigeons were rewarded with food pellets every seconds, regardless of what they did. He found that the birds tended to associate the arrival of the food with a particular action- tucking the head under a wing, hopping from side to side, or turning in a clockwise direction. About 10 seconds after the arrival of the last pellet, a bird would begin doing whatever it had associated with getting the food and keep at it until the next pellet arrived.

In the same way, baseball players tend to believe there is a causal connection between two events that are linked only temporally. If a superstitious player touches his crucifix and then gets a hit, he may decide the gesture was responsible for his good fortune and follow the same practice the next time he comes to the plate. If he should get another hit, the chances are good that he will begin touching the crucifix each time he bats and that he will do so whether or not he hits safely each time.

The average batter hits safely approximately one-quarter of the time. If the behavior of Skinner's pigeons or of gamblers at a Las Vegas slot machine is any guide, that is more than enough to keep him believing in a ritual. Skinner found that once a pigeon associated one of its actions with the arrival of food or water, sporadic rewards would keep the connection going. One pigeon, apparently believing that hopping from side to side brought pellets into its feeding cup, hopped 10,000 times without a pellet before finally giving up.

Since the batter associates his hits, at least to some degree, with his ritual touching of a crucifix, each hit he gets reinforces the strength of the ritual. Even if he falls into a batting slump, and the hits temporarily stop, he may continue to touch his crucifix in the hope that it will change his luck. If the slump lasts too long, however, he will soon change his behavior and look for a new practice to bring back his luck.

Skinner and Malinowski's explanations are complementary. Skinner's research throws light on how a ritual develops and why a particular ritual, taboo, or fetish is maintained. Malinowski focuses on why human beings turn to magic in situations of chance and uncertainty. In their attempts to gain greater control over their performance, we saw that baseball players respond to chance and uncertainty in the same way as people in tribal societies. It is wrong to assume that magical practices are a waste of time for either group. The magic in baseball obviously does not make a pitch travel faster or more accurately or a batted ball seek the gaps between fielders. Nor does the Trobriand brand of magic make the surrounding seas calmer and more abundant with fish. What both kinds of magic do is give their practitioners a sense of control and, with that, confidence, at very little cost.

## NOTE

This chapter was revised by the author from the original article that appeared in *Transaction* 8, no. 8 (1971): 39-41. Reprinted by permission of the author.

## REFERENCES

Malinowski, B. *Magic, Science and Religion and Other Essays*. Glencoe, IL., 1948.
Skinner, B. F. *Behavior of Organisms: An Experimental Analysis*. D. Appleton-Century, 1938.
_____. *Science and Human Behavior*. New York: Macmillan, 1953.

## *chapter 13*

# Into the End Zone for a Touchdown:
# A Psychoanalytical Consideration
# of American Football

## *Alan Dundes*

In college athletics it is abundantly clear that football counts highest among both enrolled students and alumni. It is almost as though the masculinity of male alumni is at stake in a given game, especially when a hated rival school is the opponent. College fund raisers are well aware that a winning football season may prove to be the key to a successful financial campaign to increase the school's endowment capital. The Rose Bowl and other postseason bowl games for colleges, plus the Super Bowl for professional teams, have come to rank as national festival occasions in the United States. All this makes it reasonable to assume that something about football strikes a most responsive chord in the American psyche. No other American sport consistently draws fans in the numbers that are attracted to football. One need only compare the crowd attendance statistics for college or professional baseball games with the analogous figures for football to see the enormous appeal of the latter. The question is, What is it about American football that could possibly account for its extraordinary popularity?

In the relatively meager scholarship devoted to football, one finds the usual array of theoretical approaches. The ancestral form of football, a game more like rugby or soccer, was interpreted as a solar ritual--with a disc-shaped rock or object supposedly representing the sun (Johnson 1929: 228)--and also a fertility ritual intended to ensure agricultural abundance. It had been noted, for example, that in some parts of England and France, the rival teams consisted of married men playing against bachelors (Johnson 1929: 230-31; Magoun 1931: 24, 36, 44). In one custom, a newly married woman would throw over the church a ball for which married men and bachelors fought. The distinction between the married and unmarried suggests that the game might be a kind of ritual test or battle, with marriage signifying socially sanctioned fertility (Johnson 1929: 231).

The historical evolution of American football from English rugby has been well documented (Riesman and Denny 1951), but the historical facts do not, in and of themselves, account for any psychological rationale leading to the unprecedented enthusiasm for the sport. It is insufficient to state that football offers an appropriate outlet for the expression of aggression. William Arens has rightly observed that it would be an oversimplification "to single out violence as the sole or even primary reason for the game's popularity" (Arens 1975). Many sports provide a similar outlet (e.g., wrestling, ice hockey, roller derby), but few of these come close to matching football as a spectacle for many Americans. Similarly, pointing to such features as love of competition, the admiration of coordinated teamwork, or the development of specialties (e.g., punters, punt returners, field-goal kickers, etc.) is not convincing since such features occur in most, if not all, sports.

Recently, studies of American football have suggested that the game serves as a male initiation ritual (Beisser 1967; Fiske 1972; Arens 1975). Arens, for example, remarks that football is a "male preserve that manifests both the physical and cultural values of masculinity" (Arens 1975: 77), a description that had previously been applied--aptly it would appear--to British rugby (Sheard and Dunning 1973). Arens points out that the equipment worn "accents the male physique" through the enlarged head and shoulders coupled with a narrowed waist. With the lower torso "poured into skintight pants accented only by a metal codpiece," Arens contends that the result "is not an expression but an exaggeration of maleness." He comments further: "Dressed in this manner, the players can engage in handholding, hugging, and bottom patting, which would be disapproved of in any other context, but which is accepted on the gridiron without a second thought" (Arens 1975: 79). Having said this much, Arens fails to draw any inferences about possible ritual homosexual aspects of football. Instead, he goes on to note that American football resembles male rituals in other cultures insofar as contact with females is discouraged, if not forbidden. The argument usually given is one of "limited good" (Foster 1965). A man has only so much energy, and if he uses it in sexual activity, he will have that much less to use in hunting, warfare, or, in this case, football. I believe that Arens and others are correct in calling attention to the ritual and symbolic dimensions of American football but that the psychological implications of the underlying symbolism have not been adequately explored.

Football is one of a large number of competitive games that involve the scoring of points by gaining access to a defended area in an opponent's territory. In basketball, one must throw a ball through a hoop (and net) attached to the other team's backboard. In ice hockey, one must hit the puck into the goal at the opponent's end of the rink. In football, the object is to move the ball across the opponent's goal into his endzone. It does not require a great deal of Freudian sophistication to see a possible sexual component in such acts as throwing a ball through a hoop, hitting a puck across a "crease" into an enclosed area bounded by nets or a cage, and other structurally similar acts. But what is not so obvious is the connection of such sexual symbolism with an all-male group of participants.

Psychologists and psychoanalysts have not chosen to examine American football to any great extent. Psychologist G.T.W. Patrick, writing in 1903, tried to explain the fascination of the game: "Evidently, there is some great force, psychological or sociological, at work here which science has not yet investigated," but he could offer little detail about what that great force might be (Patrick 1903: 370). Similarly, psychoanalyst A. A. Brill's superficial consideration of football in 1929 failed to illuminate the psychodynamics of the game (Brill 1929). Perhaps the best-known Freudian analysis of football is the parody written originally in 1955 in the *Rocky Mountain Herald* by poet Thomas Hornsby Ferril, using the pseudonym Childe Herald, but the essay is more amusing than analytical. Actually, his interpretation tends to be more inclined toward ritual than psychoanalytic theory. He suggests that

> football is a syndrome of religious rites symbolizing the struggle to preserve the egg of life through the rigors of impending winter. The rites begin at the autumn equinox and culminate on the first day of the New Year with great festivals identified with bowls aplenty; the festivals are associated with flowers such as roses, fruits such as oranges, farm crops such as cotton and even sun-worship and the appeasement of great reptiles such as alligators. (Herald 1965: 250-52)

While he does say that "football obviously arise out of the Oedipus Complex," he provides little evidence other than mentioning that college games are usually played for one's alma mater, which translates as "dear mother." Actually, a more literal translation would be "nourishing mother" (and for that matter, *alumnus* literally means nursling.)

A more conventional psychoanalytical perspective is offered by Adrian Stokes in his survey of ball games with special reference to cricket. Stokes predictably describes football (soccer) in oedipal terms. Each team defends the goal at its back. "In front is a new land, the new woman, whom they strive to possess in the interest of preserving the mother inviolate, in order, as it were, to progress from infancy to adulthood: at the same time, the defensive role is the father's; he opposes the forward youth of the opposition" (Stokes 1956). Speaking of rugby football, Stokes proposes the following description: "Ejected out of the mother's body, out of the scrum, after frantic hooking and pushing, there emerges the rich loot of the father's genital." According to Stokes, both teams fight to possess the father's phallus, that is the ball, in order to "steer it through the archetypal vagina, the goal" (Stokes 1956: 190). Earlier, Stokes had suggested the ball represented semen, though he claimed that "more generally the ball is itself the phallus" (Stokes 1956: 187). Folk speech offers some support for the phallic connotation of a ball. One thinks of "balls" for testicles. A man who has "balls" is a man of strength and determination. To "ball" someone is a slang expression for sexual intercourse (Rodgers 1972; Wepman, Newman, and Binderman 1976). On the other hand, while one might agree with the general thesis that there might be a sexual component to both soccer and American football, it is difficult to cite concrete evidence supporting Stokes' contention that the game involves a mother figure or a father surrogate. If psychoanalytical interpretations are valid, then it ought to be possible to adduce specific details of idiom and ritual as documentation for such interpretations. It is not enough for a psychoanalyst to assert ex cathedra what a given event or object supposedly symbolizes.

A useful way to begin to understand the psychoanalytical significance of American football is through an examination of folk speech, for it is precisely in the idioms and metaphors that a clear pattern of personal interaction is revealed. In this regard, it might be helpful first to briefly consider the slang employed in the verbal dueling of the American male. In effect, I am suggesting that American football is analogous to male verbal dueling. Football entails ritual and dramatic action, while verbal dueling is more concerned with words. But structurally speaking, they are similar or at least functionally equivalent. In verbal dueling, it is common to speak about putting one's opponent "down." This could mean simply to topple an opponent figuratively, but it could also imply forcing one's adversary to assume a supine position, that is, the "female" position in typical Western sexual intercourse. It should also be noted that an equally humiliating experience for a male would be to serve as a passive receptacle for a male aggressor's phallic thrust. Numerous idioms attest to the widespread popularity of this pattern of imagery to describe a loser. One speaks of having been screwed by one's boss or of having been given the shaft. Submitting to anal intercourse is also implied in perhaps the most common single American folk gesture, the so-called *digitus impudicus*, better known in folk parlance as the "finger." Giving someone the finger is often accompanied by such unambiguous explanatory phrases as "Fuck you!" "Screw you!" "Up yours!" or "Up your ass!"

Now, what does has this all to do with football? The same symbolic pattern is at work in verbal dueling and much ritual play. Instead of scoring a touchdown, one scores a touchdown. Certainly the terminology used in football is suggestive. One gains yardage, but it is not territory that is kept in the sense of being permanently acquired by the invading team. The territory invaded remains nominally under the proprietorship of the opponent. A sports announcer or fan might say, for example, "This is the deepest *penetration* into (opponent's team name) territory so far" [my emphasis]. Only if one gets into the end zone (or kicks a field goal through the uprights of the goalposts) does one earn points.

The use of the term "end" is not accidental. Evidently, there is a kind of structural isomorphism between line (as opposed to backfield) and the layout of the field of play. Each line has two ends (left end and right end) with a "center" in the middle. Similarly, each playing field has two ends (end zones) with a midfield line (the 50-yard line). Ferril remarked on the parallel between the oval shape of the football and the oval shape of most stadiums (Herald in Ferril 1965), but I submit it might be just as plausible to see the football shape as an elongated version of the earlier round soccer or rugby ball, a shape that tends to produce two accentuated ends of the ball. Surely, the distinctive difference between the shape of the football and the shape of the balls used in most other ball games (e.g. baseball, basketball, soccer) is that it is not perfectly spherical. The notion that a football has two "ends" is found in standard idiom used to describe a kick or a punt in which the ball turns over and over from front to back during flight (as opposed to moving in a more direct, linear, spiraling patter) as an "end over end" kick.

The object of the game, simply stated, is to get into the opponent's end zone, while preventing the opponent from getting into one's own endzone. Structurally speaking, this is precisely what is involved in male verbal dueling. One wishes to put one's opponent down, to "screw" him while avoiding being screwed by him. We can now better understand the appropriateness of the "bottom patting" so often observed among football players. A good offensive or defensive play deserves a pat on the rear end. The recipient has held up his end and thereby helped protect the collective "end" of the entire team. One pats one's teammates' ends, but one seeks to violate the end zone of one's opponent!

The trust one has for one's own teammates is perhaps signaled by the common postural stance of football players. The so-called three-point stance involves bending over in a distinct stooped position with one's rear end exposed. It is an unusual position (in terms of normal life activities), and it does make one especially vulnerable to attack from behind, that is, vulnerable to homosexual attack. In some ways, the posture might be likened to what is termed *presenting* among nonhuman primates. *Presenting* refers to a subordinate animal's turning its rump toward a higher-ranking or dominant one. The center thus presents to the quarterback--just as linemen do to the backs in general. George Plimpton has described how the quarterback's "hand, the top of it, rests up against the center's backside as he bends over the ball--medically against the perineum, the pelvic floor" (Plimpton 1965: 59). We know that some dominant nonhuman primates will sometimes reach out to touch a presenting subordinate in similar fashion. In football, however, it is safe to present to one's teammates. Since one can trust one's teammates, one knows that one will be patted, not raped. The traditional joking admonitions of the locker room warning against bending over in the shower or picking up the soap (this presumably offering an inviting target for homosexual attack) do not apply since one is among friends. "Grabass" among friends is understood as being harmless joking behavior.

The importance of the "ends" is signaled by the fact that they alone among linemen are eligible to receive a forward pass. In that sense, ends are equivalent to the "backs." In symbolic terms, I am arguing that the end is a kind of backside and that the end zone is a kind of erogenous zone. The relatively recently coined terms *tight end* and *split end* further demonstrate the special emphasis upon this "position" on the team. The terms refer to whether the end stays close to his neighboring tackle, fir example, to block, or whether he moves well away from the normally adjacent tackle, for example, to go out for a pass. However, both *tight end* and *split end* (cf. also *wide receiver*) could easily be understood as possessing an erotic nuance.

I must stress that the evidence for the present interpretation of American football does not depend on just a single word. Rather, many terms appear to be relevant. The semantics of the word *down* are of interest. A down is a unit of play insofar as a team has four downs in which to either advance 10 yards or score. A touchdown, which earns six points, refers to the act of an offensive player's possessing the ball in an opponent's end zone. (Note that it is not sufficient for the player to be in the end zone; the ball must be in the end zone.) In a running play, the ball often physically touches the end zone and could therefore be said to "touch down" in that area. However, if an offensive player catches a pass in the end zone, the ball does not actually touch the ground. The recent practice of "spiking" the ball, in which the successful offensive player hurls the ball at the ground as hard as he can, might be construed as an attempt to have the ball physically touch down in the end zone. In any case, the use of the word *touch* in connection with scoring in football does conform to a generally sexually symbolic use of that term. The sexual nuances of *touch* can even be found in the Bible. For example, in I Corinthians 7:12, we find: "It is good for a man not to touch a woman. Nevertheless to avoid fornication, let every man have his own wife" (cf. Genesis 20:6, Proverbs 6:29). Touching can be construed as an aggressive act. Thus, to be touched by an opponent means that one has been the victim of aggression. The game of "touch football" (as opposed to *tackle* football) supports the notion that a mere art of touching is sufficient to fulfill the structural (and psychological) requirements of the basic rules. No team wants to give up a touchdown to an opponent. Often a team on defense may put up a determined goal-line stand to avoid being penetrated by the opponent's offense. The special spatial nature of the end zone is perhaps indicated by the fact that it is not measured in the 100 yard distance between the goal lines. Yet it is measured. It is only 10 yards deep; a pass caught by an offensive player whose feet are beyond the end line of the end zone would be ruled incomplete.

Additional football folk speech could be cited. The object of the game is to "score," a term that in standard slang means to engage in sexual intercourse with a member of the opposite sex. One "scores" by going "all the way." The latter phrase refers specifically to making a touchdown (Rote and Winter 1966: 102). In sexual slang, it alludes to indulging in intercourse as opposed to petting or necking. The offensive team may try to mount a "drive" in order to "penetrate" the other team's territory. A ball carrier might go "up the middle," or he might "go through" a hole" (made by his linemen in the opposing defensive line). A particularly skilled runner might be able to make his own hole. The defensive is equally determined to "close the hole." Linemen may encourage one another to "stick it to 'em," meaning to place their helmeted heads (with phallic-symbolic overtones) against the chests of their opposite numbers to drive them back or put them out of the play.

A player who scores a touchdown may elect to "spike" the ball by hurling it downward toward the ground full force. This spiking movement confirms to all assembled that the enemy's end zone has been penetrated. The team scored upon is thus shamed and humiliated in front of an audience. In this regard, football is similar to verbal dueling inasmuch as dueling invariably takes place before one or more third parties. The term *spike* may also be germane. As a noun it could refer to a sharp-pointed, long, slender part or projection. As a verb, it could mean either to "mark or cut with a knife" (the football would presumably be the phallic spike) or to "thwart or sabotage an enemy." In any event, the ritual act of spiking serves to prolong an accentuate and all-too-short moment of triumph, the successful entry into the enemy's end zone.

The sexual connotations of football folk speech apply equally to players on defense. One goal of the defensive line is to penetrate the offensive line to get to the quarterback. Getting to the offensive quarterback and bringing him down to the ground are termed "sacking the quarterback." The verb *sack* connotes plunder, ravage, and perhaps even rape. David Kopay, one of the few homosexuals in professional football willing to admit a preference for members of the same sex, commented on the nature of typical exhortations made by coaches and players:

> The whole language of football is involved in sexual allusions. We were told to go out and "fuck those guys"; to take the ball and "stick it up their asses" or "down their throats." The coaches would yell, "knock their dicks off," or more often than that, "knock their jocks off." They'd say, "Go out there and give it all you've got, a hundred and ten percent, shoot your wad." You controlled their, line and "knocked" 'em into submission. Over the years I've seen many a coach get emotionally aroused while he was diagramming a particular play into an imaginary hole on the blackboard. His face red, his voice rising, he would show the ball carrier how he wanted him to "stick it in the hole." (Kopay and Young 1977: 53-54)

The term "rape" is not inappropriate, and, in fact, it has been used to describe what happens when an experienced player humiliates a younger player: "That poor kid, he was raped, keelhauled, he was just *destroyed*" (Plimpton 1965:195, 339). Kopay's reference to *jock* as a phallus is of interest since *jock* is a term (short for *jockstrap*, the article of underapparel worn to protect the male genitals) typically used to refer generally to athletes. Calling an athlete a jock or strap thus tends to reduce him to a phallus. A *jocker* is used to refer to an aggressive male homosexual (Wentworth and Flexner 1967: 294: Rodgers 1972). (The meaning of *jock* may well be related to the term *jockey* insofar as the latter refers to the act of mounting and riding a horse.)

Some of the football speech is less obvious, and the interpretation admittedly is a bit more speculative. For example, a lineman may be urged to "pop" an opposing player, meaning to tackle or block him well. Executing a perfect tackle or block may entail placing one's helmet as close as possible to the middle of the opponent's chest. The use of the verbs strongly suggests defloration, as in the idiom "to pop the cherry" referring to the notion of rupturing the maidenhead in the process of having intercourse with a virgin" (Randolph 1976: 9). In Afro-American folk speech, "pop" can refer to sexual penetration (Wepman, Newman, and Binderman 1976: 186). To "pop" an opponent thus implies reducing him to female-victim status. Much of the sexual slang makes it very clear that the winners are men, while the losers are women or passive homosexuals. Kopay articulates this when he says, "From grade school on, the curse words on the football field are about behaving like a girl. If you don't run fast enough to block or tackle hard enough you're a pussy, a cunt, a sissy" (Kopay and Young 1977: 57). By implication, if a player succeeds, he is a male. Thus, in the beginning of the football game, we have two sets of males. By the end of the game, one of the teams is on "top," namely, the one that has "scored" most by getting into the other team's "end zone." The losing team, if the scoring differential is great, may be said to have been "creamed."

It is tempting to make something of the fact, that originally, the inner portion of the football was an inflated animal bladder. Thus, touching the enemy's end zone with a bladder would be appropriate ritual behavior in the context of a male homosexual attack. However, it could be argued that the bladder was used simply because it was convenient, a inflatable object available to serve as a ball.

If the team on offense is perceived in phallic terms, then the quarterback could be said to be nominally in charge of directing the attack. In this context, it may be noteworthy that a quarterback intending to pass often tries to stay inside the "pocket," a deployment of offensive players behind the line of scrimmage designed to provide an area of maximum protection (Rote and Winter 1966: 130). A pants pocket, of course, could be construed as an area where males can covertly touch or manipulate their genitals without being observed. "Pocket pool," for example, is a slang idiom for fondling the genitals (Rodgers 1972: 152), an idiom that incidentally may suggest something about the symbolic nature of billiards. The quarterback, if given adequate protection by his "pocket," may be able to "thread the needle," that is, throw the ball accurately, past the hands of the defensive players, into the hands of his receiver. The metaphor of threading the needle is an apt one since getting the thread through the eye of the needle is only preparatory for the act of "sewing." (Note also that to "make a pass" at someone is a conventional idiom for an act of flirtation.) Once the ball is in his possession, the receiver is transformed from a passive to an active role as he tries to move the ball as far forward as possible.

While it is possible to disagree with several interpretations offered of the individual items of folk speech cited this far, it would seem difficult to deny the overall sexual nature of much of football (and other sport) slang. The word *sport* itself has had this connotation for centuries. Consider one of Goucester's early lines in *King Lear* when he refers to his bastard son Edmund by saying, "There was good sport at his making" (I,I,23) or in such modern usages as "sporting house" for "brothel" (Wenthworth and Flexner 1967: 511: 186) or *sporting life* referring to pimps and prostitutes (Wepman, Newman, and Binderman 1976). In the early 1950s, kissing was commonly referred to by adolescents as a "favorite indoor sport," presumably in contrast to outdoor sports such as football. It should also be noted that *game* can carry the same sexual connotation as *sport* (Rodgers 1972: 92, Wepman, Newman, and Binderman 1976: 182).

I have no doubt that a good many football players and fans will be skeptical (to say the least) of the analysis proposed here. Even academics with presumably less personal investment in football will probably find implausible, if not downright repugnant, the idea that American football could be ritual combat between groups of males attempting to assert their masculinity by penetrating the end zones of their rivals. David Kopay, despite suggesting that, for a long time, football provided a kind of replacement for sex in his life and admitting that football is "a real outlet for repressed sexual energy" (Kopay and Young 1977: 11, 53), refuses to believe that "being able to hold hands In the huddle and to pat each other on the ass if we felt like it" is necessarily an overt show of homosexuality (Kopay and Young 1977: 57). Yet I think it is highly likely that the ritual aspect of football, providing, as it does a socially sanctioned framework for male body contact-football, after all, is a so-called body contact sport is a form of homosexual behavior. The unequivocal sexual symbolism of the game, as plainly evidenced in folk speech, coupled with the fact that all of the participants are male, makes, it difficult to draw any other conclusion. Sexual acts carried out in thinly disguised symbolic form by, and directed toward, males and males only would seem to constitute ritual homosexuality.

Evidence from other cultures indicates that male homosexual ritual combats are fairly common. Answering the question of who penetrates whom is a pretty standard means of testing masculinity crossculturally. Interestingly enough, the word *masculine* itself seems to derive from Latin *mas* (male) and *culus* (anus). The implication might be for that a male to prove his masculinity with his peers, he would need to control or guard his buttock area while at the same time threaten the posterior of another (weaker) male. A good many men's jokes in Mediterranean cultures (e.g., in Italy and Spain) center on the *culo*.

That a mass spectacle could be based on a ritual masculinity contest should not surprise anyone familiar with the bullfight. Without intending to reduce the complexity of the bullfight to a single factor, one could nonetheless observe that it is, in part, a battle between males attempting to penetrate one another. The one who is penetrated loses. If it is the bull, he may be further feminized or emasculated by having various extremities cut off to reward the successful matador. In this context, we can see American football as a male activity (along with Boy Scouts, fraternities, and other exclusively male social organizations in American culture) as belonging to the general range of male rituals around the world in which masculinity is defined and affirmed. In American culture, women are permitted to be present as spectators or even cheerleaders, but they are not participants. Women resenting men's preoccupation with such male sports are commonly referred to as football widows (analogous to golf widows.) This, too, suggests that the sport activity is, in some sense, a substitute for normal heterosexual relations. The men are "dead" as far as relationships with females are concerned. In sport and ritual, men play both male *and* female parts. Whether it is the verbal dueling, tradition of the circum-Mediterranean (Dundes, Leach, and Ozkok 1970: 325-49) in which young men threaten to put opponents into a passive homosexual position, or the initiation rites in aboriginal Australia and New Guinea (and elsewhere) in which younger men are subjected to actual homosexual and intercourse by older members of the male group (cf. Dundes 1976: 220-38), the underlying psychological rationale appears to be similar. Professional football's financial incentives may extend the playing years of individuals beyond the late adolescent masculinity initiation ritual in which the winner gets into the loser's end zone more times that the loser gets into his!

## NOTE

This chapter previously appeared as "Into the Endzone: A Psycho-analytical Consideration of American Football," by Alan Dundes, from *Interpreting Folklore* edited by Bloomington: Indiana University Press Publisher, 1988. Reprinted with permission of the University of Indiana Press.

## REFERENCES

Arens, William. "The Great American Football Ritual." In *The American Dimension: Cultural Myths and Social Realities*, edited by W. Arens and Susan Montague. Port Washington: 1975.

Beisser, Arnold R. *The Madness in Sports*. New York: 1967.

Brill, A. A. "The Why of the Fan." *North American Review* 228 (1929): 429-34.

Dundes, Alan. "A Psychoanalytic Study of the Bullroarer." *Man* 11(1976): 220-38.

Dundes, Alan, Jerry Leach and Bora Ozkok. "The Strategy of Turkish Boys' Verbal Dueling Rhymes." *Journal of American Folklore* 831 (1970): 325-49.

Fiske, Shirely. "Pigskin Review: An American Initiation." In *Sport in the Socio-cultural Process*, edited by Marie Hart. Dubuque, IA: 1972.

Foster, George M. "Peasant Society and the Image of Limited Good." *American Anthropologist* 67 (1965): 293-315.

Herald, Childe [Thomas Hornsby Ferril]. "Freud and Football." In *Reader in Contemporary Religion,* 2d ed, edited by W. Lessa and E. Vogt. New York: 1965.

Johnson, Branch. "Football, A Survival of Magic?" *The Contemporary Review* 135 (1929):228.

Kopay, David and Perry Deane Young. *The David Kopay Story*. New York: 1977.

Magoun, Francis P., Jr. "Shrove Tuesday Football." *Harvard Studies and Notes in Philology and Literature* 13, no. 24 (1931): 44.

Patrick, G. T. W. "The Psychology of Football." *American Journal of Psychology* 14 (1903): 370.

Plimpton, George. *Paper Lion.* New York: 1965.

Randolph, Vance. *Pissing in the Snow and Other Ozark Folktales*. Urbana, IL: 1967.

Riesman, David, and Reuel Denney. "Football in America: A Study in Cultural Diffusion." *American Quarterly* 3 (1951): 309-325.

Rodgers, Bruce. *The Queen's Vernacular: A Gay Lexicon*. San Francisco: 1972.

Rote, Kyle, and Jack Winter. *The Language of Pro Football*. New York: 1966.

Sheard, K. G. and E. G. Dunning. "The Rugby Football Club as a Type of 'Male Preserve": Some Sociological Notes." *International Review of Sport Sociology* 3-4 (1973): 5-24.

Stokes, Adrian. "Psycho-Analytic Reflections on the Development of Ball Games, Particularly Cricket." *International Journal of Psycho-Analysis* 37 (1956): 185-92.

Wenthworth, Harold, and Stuart Berg Flexner. *Dictionary of American Slang*. New York: 1967.

Wepman, Dennis, Ronald B. Newman and Murray B. Binderman. *The Life: The Lore and Folk Poetry of the Black Hustler*. Philadelphia: 1976.

# Index

# About the Editor and Contributors

**Robert R. Sands** is an Anthropology Professor at Community College of Southern Nevada. His research has focused on sport and culture, sport ethography, and anthropology theory. His intensive ethnography has included fieldwork on college sprinting, college basketball, and junior college football. He is the author of *Instant Acceleration: Living in the Fast Lane*. He has two works in progress, a primer on anthropology of sport, *Sport and Culture: At Play in the Fields of Anthropology,* and *Gutcheck!: An Anthropologist's Wild Ride into the Heart of College Football*, which is based on Sands' two-year participation, while an anthropology professor, as a wide receiver for the Santa Barbara City College football team. Sands is currently doing fieldwork on the Southern California surfing culture.

**David Andrews** is an Assistant Professor in the Department of Human Movement Sciences and Education at the University of Memphis, where he teaches courses on Sport as Promotional Culture, Sport and Critical Theory, and Sport and Gender. His research interests include sport and postmodern theory, sport and the politics of suburban space, and sport and consumer culture. An avid Fulham F.C. supporter, he is a member of the editorial board for the *Sociology of Sport Journal*.

**John Bale** is Reader in Education and Geography at Keele University, England. His academic specialty lies in the geography of sport, a subject that he has pioneered over the past few decades. Among his books are *The Brawn Drain, Landscapes of Modern Sport* and (with Joe Sang) *Kenyan Running*. He is currently researching the representation of African corporeality and athleticism in early twentieth-century texts and photographs.

**Hillary McD. Beckles** is a Professor of History and Dean of the Faculty of Humanities at the University of the West Indies, Barbados. He has published more than a dozen books, including *Liberation Cricket: West Indies Cricket Culture* (New York: Manchester University Press, 1995).

**Kendall Blanchard** is one of the pioneers in the study of sport and culture. Author of *The Mississippi Choctaws at Play: The Serious Side of Leisure* and co-author with

Alyce Cheska of the *Anthropology of Sport*, the first, and still only, text on anthropology of sport, Blanchard has also written numerous articles and presented several papers on the anthropology of sport and play. Blanchard was one of the leaders in the formation of TAASP (the Association for the Anthropological Study of Play).

**Amby Burfoot** is the Executive Editor of *Runner's World Magazine*, the world's leading running magazine. While at Wesleyan University, he was undefeated in four years of dual-meet competition in cross-country, and twice placed sixth (1966 and 1967) in the National Collegiate Athletic Association (NCAA) Division I Cross-Country Championships. Two months before his graduation, Burfoot won the 1968 Boston Marathon--the first American in 11 years to win the world's most prestigious marathon. Later in 1968, he recorded a personal best marathon time of 2:14:28 at the Fukuoka (Japan) Marathon. While at Wesleyan, Burfoot was a roommate with, and mentor to, Bill Rodgers, who went on to international running fame, including four Boston Marathon wins and four New York City Marathon wins. In 1981 Burfoot was given the Journalism Award from the Road Runners Club of America (RRCA). In 1993, he was inducted into the RRCA's "Hall of Fame." The same year his controversial "White Men Can't Run" article was nominated for a National Magazine Award by the American Society of Magazine Editors.

**Cheryl L. Cole** is an Assistant Professor in Kinesiology, Women's Studies, and Criticism and InterpretiveTheory at the University of Illinois at Urbana-Champaign. Her teaching and research examine how social categories of deviance become associated with particular bodies and the relationship between embodied deviance and national identity. Her research has appeared in a wide range of journals and anthologies, including *Critical Sociology, Cultural Studies, Immigrants and Minorities, International Review of the Sociology of Sport, Journal of Sport and Social Issues, Masculinities, Sociology of Sport Journal,* and *Queer Theory/ Sociology.* She is coeditor of *Women, Sport, and Culture*, the SUNY book series *Sport, Culture, and Social Relations,* and two forthcoming anthologies entitled *Exercising Power: The Making and Remaking of the Body* and *Nike Nation: Technologies of an American Sign.*

**Scott Crawford**, a Scottish New Zealander, is a Professor and Graduate Coordinator, Department of Physical Education, College of Education and Professional Studies, Eastern Illinois University, Charleston. He has written for the *International Review of Sport Sociology*, the *International Journal of Sport*, the *Journal of Sport History*, the *Journal of Sport and Social Issues,* and other professional and academic journals. He is a book review editor of the *International Journal of Sport History.* His most recent works are entries for the *Oxford University New Dictionary of National Biography* and a 7,000-word essay on the Ring publisher/editor Nat Fleischer for the forthcoming *Dictionary of Literary Biography: American Sportswriters.* He is currently active in a move to make women's rugby a college sport at EIU.

**Alan Dundes** is a psychoanalytical folklorist and anthropologist at the University of California, Berkeley. Dundes is the author of numerous books, including *Parsing through Customs: Essays by a Freudian Folklorist* (1987) and *Folklore Matters* (1989); coauthor of many books, including, most recently, *Sometimes The Dragon Wins: Yet More Urban Folklore from the Paperwork Empire* (1996). He has also edited or coedited an extensive number of volumes on folklore and myth. Dundes' professional goals are to "make sense of nonsense, find a rationale for the irrational and seek to make the unconscious conscious."

**George Gmelch** is Chair and Professor of Anthropology at Union College in upstate New York. He and has done field research and written about Irish Travelers, return migrants in Newfoundland, Ireland, and Barbados, Alaskan fishermen, and professional baseball players. He is the author of seven books, most recently *In the Ballpark: The Working Lives of Baseball People.*

**John Hoberman** has been active as a sports scholar and sports journalist for the past 20 years. He is the author of *Sport and Political Ideology* (1984), *The Olympic Crisis: Sport, Politics, and the Moral Order* (1986), *Mortal Engines: The Science of Performance and the Dehumanization of Sport* (1992), and *Darwin's Athletes: How Sport Has Damaged Black America and Preserved the Myth of Race* (1997). He has taught sports studies courses at Harvard University, the University of Chicago, and the University of Texas at Austin, where he is Professor of Germanic Languages.

**Steven Jackson** is a Senior Lecturer in the School of Physical Education, University of Otago, New Zealand, where he teaches courses in Sport, Media and Culture and Sociology of Sport. His research interests include sport and the media, sport and globalization of culture, sport violence, and sport and advertising. Jackson has published articles in *Sociology of Sport Journal* and *Journal of Sport and Social Issues*. He is member of the editorial board for the *Sociology of Sport Journal*.

**Samantha King** has published on AIDS and popular culture and the politics of race, sport, and the inner city. She is currently writing on philanthropy, sport, and citizenship.

**Michael Malec** is Associate Professor of Sociology at Boston College, where he teaches courses in the Sociology of Sport, Caribbean Cultures, and Statistics. He has published three books, including *The Social Roles of Sport in Caribbean Societies* 1995).

**Klaus Meier** is a Professor in the Faculty of Kinesiology at the University of Western Ontario. He served as the editor of the *Journal of Sport Philosophy* from 1977 to 1994 and has been coeditor of *Olympika: The International Journal of Olympic Studies*. He was elected International Fellow in the American Academy of Kinesiology and Physical Education in 1991.

**Sally Ann Ness** is a Certified Movement Analyst and currently teaches in the Department of Dance at the University of California, Riverside.

ISBN 0-89789-599-1